THE ODYSSEY
OF THE AMERICAN RIGHT

MICHAEL W. MILES

THE ODYSSEY
OF THE
AMERICAN RIGHT

New York   Oxford

OXFORD UNIVERSITY PRESS

1980

FOR MARY

Copyright © 1980 by Michael W. Miles

Library of Congress Cataloging in Publication Data

Miles, Michael W   1945–
The odyssey of the American right.

Includes bibliographical references and index.
1. Conservatism—United States.   2. United States—
Politics and government—1945–   I. Title.
JA84.U5M62   320.5'2'0973   80-14532
ISBN 0-19-502774-4

Printed in the United States of America

CONTENTS

INTRODUCTION

It is a truism that the Great Depression of the 1930s gave birth to the "Roosevelt coalition" in American politics. President Franklin D. Roosevelt took a minority party, the Democratic party, and made of it a stable ruling coalition by welding together the rural South and the Northern industrial cities under crisis conditions. E. E. Schattschneider called this event the "revolution of 1932." Political scientists consider the "Roosevelt revolution" as only one of several "critical elections" that have redirected American history. These critical elections have come at times of deep social crisis, such as economic depressions and/or new stages of economic and social development, such as the American Civil War. They have "realigned" the political parties by tearing apart old political coalitions and putting together new ones.

In responding to the needs of the unemployed, Roosevelt abandoned *laissez-faire* economics for policies of state intervention. In laying the groundwork for the "welfare state," he also moved toward state capitalism. But the crisis of American capitalism, while peculiarly severe, was not merely national in character; it reflected a crisis in the international system brought on by the recession of the British free trade imperium. Slowly, the Roosevelt Administration abandoned economic nationalism for policies promoting a freer trade. In waging war on the Fascist states, Roosevelt also committed the United States to a far-reaching international program which, in the post-war era, actively promoted international trade and development and "contained" a Communist system which not only posed a potential military threat and eschewed democratic values but appeared to restrict the developmental possibilities of Western capitalism. Thus, in both the domestic and international spheres, in both the New Deal and internationalism, a new idealism rose with a new structure of power which exhibited a profound ambivalence between social democracy and state capitalism, progressive internationalism and a new free trade imperium.

But, if there was a world crisis of 1929–45 consisting of world depression and world war and if in the United States this crisis created a new democratic hegemony, what became of the political *losers* in this process? In America, some political constituencies broke up in the face of the new circumstances; others went over to the Roosevelt coalition, either conditionally or unconditionally. But the late nineteenth- and early twentieth-century world of hegemonic Republicanism did not abruptly or entirely disappear in 1932. Stripped of many of its working-class and black allies, uncertain even of the allegiance of the metropolitan upper class and many farmers, classical Republicanism retained the loyalties of unreconstructed Republicans in the provincial Midwest—the core of the American right wing in subsequent decades. The cultural traditions of political Republicanism and white Anglo-Saxon Protestantism were decisive, usually in combination with economic interest but sometimes against it. Small business was the nucleus of reactionary Republicanism.

The basic impetus of this core constituency was to restore the old *laissez-faire* capitalist order and its foreign policies of protectionism and Pacific First. In this project, the right could not always count on the support of the metropolitan upper class, which gravitated toward the internationalist and developmental aspects of the Democratic program, even though it was put off by signs of class conflict and popular idealism. The first opportunity for the right came in 1937. The apparent failure of the New Deal's economic policies, its tolerance of labor radicalism, and its effort to alter the Constitutional balance allowed the Republican right to recover strength among both the middle class and the working class, especially in provincial areas of Republican tradition. But the attempts of the right to move on to the offensive against the New Deal were put off by World War II, which imposed a policy of patriotic unity on the political parties. After the war, the right-wing Republicans were unable to unite. An old "isolationist" group opposed an American commitment to Western Europe, while a new interventionist group supported it. When the scene shifted to Asia, the right was finally able to coalesce around the symbolic figures of Douglas MacArthur and Joseph McCarthy. Senator McCarthy denounced the New Deal and internationalist foreign policy as equivalents of treason.

McCarthyism was a failure. The Senator was censured by the same broad coalition of liberal Democrats, Southern Democrats, and moderate Republicans that had defeated the "isolationists"—that is, the nationalists—in Congress before World War II. For the right-wing core, there was one consolation in McCarthy's defeat. An Irish-German Catholic himself, McCarthy demonstrated real strength with American Catholics who for reasons of ethnic origin were disillusioned with Democratic foreign policy. The old right began to develop new allies.

Two other post-war forces redounded to the benefit of the Republican reaction. The economic boom in the West and parts of the South gave a new lease on life for *laissez-faire* philosophy; and the Democratic party's advocacy of civil rights for black Americans in the early 1960s alienated many whites, especially Southern whites. A Western Senator, Barry Goldwater of Arizona, made a special appeal to the West and South in his Presidential campaign of 1964. But he strayed too far from traditional Republican constituencies, and he found that the Kennedy Presidency had reversed the Catholic shift to the right.

In many political quarters, both left and right, the 1960s

gave rise to the hope that a new critical election and realignment of parties was at hand. Under the pressure of racial issues and the Vietnam War, the Roosevelt coalition of the Democrats came unstuck. Richard Nixon was the first President to pursue self-consciously a policy of burying the Roosevelt coalition. Nixon's grand strategy was to attract Catholics, the West, and the South to the Republican minority by exploiting the issues of race and war. Such moderation as he exhibited on these questions was in large part dictated by the chastening precedents of McCarthy and Goldwater. Nixon failed to dent the Democratic majorities in Congress. Although he won reelection by a large majority in 1972, he was later forced to resign from office by the same coalition of Democrats and moderate Republicans that previous right-wing emergencies had called into being.

Nixon's internationalist attitude in foreign policy, which led him to assume the burden of an Asian war inherited from the Democrats, was not representative of the right wing of his party. A paradox of Nixon's internationalism was that, as a committed partisan, he retained all of the traditional conservative fears of internationalist institutions, such as the Central Intelligence Agency, which would have been appropriate to a Republican nationalist. A second paradox was that, while himself withdrawing ground troops from Vietnam, he wished to exploit public hostility to the anti-war movement. This curious complex of attitudes created Nixon's peculiar vulnerability to the Watergate incident. As a Republican internationalist, Nixon reacted harshly to the anti-war candidacy of Senator George McGovern. As a conservative Republican, he bypassed the security agencies in an effort to undermine that candidacy. The first attitude led to the Watergate apartment complex. The second eventually led back into the White House.

When his day of destiny came, he looked around, innocently, saw the gargoyles of Anti-Christ staring and sneering at him from everywhere, and innocently he reached out to crush them.

•   •   •

In this grave we have put, for whatever future God has in His mind, a young man who, in five gruesome years, was stoned by the genteel into an ultimate fatigue. We do not crave his fate. We dread it. But we are ready to face it. We, too, have seen the gargoyles stare and sneer at us. We, too, are reaching out to crush them. We mean it. We are McCarthyites.

William S. Schlamm
"Across McCarthy's Grave"
National Review, May 18, 1957

I

THE SPECTRE
OF THE NEW DEAL

1

THE
REPUBLICAN HEGEMONY

"The crystallization in the past dozen years or so of an American conservative movement," Frank S. Meyer, an editor of the *National Review*, wrote in the mid 1960s, "is a delayed reaction to the revolutionary transformation of America that began with the election of Roosevelt in 1932."[1] Although it is debatable whether there was a "revolutionary transformation" of the United States in the 1930s, the right wing of the Republican Party insists that there was such a development, that it commenced with the Great Depression and the election of Franklin D. Roosevelt as President, and that it was called the New Deal.

From the beginning, a section of the G.O.P. viewed the Roosevelt Administration as a "collectivist" offensive against a free America. In *The Challenge to Liberty*, serialized in the *Saturday Evening Post* and published as a book in 1934, former President Herbert Hoover attacked the Democratic Administration for promoting "national regimentation" in the style of Fascist and Communist states. At the Republican Convention in 1936, party orators castigated the "Un-American attitude of setting class against class." On his election to the U.S. Senate in 1938, Robert A. Taft began his sustained critique of "New Deal Socialism"—a notion that became basic to right-wing Republican thinking.

The reaction to the New Deal was delayed, first, because the

3

Republican Party was reduced to impotence in a series of crushing electoral defeats from 1930 to 1936. After the Presidential election of 1936, the Republicans held only eighty-nine seats in the House of Representatives and sixteen in the Senate of which only ten were in conservative hands. The immediate response of most Republican politicians to this deluge was to retreat into silence or make an expedient accommodation to political reality. From this traumatic period, conservative Republicans, particularly in the Midwest, were to emerge the same yet different. They did not change their basic principles, which remained the ones in which they had always believed. But "conservative" Republicans often became "right-wing" Republicans. Where they had once ruled the country with supreme confidence from the Civil War to the Great Crash, they now plotted their return to power and the restoration of the old regime as a bitter faction determined to revenge themselves on the enemies who had deprived them of their heritage.

Over the question of the New Deal, the Republican Party ultimately split three ways. The "Western Progressives" tended to support the Roosevelt Administration on domestic social policy, although many later opposed intervention in World War II. The "Eastern" wing at first opposed the New Deal, but once the reform wave had passed, adjusted to the new order and, in addition, actively endorsed the "internationalist" foreign policies of the Roosevelt and Truman Administrations. Actually, this "Eastern" sentiment was metropolitan in character[2] and sometimes found an echo in Republican constituencies in the larger cities outside the Northeast. As the Progressives either moved out of the party in support of the New Deal or in some cases moved to the right in opposition to it, the "regular Republicans" in the Midwest and West consolidated their control of the party apparatus and became the nucleus of right-wing Republicanism for the next two decades. This tendency was strong in the rural areas, small towns, and smaller cities of these regions and in the provincial areas of the Northeast as well. Among themselves, the regulars varied in their attitude from tolerance for mild reform through standpat conservatism to outright reaction. For many, a return to power would suffice to restore their equanimity and a posture of responsible conservatism. During subsequent Republican Administrations, however, there would always be irreconcilables who would demand the repeal of the New Deal.

After Roosevelt ran into difficulties in his second term, the Republican Party recovered its fortunes in the 1938 election, and continued to make steady progress in the off-year elections of 1942, 1946, and 1950. But there was no major reactionary offensive mounted against the New Deal in the 1930s. After 1938, there were the first stirrings of such an effort in the operations of the Dies Committee and the "conservative coalition" in Congress. But the Roosevelt Administration soon regained the initiative over the question of intervention in World War II. After a promising beginning in the 1946 elections, right-wing Republicanism was again thrown on the defensive in the immediate post-war years over foreign policy. Not only the "Eastern internationalist" wing of the party but also a conservative element led by Senator Arthur Vandenberg of Michigan rendered "bi-partisan" support to the foreign policy of the Truman Administration. The right wing of the party was divided internally by the dilemma posed by the Cold War for its "isolationist" heritage—actually better described as an hostility to European intervention. But the central question of the day concerned intervention in Europe against the Soviet Union. It was not until the victory of the Chinese Revolution in 1949 that the right was able to establish internal unity and to operate effectively on a major foreign policy question. Once this "Who lost China?" campaign was launched, it became the occasion for the great assault, long delayed and somewhat veiled, on the New Deal and all its works. This was "McCarthyism."

Now that the New Deal reforms have been assimilated and corporate capitalism has been reconciled in a grudging manner to the role of the federal government as an instrument of economic stabilization, it takes an effort of imagination to recreate the social crisis of the 1930s. Not only contemporary historians of leftist persuasion but many observers of the time including Franklin Roosevelt himself argued that the primary mission of the New Deal was to "save capitalism." Yet the right regards the 1930s as its Gethsemane. There was no revolution, but clearly *something* of importance occurred to release a reactionary social force which persists into the present.

There was the Great Depression. By 1933, the unemployment rate was 25 per cent; industrial production had fallen by 50 per cent; the gross national product by 40 per cent. A deflation of these proportions was more than an economic problem; it called into question the legitimacy of the social system. Marxists argued that American capitalism had finally exhausted its ability to find domestic outlets for capital investment and have maintained since that this problem was solved only by rearmament for war and by post-war imperialist expansion. The Marxists saw a way out of the depression in Socialism—a system of planned development and public control of the means of production, presumably under working class hegemony.

The Keynesians also believed that American capitalism had reached "maturity" and therefore stagnation with the closing of the frontier and the decline in population growth, but were content to recommend compensatory federal spending as a means to force economic growth.

The old Progressives denounced the "monopolies" which they believed had induced a depression through high and exploitative "administered prices." The monopolies, they maintained, had brought about oversavings, underconsumption, and a maldistribution of income. In their judgment, American capitalism would recover much of its vitality if the monopolies were broken up, industries regulated by government, and income redistributed through progressive tax measures. Even big business lost its faith in the "American System" and favored for a time the creation of a "business commonwealth" which would undertake "national planning" for the common good under the auspices of the National Recovery Act.

When the depression finally passed, so did most of the explanations that located the crisis in inherent structural deficiencies in American capitalism. With varying emphases, economic historians have since given more stress to the dislocations of World War I. In this account, the European economy was weakened by the prostration of the losers of the war in Central Europe, especially Germany, and by the withdrawal of the Soviet Union into a form of autarchy. Great Britain was no longer economically strong enough to guarantee an international system characterized by a free flow of trade and investment, and the United States was too immature politically to take its place. Consequently, when the business cycle turned down, a normal deflation quickly turned into a disastrous world-wide depression in which international trade collapsed and nations engaged in an economic war of competitive tariff increases, currency depreciations, and bilateral trade agreements.

Herbert Hoover himself endorsed this explanation and added that the mild upturn of 1932 would have been the beginning of a general recovery if the Roosevelt Administration had not frightened business by abandoning the gold standard and wrecking the World Economic Conference of 1933. Hoover, however, was much more of an internationalist than the right wing of the party with which he subsequently became identified. The right was content to stress the domestic policies of the New Deal which, it said, destroyed business confidence and discouraged private investment, particularly after the conclusion of the NRA phase of the New Deal. Had it not been for the demagogic attacks of the Democrats on business and their irresponsible fiscal policies, the right maintained, economic recovery would have been achieved before World War II through the normal recuperative processes of the business cycle.

Not much given to theoretical speculation or ideological commitment, the American people simply rejected the ruling party in 1932. This was the Republican Party, which had controlled the White House, except for the tenures of Grover Cleveland and Woodrow Wilson, since its victory in the Civil War. Before the 1890s, there was a relatively even balance between the parties. Presidential elections were extremely close, and the Democrats often had control of at least one house of Congress. But the Democrats had the misfortune of occupying the White House at the time of the "panic of 1893"—a massive depression in which unemployment was estimated to run as high as 20 per cent. Grover Cleveland, a "Gold Democrat" responsive to Eastern business interests, was in 1896 repudiated by his own party, which nominated William Jennings Bryan, a monetary inflationist who advocated "free silver." The nomination of Bryan and the absorption of the Populist movement into the party only made matters worse for the position of the Democrats in the industrial centers of the East and Midwest. Although the Populists have been accused of a multitude of sins they did not commit in the way of ethnic prejudice, they certainly had a Protestant fundamentalist cast which could not endear them to the Catholic and Jewish immigrant working class that constituted the party's base east of the Mississippi and north of the Mason-Dixon line. Bryan's program of inflation was geared to the farmer and the debtor and offered the prospect of higher prices for the worker and consumer. Repudiating both the Cleveland Administration and the Bryan candidacy, the American people elected William McKinley by a substantial majority in 1896.

What ensued until the election of Roosevelt is what has been called the "system of 1896."[3] The Republican Party appealed not only to the provincial Midwest and the upper and middle classes of the metropolitan centers but made inroads among the "new immigrants" from Southern and Eastern Europe in the cities. For the next several decades, the Republican Party was the majority party in the United States and dominated the great cities and the Northeast and Midwest regions as a whole. More than ever, *both* parties developed sectional bases. Where competitive two-party politics had once existed in thirty-six states, this number fell by half after 1896. Wilson was elected in 1912 only when the Republican vote was divided between William Howard Taft, the Republican President, and the Progressive Party candidacy of Theodore Roosevelt. Enjoying the advantages of incumbency and the peace issue, Wilson was reelected in 1916 by carrying the South, the Border states, and the West; the Republicans continued to hold most of the East and Midwest. For most of the period, the Republican conservatives had as many difficulties from their "insurgent" wing in the trans-Mississippi West—the sparsely populated Great Plains and Rocky Mountains—and the Progressive movement in the East as from the Democratic Party. The system of 1896 was an historic irony; the party of business and the American Protective Association, the anti-Catholic secret society in the Midwest, was the political beneficiary of an economic depression and a shift in the immigrant vote.

The Republican regime did not rigidly pursue a policy of *laissez-faire* since it was willing to provide indirect subsidies to business. But it did avoid massive federal expenditures, particularly for social welfare, and therefore minimized taxes and kept the budget in balance and the national debt low. According to Republican doctrine, the best guarantee of popular well-being was a healthy economy organized by private capital. This was bourgeois government in a rather pure form. The party was dominated by Americans of Anglo-Saxon and North European heritage. Although big business was opposed to a cut-off of its supply of cheap labor, most of the party joined with Southern and Western Democrats to pass immigration restriction legislation in the early 1920s. The quota system of these laws was devised as a covert means of enforcing a racialist theory of a hierarchy in descending order of Anglo-Saxons, North Europeans, East and South Europeans, and Orientals. Foreign policy was expansionist but did not require large military expenditures, since it was designed to avoid war with major powers.

Until the 1930s, this system was harassed but not overthrown by its opponents. Seen from a national perspective, the struggles of the labor movement and the campaigns of the Socialist Party were not decisive. Though run primarily by men of German and Irish heritage, the American Federation of Labor was partially Anglo-Saxon and Republican in sentiment, and opposed to immigration. The important opposition to Republican hegemony was agrarian and sectional. Defeated, impoverished, and resentful, the South stood apart in an incongruous alliance with urban immigrant political machines in the North run by Irish Catholics. Farmers in the Great Plains and miners in the Rocky Mountains sometimes turned radical. The Progressive movement organized in some areas a "farmer-labor" opposition, but was essentially middle class in spirit, amorphous and contradictory, with metropolitan and provincial wings. The Progressives had their day when Wilson was able to combine several of these streams of opposition against a divided Republican Party.

In 1932, the Democratic Party had better luck than in 1896. Recovering from the cultural reaction against Bryan, the party regained much of its strength among Catholic immigrant workers in the cities by nominating Al Smith, governor of New York, who was of German/Irish heritage, for President in 1928. The depression consolidated these gains and also set the stage for a gradual abandonment of a historic commitment to the Republican Party since the Presidency of Lincoln by the black population. The nomination of Roosevelt in 1932, who had been influenced by the Progressive movement and had a liberal record as governor of New York, appealed to the urban middle-class Progressives. Roosevelt was also attractive to Western Progressives in the Republican Party. To these advantages, Roosevelt could add the traditional base of the Democratic Party in the South and Border states and in the urban immigrant machines of the North. He was elected with almost 60 per cent of the two-party vote. Only six *Eastern* states went Republican.

The "New Deal coalition" put an end to the Republican system of 1896. In composition, this coalition was incongruous, but uniformly repugnant to the Republicans. Its more traditional and more conservative elements, the South and the urban immigrant machines, were offensive to the party that had preserved the Union and restricted immigration. The urban middle-class liberals and Western Progressives had harassed Republican conservatives from within and without the party for several decades. What was actually frightening, however, was the central role in the new Democratic coalition of a militant labor movement. The Congress of Industrial Organizations, begun on the initiative of John L. Lewis of the United Mine Workers in 1935 as a committee of the AFL, organized millions of workers and carried out a campaign of militant strikes in the middle and late 1930s. Labor's Nonpartisan League, an arm of the CIO, played a substantial role in the reelection of Roosevelt in 1936. And operating on the left wing of the New Deal and the CIO was the Communist Party. After abandoning the left sectarianism of the "Third Period" in 1934 and inaugurating its "Popular Front" policy of cooperation with reform forces, the Communist Party became a significant factor in American politics. With a peak membership of 100,000, the party was influential in middle-class reform and foreign policy organizations. It controlled some important immigrant associations. Its impact on the intelligentsia helped to disseminate a congenial viewpoint through the schools, the press, entertainment industry, and other organs of culture. Approximately one quarter of the CIO unions were led by Communists.

For traditional Republicans, the 1930s was a world turned upside down. Joseph W. Martin, Jr., for many years the Republican leader in the House, later explained:

> Now, with the battles of the Thirties far behind us and the reforms forged in those controversies accepted as a normal part of our life, one cannot so easily understand what a wrench many of the innovations of the New Deal caused Republicans of my bent and background. American society as it had existed for a generation or so before the Depression was certainly not a perfect society, as anyone knew who had, like myself, lived close to the hardships of New England mill towns. Nevertheless it was a good society and, at its own peculiar pace, a progressive society. Above all, in a world that was flying faster than anyone realized into the clutches of regimentation it was a society that cherished the individual and fostered his enterprise.[4]

The Democratic Party was no longer a sectional party with a beachhead in the cities; it was a national party which controlled the cities. The new immigrants, which had been distributed between the two major parties, were now largely concentrated in what was the ruling party. The baneful cultural influences of the metropolis, which had been held in check by the hegemony of the better elements, now had direct access to the seats of power. Class conflict, which had been diffused by Republican dominance in a context of sectional, agrarian, and ethnic antagonisms, was now the central issue of national politics. Republican politicians denounced Roosevelt for promoting "class hatred" from the White House. In his famous speech accepting the Democratic nomination for President in 1936, Roosevelt devoted himself exclusively to an attack on the "economic royalists":

> For too many of us the political equality we once had won was meaningless in the face of economic inequality. A small group had concentrated into their own hands an almost complete control over other people's property, other people's money, other people's labor—other people's lives. For too many of us life was no longer free; liberty was no longer real; men could no longer follow the pursuit of happiness.
>
> Against economic tyranny such as this, the American citizen could appeal only to the organized power of Government. The collapse of 1929 showed up the despotism for what it was. The election of 1932 was the people's mandate to end it. Under that mandate it is being ended.[5]

Actually, Roosevelt was using the Progressive rhetoric of opposition to the monopolies rather than a rhetoric of class struggle. Roosevelt complained:

> There was no place among this royalty for our many thousands of small business men and merchants who sought to make a worthy use of the American system of initiative and profit. They were no more free than the worker or the farmer. Even honest and progressive-minded men of wealth, aware of their obligation to their generation, could never know just where they fitted into this dynastic scheme of things.[6]

Nonetheless, not all of the opponents of the Administration would forgive Roosevelt's reference to America's greatest capitalists and most substantial citizens as the "resolute enemy within our gates."

The Republicans' perception of the political situation in the 1930s, though often exaggerated by their fears for the worst, was grounded in the reality. It is a fair inference that class conflict in America in that decade was more intense than at any other time in the twentieth century. Although reliable empirical surveys of the class base of the electoral vote in the 1930s do not exist, the Survey Research Center of the University of Michigan found that class-based voting in the post-war period was strongest in 1948 when Truman ran a New-Deal-style campaign based on denunciations of Wall Street and the fear of a renewed depression. In that election, Truman received almost 80 per cent of the blue collar vote, and among workers those most likely to vote Democratic were those who had grown to maturity in the 1930s.[7]

The policies of the New Deal were no more agreeable to conservative Republicans than the social forces that supported them. The New Deal alternated between, and often combined, policies promoting state capitalism and social democracy. Judging them against the standards of the Republican Era, unreconstructed Republicans opposed both tendencies. In the "First New Deal," Roosevelt based his government on a policy of national unity and cooperation with big business. The keystone to this policy was the National Recovery Administration of which the model was the collaboration of government and industry during the First World War. The NRA employed wartime methods of patriotic mobilization in "Blue Eagle" campaigns and marches, and allowed industrial groups and trade associations to restrict the "unfair competition" of price reductions and to establish codes of "industrial self-government" controlling prices and output in their industries. In effect, the NRA sponsored cartels. Its operations were retarded by opposition from organized labor and anti-monopoly Progressives, while its policies of maintaining prices and restricting competition underwrote economic scarcity rather than full production and economic recovery. The NRA was all but a dead letter when the Supreme Court declared it unconstitutional in 1935.

While large corporations embraced the NRA, rank-and-file Republicans were often skeptical and viewed it as a venture into state capitalism and even Fascism in violation of classical capitalist principles. Their opposition to the ruling party intensified when Roosevelt dropped his policy of national unity and turned his Administration sharply to the left in the "Second New Deal" beginning in 1935. In large part, Roosevelt was forced to the left by the failure of the NRA and the desertion by business of the Democratic Administration. From the beginning, businessmen were put off by the social forces expressing themselves through the Democratic Party and by the relatively slight representation of businessmen, apart from the NRA, in the Administration. They viewed with distaste the New Deal's early reform measures in the areas of public power and relief, not to mention investigations and reforms of banking and the stock market. As the economy began a slow recovery, unbalanced budgets were regarded with more suspicion. In 1934, conservative Democrats and wealthy businessmen founded the American Liberty League which began a large-scale propaganda campaign against the New Deal. Responding in kind, Roosevelt began to see himself as a latter-day Andrew Jackson fighting the forces of "entrenched greed."

Roosevelt was also pressed to the left by the inherent logic of his political coalition. He could not maintain the support of middle-class liberals and organized labor without enacting programs agreeable to them. The election of 1934 strengthened the liberal/labor forces in Congress. Operating outside of the orbit of the Administration were politicians and movements of the left or pseudo-left, such as Huey Long, who were ready to move into any political vacuum. Accordingly, the Administration obtained legislation in 1935 for social security, progressive tax reform, and collective bargaining. These excursions into social democracy confirmed the worst fears of the Republican right.

One of the several ironies of the New Deal was that its turn to the left was carried out under the banner of Wilsonian Progressivism. Unlike the "New Nationalism" of Theodore Roosevelt's 1912 campaign, Wilson's "New Freedom" rejected the idea of state intervention as a positive good in favor of restoration of competitive capitalism through selective reform. During its second term, the Roosevelt Administration pressed forward the Progressive conception of free enterprise through revival of anti-trust suits by the Department of Justice and through the hearings of the Temporary National Economic Committee. At one point, the good news was carried to a conference of small businessmen, which dissolved farcically into Red-baiting and right-wing denunciation of the Administration. Despite this ideological façade, the right was correct to evaluate the Second New Deal as centralizing in its main tendencies—the "welfare state" and federal spending programs to counteract depression. This result was some distance from Socialism. Even the Tennessee Valley Authority, the nearest thing to a federal takeover of productive enterprise, was justified in Progressivist terms as a competitive "yardstick" which could be used to measure the real efficiency of private utilities.

The right also had some grounds for its suspicions of the social forces working through the Democratic Party. The leadership of the Administration was always in the hands of middle-class—or in the case of Roosevelt himself upper-class—reformers. Its "class rhetoric" was the rhetoric of middle-class Progressivism. Its massive vote had many conservative, as well as docile and politically unaware, components. But the most dynamic force working during the decade was a relatively class-conscious labor movement in direct conflict with capital. The relations between Roosevelt and John L. Lewis were never good, but the CIO was an essential element in the New Deal scheme of things. The AFL was forced by competitive pressure to imitate the CIO's methods of industrial organization and political activism. The CIO was not officially Socialist, much less Communist, but left-wing organizers were many and influential, and "progressive" ideas were in the air. Left-oriented trade unionism did not always command the largest voting bloc, but it did command industrial workers, organization, money, and political will. For a time, it also seemed to have a decisive position in the logic of events.

In *The Decline of the American Republic,* John T. Flynn, who was in the early 1930s a liberal reformer of the malfeasance of high finance on the staff of the Pecora Committee but later became a right-wing writer and professional critic of Roosevelt and the New Deal, summarized the extreme conservative response to the turn of events represented by the New Deal:

> What had gone before was a confused hodgepodge of measures—some socialist, some fascist, most of them mere devices for keeping people on the dole. The student of this epoch must never lose sight of this fact—that the so-called first New Deal was not in any sense a communist or socialist operation. It had actually found little favor with the communists or socialists, in spite of the fact that large numbers of them managed to insert themselves into the numerous collectivist agencies set up in 1933.
>
> The crackpot schemes had failed; most were liquidated. And recovery remained aloof. The socialist cabal, now well schooled in the stratagems of a socialist Europe—in Germany, France, Italy and England—saw its opportunity here. They now appeared in Washington to confront a triumphant but frustrated and planless President with a workable plan.
>
> This was the hour of fate for America. We can see now and understand clearly the overall program of the socialist revolutionaries to make a socialist America—without making any *lawful* change in our great charter of freedom, the Constitution of the United States.[8]

2

TRUE LIBERALISM
AND AMERICANISM

For the right, it was a sacrilege for New Deal "collectivism" to call itself "liberal." The liberal democracy of the welfare state and aggressive trade unionism was a "false liberalism." It was, rather, the right wing of the Republican Party which stood for "true liberalism." The basic viewpoint of true liberalism derived from, as Herbert Hoover put it, the "deep realization that economic freedom cannot be sacrificed if political freedom is to be preserved."[1] In other words, political freedom was a function of the decentralization, independence, and individualism promoted by pure capitalist economy. Any deviation in the direction of central planning, bureaucracy, and federal activity would necessarily involve some degree of abridgement of political liberty. Indeed, such a trend would be truly reactionary since it would be a throwback to the economic policies of the absolute monarchies. It also followed that a defense of property rights and the unregulated market mechanism was a defense of "Liberty" as such, a term which the right preferred as suggesting better than "freedom" the organic relationship between principles in the economic and political realms.

This view is sometimes referred to as "19th century liberalism" or "classical liberalism." In the founding editorial of *The Freeman*, a leading right-wing intellectual magazine of the postwar period, John Chamberlain and Henry Hazlitt invoked this tradition: "It will be one of the foremost aims of the *Freeman* to clarify the concept of individual freedom and apply it to the problems of our time. Its basic principles and broader applications have long been embodied in the classic liberal tradition. That tradition has always emphasized the moral autonomy of the individual. Real morality cannot exist where there is no freedom of choice."[2] This doctrine was built on the foundations of English political economy which maintained that not only maximum efficiency and full production but the common good was served by the rational pursuit of self-interest in a competitive environment of free markets. If morally autonomous, "economic man" was also characterized by a perfect rationality, selfishness, and materialism. The "Manchester school" in England showed the same spirit of capitalist militancy that right-wing Republicanism was later to exhibit.

In America, true liberalism meant true Republicanism. It was not actually a theory rigorously deduced from a set of premises, but an ideology originating in a tradition. The tradition was inherited from the period of Republican political dominance from the Civil War to the turn of the century—the "Gilded Age" as Mark Twain christened it. Thus, classical English liberalism might demand international free trade but true liberalism was compatible with protective tariffs, which had been a key element in American industrialization after the Civil War. *Laissez-faire* might forbid government subsidies as conducive to inefficiency, but true liberalism countenanced not only the tariff but huge land grants, tax benefits, and other subsidies to business which ate its fill at what Vernon Louis Parrington called the "Great Barbecue." Although government was allowed to provide business with indirect subsidies, it was discouraged from undertaking direct expenditures for economic development under its own aegis as the propertied classes turned away from the Hamiltonian doctrine of state-sponsored development which no longer seemed necessary.

The Gilded Age celebrated the major traditions of conservative implication in American history. The Constitution's restrictions on popular democracy were one such tradition, particularly after the interpretation given it by the late 19th-century Supreme Court. The separation of powers, states' rights, and judicial review could be seen as protections to "individual liberty" against the tyranny of popular majorities. The tradition of the Protestant Reformation was the source of the religious convictions of most of the Republican constituency which was Anglo-Saxon and North European in origin. English Puritanism in particular stood for an austere individualism which accorded well with capitalist activity. The Protestant Reformation, indeed, supplied the English bourgeoisie—at the time mainly merchants and commercially oriented landed gentry—with an ideology in the English Revolution of the 17th century. In his *Second Treatise of Government,* John Locke developed a more secular rationale for the ultimate triumph of the substantial and moderate elements of the English gentry in the "Glorious Revolution" in 1689, which was incorporated into the American political tradition through the American Revolution.

Locke's doctrine of "natural rights" was firmly rooted in commitments to the propertied classes. These rights were derived from a hypothetical "state of nature" in which society and the social compact had their origins. In this condition, man enjoyed unrestricted freedom. The original and primary right was the right to property in any part of nature in which a man invested his labor. In the formation of society, man limited his freedom only to the extent required by agreed-upon social purposes. His essential control over his own person remained, since the reason for the formation of society was not to surrender this control, but only to accomplish common tasks not otherwise possible. Locke's approach was "scientific" since it claimed to derive *rights* from hypothetical *facts* of nature. Property rights were primary because they were originally exercised in the state of nature, and in a sense other human rights only represented a man's reserved property right in his own person. In Locke's scheme, freedom was not the fulfillment of man's essence, as in Aristotle's concept of virtue, but his freedom of action, for good or ill, in a precivilized state.

In *The Liberal Tradition in America,* Louis Hartz argues that

both left and right have been absorbed into a common mainstream of "irrational Lockeanism" in American history. The
meaning of this claim is that no decisive political force in American history has operated beyond the parameters of "democratic capitalism" of which Locke is the classical theorist. However, there is a tension, both historical and theoretical, in the
tradition of democratic capitalism. Robert Green McCloskey
has pointed to a dualism in the heritage of the English and
American Revolutions and placed Republican conservatism and
popular democracy on opposite sides of the division. Essentially, the thesis that personal liberty depends upon property
rights is the revolutionary bequest of the "sober-sided English
middle class." At its inception, the theory justified property restrictions on the franchise, which placed Parliament under the
control of a narrow stratum of propertied wealth until the Reform Act of 1832; England did not have universal suffrage
until the 20th century. The idea of pure political democracy
was advanced in the English Revolution not by the commercial
leaders but the "people"—the workers, artisans, and free-
holders supporting the "Leveller" movement. Their ideas were
based not on Locke or any other 17th-century "scientific"
thinker but on the Christian Protestant doctrine of the equality
of men in the eyes of God, based on the common possession of
an immortal soul.

In the United States, Jeffersonian democracy drew on this
tradition of radical Protestantism and on a similar constituency
of workers, artisans, and small farmers. At the end of the 18th
century, radical democracy in America was distinctly more secular in tendency and was inspired not only by Locke but by a
"natural rights" tradition going beyond the English political
theorists to Greek and Medieval civilization. According to the
latter, the rights of man were "natural" not because they originated in material causes but because they followed from the *essence* of man as rational and capable of self-determination. The
doctrine of natural rights and the heritage of the left wing of
the Reformation were the foundation for a democratic human-

ism which did not derive from a Newtonian scientific perspective or regard property rights as original and fundamental.

True liberalism took its stand on the more strictly bourgeois side of the democratic capitalist dichotomy. Its primary moral commitment was to "individual liberty" not to popular government, which was seen as an actual threat to liberty. While democratic humanism could fade into a spiritual ionosphere or be crushed beneath the weight of state bureaucracy, economic necessity, and class divisions, Republican "liberalism" frankly attempted to base itself in economic reality. Justice was achieved not through substantive equality but through the opportunity, if not always strictly "equal opportunity," which a system of free markets, competition, and individual liberty afforded. Ultimately, social standing was a rough indicator of moral standing, as hard work, self-denial, and individual merit led necessarily to material improvement. Failure was generally deserved.

Not surprisingly, the Gilded Age embraced Social Darwinism as a scientific confirmation of its political attitude. The fate of animal species in biological evolution, the "survival of the fittest," was roughly analogous to individual man's fate in the competitive struggle under free-market capitalism. William Graham Sumner, a social scientist at Yale, popularized the new marriage of capitalism and Social Darwinism: "Let it be understood that we cannot go outside of this alternative: liberty, inequality, survival of the fittest; not—liberty, equality, survival of the unfittest. The former carries society forward and favors all its best members; the latter carries society downwards and favors all its worst members."[3] From the application of Darwinian ideas to society, it was a relatively short step to the stereotyping of certain classes, ethnic groups, and races as losers in the competitive struggle. These theories did not necessarily share the same premises and were not always consistent with one another. Republican liberalism stressed the moral qualities of the individual as the decisive factor in success. Social Darwinism was based on an environmental/genetic interpretation of society.

Still, the apparent failure of whole races and ethnic groups opened the way to a more strictly racist and genetic argument. Henry Cabot Lodge, Sr., for one, did not blanch at this possibility. While the Republican Party remained the trustee of the black population, it would be inhibited from any official endorsement of racist views. The party, which had inherited much of the constituency of the anti-Catholic American Party of the 1850s, was suspicious of foreign immigration, but on "nativist" or anti-foreign rather than formally racist grounds. But just as Social Darwinism lay in the background of true liberalism, so racialism stood close behind Social Darwinism.

True liberalism, then, faded into a nativist "Americanism." It was not identical with it as Louis Hartz suggests. Beginning with its espousal by the Know-Nothings in the 1850s, "Americanism" was a nationalist and xenophobic ideology and not merely a commitment to liberal capitalism. In the 19th century, it stood for opposition to the influx of foreign populations of non–Anglo-Saxon heritage. As a corollary, it was anti-Catholic, although anti-Catholicism also had roots in the religious struggles of the Reformation and popular suspicion of Catholicism as an authoritarian and anti-democratic force. As the major cities absorbed the foreign immigration, Americanism had its strongholds in provincial areas and tended to merge with a general suspicion of the cosmopolitanism and moral laxity of metropolitan culture.

The Republican Party had no monopoly on Americanism which was equally popular with the nonmetropolitan and nonimmigrant constituents of the Democratic Party. As World War I approached, Woodrow Wilson denounced "hyphenism"—that is, "hyphenated Americans" of recent foreign descent—from the White House. The world war brought tremendous pressure to bear on German-Americans and condoned the identification of nativism with patriotism. The build-up of nationalist and anti-foreign feeling during the war was deflected onto American radicals and East European immigrants in the great "Red Scare" when a strike wave in 1919 seemed to confirm the vague fear of revolution unloosed by the Russian Revolution in 1917.

The spearhead of Americanist reaction was the American Legion, a veterans organization founded at the end of World War I by American army officers in France as an anti-Communist bulwark to revolutionary unrest which was then sweeping through Europe and its armies. Anti-radicalism had always gone hand in hand with nativism, since radicalism was considered a "European disease" carried by immigrants. The repressive spirit of Americanism was also evident. If the respectable Anglo-Saxon provincial family, preferably running its own business, was quintessentially "American," then the urban immigrant, radical proletarian was surely "Un-American." The effort to connect radicalism with alien influences and to repress both had a long history going back to the Alien and Sedition Acts of the Administration of John Adams.

Beginning with the New Deal, modern Republican reaction had little to add to this scheme of true liberalism and Americanism, which combined the celebration of "individual liberty" with a repressive animus against Un-American elements. The right relied upon economists of the "Austrian school" and the "Chicago school" to keep alive the classical liberal tradition in economics and upon clever publicists to carry on the defense of Liberty. There were many unschooled volunteers ready to advance the spirit of Americanism. In *The Road to Serfdom,* published at the end of World War II and condensed in *The Reader's Digest,* Friedrich A. Hayek added a new string to the bow by applying the concept of "totalitarianism" to any economic system incorporating aspects of economic planning and government intervention. Developed by European intellectuals of the center to describe both Communism and Fascism, the idea of totalitarianism was taken up by liberal-Democratic intellectuals after the war and applied to "totalitarian liberals" who cooperated with Communists in Popular Front organizations. Hayek, however, saw totalitarian tendencies in any proponent of the welfare state, including anti-Communist liberals.

What was truly distinctive about the Republican reaction after 1932 was the rededication to old ideals and a new spirit of vengeance. The principles of true liberalism and Americanism were thrown on the defensive in the 1930s. Possibly, they had been permanently vanquished. These ideals were no longer held in the spirit of complacency and natural superiority of a ruling party. In the post-war period, they were believed defensively and consciously. If the proponents of these principles were to regain their old ascendancy, they would have to find new strategies and a new political will. If the ideals were to be accepted, they would have to be actively propagated in magazines, syndicated columns, lectures, and campus organizations.

Where the Republican right was most original was in the development of theories to explain its defeat and provide guides for its return to power. The theories invariably orbited around the questions of Socialism and Communism. While the Democratic Party later denied any association with either, these denials were disingenuous. We have noted that the Communist Party was a politically active force in the 1930s, often acting in concert with trade unions and reformers closely associated with the Democratic Party. A fair appraisal of the political line-up would have assigned the Communists a role as an important faction on the left wing of the New Deal coalition but certainly not a role as the hidden directorate of the Democratic Party. The later claim was made ever more insistently in Republican campaigns, and by 1944 it was trumpeted that "CIO-Communists" ran the party. Partly, the Republican right made this claim cynically as a presumably effective campaign tactic; and partly, as often happens, this claim was believed literally as projection of collective fears. The Democratic Party could be regarded as the Trojan horse of a militant labor movement and an Un-American intelligentsia and the latter, in turn, as the Trojan horse of Communism. By making several logical inferences of this kind, which had a certain air of inside knowledge, it was possible to take leave of political reality altogether.

This was a theory of "interlocking subversion" which held that Communists dominated whatever they contacted, either by superior organization and dedication or by the logic of events. If it was assumed, in making the journey from the left back to the center, that marginal contact with a Communist or even a fellow traveler was identical with, or the functional equivalent of, Communism, then one had a theory of "guilt by association." Possessing a surface logic, this theory proved a powerful political instrument. It could be difficult to handle, however, since the series of associative links might, in the minds of the even less sophisticated, continue their devastating march right into friendly territory. In *The Red Network* and other tracts, Elizabeth Dilling began in the 1930s and 1940s to raise questions about Robert Taft, H. L. Mencken, and other conservatives whose anti-Communism was not, perhaps, above suspicion. The more obvious target was the Eastern wing of the Republican Party which was willing to live with the New Deal. By such logic, Robert Welch, founder of the John Birch Society, concluded in the 1950s that Dwight Eisenhower, who, after all, had served under Roosevelt and had been the Eastern Republicans' candidate for President, was in fact a Communist. In effect, the counterrevolution could devour its children or at least its distant cousins.

A more moderate approach was the theory of "creeping Socialism." This concept had the virtue of concentrating on the mainstream of the modern Democratic Party rather than on the Communist Party. Its main premise was that the coalition of urban liberals and trade unions was actually working for the welfare state only as the prelude to a Socialist state. In *The Road Ahead*, widely distributed by the Republican National Committee in the 1950 elections and serialized in *The Reader's Digest*, a publication sympathetic to right-wing perspectives, John T. Flynn warned against a Communist fixation:

> In any case, the Cold War has had one significant effect. It has forced us to look at Russia for what she is and not as she was pictured to us when she was "our noble ally." And this has forced us to turn our attention to our American Communist movement. We have, as a consequence, been making war on the Communists. This has had one very serious by-product. It has dramatized the American Communist Party and its dupes as the chief internal enemy of our economic system and our form of government. And it is widely feared that a crisis here would present our native Communists with their great opportunity.

> This I hold is a mistake of the first magnitude. I insist that if every Communist in America were rounded up and liquidated, the great menace to our form of social organization would be still among us.[4]

Flynn explained that the other menace had its source not in Moscow but in London:

> Most of the countries in Europe have moved into the Socialist camp. The two which concern us most are Russia and Great Britain. Each has moved into Socialism by a different route. Each has organized its Socialist society upon a different model. But both are Socialist. Russia was conquered overnight by a sudden, violent revolutionary convulsion. Great Britain managed its revolution upon a peaceful and gradualist pattern. It moved into socialism a little at a time. The journey took almost 40 years.
> We are following not in the footstep of Russia, but in the footsteps of England. We are being drawn into socialism on the British gradualist model. We are well on the road—much further along than our people suspect.[5]

According to Flynn, American Socialists were following a gradualist strategy on the model of the Fabian Society. Just as the Fabian Socialists in Britain first worked with the Liberal Party and the trade unions for limited goals, such as the welfare state, so American Socialists worked within the Democratic Party and the labor unions for similar objectives. Just as the Liberal Party was ultimately superseded by the Labor Party and Socialist policies pursued, so the Democratic Party would suffer a similar fate and Socialism eventually come into the open. If anything, American Socialists were more clever than their British counterparts, since they did not admit to Socialist convictions and even claimed to be militant anti-Communists:

> The leaders of this movement now actually seek to outdo us in berating the Communists with whom they were marching together but two or three years ago. They are more dangerous because, as a matter of fact, they are now occupying positions of great power, have in their hands immense sections of our political machinery and are actually hailed as our brothers in the battle

against the Reds. Every day that passes reduces the power of the Communists to mislead us or to promote their program among us. But every day that passes enlarges the opportunities of our real internal enemies to confuse us, to arouse us and to entice us to travel the dark road that has led every country in Europe to its doom. Acting under false colors and a name designed to conceal their real purpose and using words chosen to deceive, they are now well advanced in a sneak attack upon our whole way of life.[6]

The masterminds of this "sneak attack" could be found among the Americans for Democratic Action, the AFL and the CIO, the Truman Administration, and the architects of the Fair Deal.

Flynn's version of the Un-American danger had the advantage of not depending upon the vitality of the Communist Party for its plausibility. It could therefore weather the 1950s and 1960s somewhat better than McCarthyism. It was more moderate in focusing upon the central forces in the Democratic Party, but at the same time less concrete, since the Socialists were in disguise. Like its Red variation, the creeping Socialism theory attempted to organize all of social reality to conform to the resentments of provincial Republicanism. If there was some pleasure for the right in the discovery that East European immigrants, and in particular Russian Jews, were the carriers of the Red infection, there was equal satisfaction in the knowledge that the Eastern upper class and the metropolitan intelligentsia had once again succumbed to their deranged Anglophilia which this time involved Socialist subversion. Both Communism and Socialism became symbols for whatever oppressed and displeased the Republican right. Anti-Communism and anti-Socialism could serve as outlets for *petit-bourgeois* resentment of the upper class or provincial envy of metropolitan opportunities. Writing in *The American Mercury* in 1936, Harold Lord Varney already sounded this chord:

Another interesting sidelight upon the inner dualism of the Roosevelt radicalism is shown by the marked preference of the Presidential family for revolutionists who come with the reassuring stamp of the prep school, college, and *Social Register*. For, try as they may to disguise the fact, the Roosevelts are never entirely comfortable with the rabble which they lead. Theirs is always the radicalism of the elite—a reaching down from on high to uplift the proletariat. Thus there has been a growth of a little coterie of Palm Beach Jacobins and coupon-clipping sans-culottes in the New Deal inner councils, bringing to the Roosevelt Revolution the warm glow of *richesse oblige* and the reassuring atmosphere of accepted clubs.[7]

Such people existed, but they were hardly representative of their class's reaction to the Roosevelt Administration. The right engaged in this attack on the "radical elite," which became a right-wing perennial, for its own internal reasons.

3

THE CRISIS OF THE NEW DEAL

A coherent right-wing Republican response to the New Deal was slow to develop in the 1930s. First, the right itself had to take form. A further reason for the delay was that the "First New Deal" offered a diffuse target for political attack. Another was that the political hegemony of the Democratic Party was so complete as to be dangerous to challenge directly. Several Senators who openly opposed the New Deal were swept away in the elections of 1934 and 1936. Major shifts within the Republican Party were taking place in response to the new political circumstances. Many Republican Progressives were appalled by the statist tendencies of the New Deal and began to shift to the right. However, the Progressive faction in Congress generally supported the social reforms of the 1930s, and the Roosevelt Administration made strenuous efforts to appeal to this group in its policies and in its appointments, such as Henry Wallace as Secretary of Agriculture and Harold Ickes as Secretary of the Interior. Some Progressives were later alienated from the Roosevelt Administration over the Constitutional issue posed by the Supreme Court plan and over the question of intervention in the war in Europe. After World War II, Progressivism, which had been in decline since World War I, disappeared from the Western wing of the party, as the old Progressives turned conservative, lost their political base, or moved into the Democratic

Party. Although some Progressives did find their way into right-wing politics, there was no genetic connection between the Progressive movement and the right. Rather, the movement broke up when confronted with the new issues posed by the Great Depression, issues which did not lend themselves to the moralizing style of the old reformers. In provincial areas, the base of the movement was also drying up as the mechanization of agriculture led to drastic reductions in the agricultural labor force and thus in the Progressive constituency.

Increasingly, the regulars were in control of the party both in the Midwest and the trans-Mississippi West. In provincial areas, including the Northeast, the regulars were the true nucleus of right-wing politics, defined as uncompromising opposition to the New Deal and a desire to govern by the principles of true liberalism and Americanism. Even in these areas, many Republicans subscribed to conservative or moderate views. Republican leaders with state-wide constituencies, such as governors and U.S. Senators, usually had to take a more moderate position in order to attract a broader vote, particularly during the heyday of New Deal popularity. Undiluted right-wing views first appeared in the U.S. House of Representatives among Congressmen with provincial Republican constituencies which held firm even during the Democratic sweeps of the 1930s. Harold Knutson of Minnesota, Leo Allen of Illinois, and Bartel Jonkman and Clare Hoffman of Michigan were representative of this tendency. Republican leaders in the House, such as Joseph Martin of Massachusetts and Charles Halleck of Indiana, were sympathetic to it.[1]

Before the Great Depression, the stronghold of Republican conservatism was in the East. During the 1930s, it was no longer possible to win elections in Eastern metropolitan areas without some modification of fundamental doctrine, although old-line Republicanism could still be maintained in provincial areas. The "Old Guard" political leadership and the corporate wealth to which it was responsive were thoroughly discredited by the depression and temporarily lost much of their influence. During the NRA, big business demonstrated that it was willing to drop *laissez-faire* for state capitalism and, after the New Deal passed, gingerly shifted toward a New Hamiltonian position. World War II completed the conversion, just as World War I had begun it.

There was, however, a faction of the national upper class, based on corporate wealth, which refused to adjust to the new realities. The leaders of this group were the masters of publishing empires. William Randolph Hearst supported Roosevelt in 1932, but he shifted the weight of his twenty-eight newspapers, various news services, thirteen magazines, and eight radio stations to the side of the Republicans in 1936. Right-wing columnists such as George Sokolsky and later Westbrook Pegler were syndicated by the Hearst enterprises. In the East, the most influential Hearst paper was the New York *Journal,* later the *Journal-American,* while Colonel Robert R. McCormick published the Chicago *Tribune,* the flagship of the right-wing press in America. The Chicago Tribune Company, controlled by a family trust, also owned the New York *Daily News,* published by McCormick's cousin, Joseph Patterson, and the Washington *Herald,* later *Times-Herald,* published by Eleanor Patterson. The *Daily News* supported the New Deal but broke with the Roosevelt Administration over intervention in World War II and, after the war, joined the *Tribune* in right-wing denunciation of the Democratic Administration. Eventually, the Roosevelt Administration retaliated against McCormick by encouraging Marshall Field III to publish a morning competitor to the *Tribune,* the Chicago *Sun.*

In 1935, the Hearst and McCormick-Patterson press controlled between them 20 per cent of the daily circulation and 36 per cent of the Sunday circulation in the United States.[2] The Hearst enterprises, however, almost suffered financial collapse in the 1930s, and many of the daily papers were subsequently sold off, although the Hearst interests continued to be the country's largest communications group as they diversified into magazines, television, and radio. The Chicago Tribune Company also had radio interests and in 1934 helped to organize the Mutual Broadcasting System. Mutual broadcast the right-wing commentator Fulton Lewis, Jr., who had a listening audience of 16 million, the largest in the country. The Hearst and McCormick interests were supported in their bitter opposition to the New Deal by smaller newspaper chains, such as that of Frank Gannett, which was based in upstate New York. Gannett was a darkhorse Presidential candidate in 1940 and founded the National Committee To Uphold Constitutional Government, later the Committee for Constitutional Government, to oppose Roosevelt's Supreme Court plan.

Another political instrument of the bourgeois right in the 1930s was the American Liberty League. Founded in 1934, the league was a bipartisan organization of conservative Democrats including the DuPont family and the Presidential nominees of 1924 and 1928, John W. Davis and Alfred E. Smith, allied with conservative capitalists of Republican views, such as J. Howard Pew, president of the Sun Oil Company. Among many other influential figures in the league, which had grown out of the Association Against the Prohibition Amendment, were Alfred P. Sloan of General Motors, then controlled by DuPont, and Ernest T. Weir of National Steel. The main effort of the league was to mount an anti–New Deal propaganda campaign which expounded the virtues of the Constitution, individual liberty, and free-market capitalism. The effort of corporate wealth to assume public leadership of opposition forces proved to be a political blunder, and the Roosevelt Administration speedily turned the Liberty League into a symbol of monied arrogance in the 1936 Presidential campaign. According to James A. Farley, the "Democratic National Committee's first 'battle order' was to ignore the Republican Party and to concentrate fire on the Liberty League." Alf Landon, the Republican Presidential candidate, denied any association with the league, but in fact consulted some of its members regularly. The DuPont and Pew families alone contributed over $1 million to the Republican campaign and one third of the members of the Republican finance committee were associated with the league. The Republican platform bore a family resemblance to Liberty League Document No. 83, *A Program for Congress,* and several members of the league served on the platform committee at the Republican Convention.[3]

Among the inhibitors of the development of a coherent right-wing political force was Herbert Hoover. A political liability of the first order, Hoover attempted to maintain party leadership during the 1930s and, as George Mayer has pointed out, "by provoking a large part of the party to organize against him, the ex-president delayed the rebirth of factionalism along clear cut ideological lines."[4] Hoover successfully put across his candidate for chairman of the Republican National Committee, Henry P. Fletcher, in 1934 and much to the chagrin of cautious candidates for political office, the committee issued ideological broadsides against the New Deal in the off-year elections. After the Democrats gained nineteen seats in the House and ten in the Senate, the way was cleared for a more moderate strategy in the 1936 campaign. Governor Landon, a moderate Progressive from Kansas, attempted to disassociate himself from Hoover, the Liberty League, the Eastern Old Guard, and big business. As the campaign progressed, however, the tone was increasingly set by denunciations of Socialist tendencies in the New Deal by the Hearst and McCormick press and by Republican politicians, in the end including Landon himself.

After Landon's defeat, Hoover once again tried to reassert political leadership by calling for a mid-term convention to set party policy. Landon and political realists in Congress blocked this move, and the outcome was a compromise policy committee which issued an innocuous report. The real breakthrough for the Republican right came from a crisis within the New Deal itself which seemed to confirm all that the right wing had been claiming, without much effect, throughout the 1930s. Although the Administration's economic policies during Roosevelt's first term had not obtained spectacular results, their effect seemed to be positive. By 1937, industrial production and the gross national product had regained 1929 levels, although unemployment was still 14 per cent because of the growth of the labor force in the intervening period. Since GNP and industrial production had fallen almost in half by 1933, progress was substantial. Then in 1937, these indices fell by 20 per cent. The Democratic Administration was now confronted with the "Roosevelt recession" which could not be pinned on Hoover. The result was a weakening in support for the Administration among lower and middle income groups.

At the same time, the CIO was engaged in militant "sitdown strikes" in an organizing drive in the automobile industry in Detroit. Neither Frank Murphy, Democratic Governor of Michigan, nor Roosevelt would intervene with force against the strikes despite intense pressure to do so. Middle-class Americans, many of them Roosevelt supporters, were clearly alarmed by these militant strikes, and according to the Gallup Poll, two-thirds of the public favored legislation and the use of force against them.[5] Finally, Roosevelt chose to present a plan to "pack" the Supreme Court, which had consistently declared New Deal social and economic legislation unconstitutional. The plan called for an additional justice for every Supreme Court justice over seventy years of age up to a number of six. The Republicans in Congress kept their peace and encouraged the Democrats to come apart over the issue. Senator Burton K. Wheeler of Montana, an old Progressive who had run for Vice President with Robert LaFollette on the 1924 Progressive ticket, emerged to lead the opposition to the plan from within the Democratic Party. Conservative Democrats, strongest in the South but also represented in the West and other sections, now had a safe issue on which to take a stand against an Administration they had long disliked. In the opinion polls, a slight majority of the public was opposed to Roosevelt's plan.[6] Even moderate liberals in the Democratic Party were disturbed by the plan's Caesaristic flavor. In the end it was defeated by a coalition of Republicans and conservative and moderate Democrats. The "Constitutional issue" was finally good politics.

In the first half of 1937, Roosevelt's popular support fell by five percentage points and in the first half of 1938 by another five points.[7] Faction-fighting within the Democratic Party intensified when Roosevelt attempted to purge powerful committee chairmen of conservative Democratic persuasion by supporting their opponents in the Democratic primaries of 1938. The Democratic Party was divided. Its working-class and lower-class support was demobilized by the recession. The sitdown strikes and Supreme Court plan intensified upper-class and middle-class opposition. In the 1938 elections, the Republicans gained six seats in the Senate and eighty in the House. The party reclaimed much of its old strength, particularly outside metropolitan areas, in the Midwest and East, although it remained weak in the Plain states and Far West. In Michigan, Governor Murphy was defeated for reelection. In Ohio and Pennsylvania, both major industrial states and locales of CIO activity, the Republican Party surged forward. Robert A. Taft was elected to the U.S. Senate from Ohio and in short order assumed leadership of the conservative wing of the party in the Senate and in the country as well.

The crisis of the New Deal prepared the way for an anti-Communist offensive, the dual purpose of which would be to affirm the principles of Americanism while rolling up the left flank of the Democratic Party. Earlier efforts along these lines had been relatively without effect. In the 1936 campaign, Roosevelt had shrugged off charges of Communist infiltration of his Administration. In 1934, James H. Rand, Jr., of Remington, Rand had claimed before a Congressional committee that pending legislation to regulate the stock exchange would move the country "along the road from Democracy to Communism." Rand was associated with the Committee for the Nation, which advocated a solution to the depression through monetary inflation. Rand cited the authority of Dr. William Wirt, an Indiana educator, who, when called to testify, could only point to the dinner party chatter of some middle-level federal officials whom he said referred to Roosevelt as the "American Kerensky." In 1935, the Hearst press orchestrated a national campaign against Communist subversion in the universities, with occasional local backing from the American Legion, but nothing much came of it.

When the New Deal was put on the defensive in 1937, there was a serious development on the anti-Communist front. In the spring, Martin Dies, a rightist Democrat from Texas, introduced a resolution, which almost passed, calling for an investigation of the sit-down strikes. He later followed up this initiative with a resolution to create a Special Committee on Un-American Activities. In 1938, this resolution was passed with bipartisan conservative support as well as some support from liberals who hoped to use the committee against native Fascist sects. In fact, the ideology of Americanism had been raised to the dignity of a special committee of the House. When elected to Congress in 1931, Dies's first act was to introduce a bill to suspend immigration to the United States for five years. Although led by a right-wing Democrat, the committee included two right-wing Republicans, Noah Mason of Illinois and J. Parnell Thomas of New Jersey. Thomas was immediately active in demanding an investigation of the Works Progress Administration's Federal Theatre and Writers Project, which he claimed was a "hotbed of Communists." The committee soon took after the project, and the next year it was killed by Congress.[8]

Although it made occasional passes at pro-Nazi groups, the Special Committee, whose mandate was annually renewed by Congress, devoted itself for the most part to attacks on the New Deal and New Deal allies with the intent of showing a connection to Communism. While the LaFollette Civil Liberties Committee in the Senate investigated the use of labor spies and goon squads against the unions, the Dies Committee tried to counter its impression by investigating Communism in the unions. In 1939, the committee moved in on the Communist Party, and the admission of its leader, Earl Browder, that he had traveled on false passports led to a federal conviction. After the conclusion of the Hitler-Stalin Pact in 1939, the Communist Party was vulnerable since it was in harsh opposition to the foreign policy of the Roosevelt Administration. Although it made some contribution to the passage of the Alien Registration Act of 1940 or Smith Act, which was directed at subversive aliens in the context of impending war, the Dies Committee much preferred to air the membership list of the American

League for Peace and Democracy, an anti-Fascist relic of the earlier Popular Front, since it included the names of prominent New Deal bureaucrats. In the following years, the committee looked into the WPA, the Tennessee Valley Authority, and wartime agencies, such as the Board of Economic Warfare, which were suspected of harboring New Dealers.

The Roosevelt Administration used various tactics to counter the Un-American activities investigations—infiltration of the committee with liberals, reduction of appropriations, preemptive investigations by the bureaucracy. None of these met with conspicuous success as long as Democratic majorities in Congress were steadily declining and the drift of domestic political events was in an unfavorable direction. The most promising moment for a counterattack came in 1944 after the CIO Political Action Committee's successful offensive against the Dies Committee in the Democratic primaries and Roosevelt's reelection in the fall. Roosevelt directed his House leaders to kill the committee, but John Rankin, an anti-Semitic Democrat from Mississippi, successfully executed a parliamentary maneuver which established it as a permanent standing committee of the House.

The election of 1938 marked the beginning of right-wing Republican reaction against the New Deal. As a result of the election, the party had sufficient strength to oppose the New Deal openly rather than covertly and had a new generation of leaders not directly associated with the Hoover Administration. The party also won on conservative issues—the Constitution, labor conflict, and New Deal economic policy. The Republican right was becoming more coherent and more confident. Working in harness with conservative Democrats in 1939, the Republicans put a halt to all social legislation, skirmished with the Administration over budgetary appropriations and economic policy, and went on the offensive for the first time in the Roosevelt tenure by investigating the WPA and the National Labor Relations Board. These investigations resulted in the Hatch Act, which made partisan political activity by federal employees unlawful, and a purge of left-wing members of the staff and board of the NLRB. These moves were directed at what the Republicans regarded as the heart of New Deal power—the labor movement and the political machine which they believed Harry Hopkins, the WPA administrator, was building through federal relief expenditures. Although the "Roosevelt recession" hurt the Administration, it did not necessarily vindicate the right's economic views, since Roosevelt did not follow a strictly Keynesian policy. As the economy seemed to recover, the Administration reduced the budget deficits from 1936 to 1938. While the sources of the renewed decline in the economy were not in government policy alone, the inauguration of a new $3 billion spending program for relief and public works in 1938 did have a positive effect. In the view of John Maynard Keynes himself, the Administration erred in attempting to achieve a balanced budget before the economy was fully recovered and did not ever attempt a spending program of the massive scale required by the Great Depression.

Republican political tactics in Congress were based in the 1930s on a low-profile posture which would give maximum play to internal divisions within the Democratic Party. The "conservative coalition" functioned on a tacit agreement on fundamental principles, principally the integrity of private enterprise and individual liberty, among conservatives of both parties. The South was the stronghold of what was called "Jeffersonian Democracy," but half of the conservative Democrats were actually from other regions, particularly the Border states and West. Essentially, the Jeffersonian Democrats were heirs of the old Democratic Party before its transformation by the New Deal. Like the Republican right, this wing of the party was provincial in its base and dominated by the upper class within those areas. The Democratic right tended to agree with the Republicans on the fundamental principles of social and economic policy and sometimes shared a xenophobic Americanist outlook. They often differed, on the other hand, on issues of race, regional economic policy, tariffs, foreign policy, and party loyalty. Consequently, the coalition was shifting in composition and informal in structure, functioning most effectively through the Rules Committee in the House in an alliance between Eugene E. Cox, the Democratic chairman, and Joseph Martin, the Republican floor leader. In the Senate, an attempt in 1937 by Senator Josiah W. Bailey, Democrat of North Carolina, and Senator Arthur Vandenberg, Republican of Michigan, to formalize the alliance with a "conservative manifesto" affirming free enterprise was a failure. After the 1938 elections, the Republicans felt strong enough to operate more independently.

As reaction began to take the offensive in 1939, it was almost immediately smothered by a larger issue—the war in Europe. The Republican right was strongly opposed to intervention in the European war and lined up behind the America First Committee. Although the right was able to maintain internal unity on the war issue, it could not control events. The Southern Democrats in Congress were interventionist and helped once more to deliver majorities for Roosevelt. After the Fall of France and the Battle of Britain, public sentiment was increasingly interventionist. In 1940, Roosevelt was again the nominee of the Democratic Party, although the weakness of Democratic liberalism was demonstrated by the difficulty which he had in obtaining the Vice Presidential nomination for Henry Wallace. In the Presidential election, the Democrats recouped little of the losses of 1938. In 1941, Pearl Harbor settled the war issue.

While the focus of events shifted to the military prosecution of the war and the prospects for the post-war world, an underground struggle over the New Deal reforms continued. Although the war had given the Roosevelt Administration a new lease on life, it also strengthened the long-run position of both wings of the Republican Party. Full production and the renewal of prosperity were removing the depression economic issues, the memory of Republican failures, and the spirit of class conflict. Corporate executives poured into Washington to take command of the war effort, thereby digging themselves in politically and renewing the popular Mandate of Heaven which they had lost in the depression. Patriotic mobilization was the order of the day, and as after World War I, anti-German and anti-authoritarian war aims were quickly converted in the post-war period into hostility to the Soviet Union and an anti-Communist offensive.

In the 1942 elections, the Democrats suffered losses in Congress from low voter turnout which disproportionately affected their working-class and lower-class constituencies. Millions of voters failed to register or vote as they went into military service or migrated to take jobs in war industries. The Republicans also capitalized on initial defeats in the Pacific, difficulties in organizing war production, and popular discontent with wartime economic controls and regimentation. The Republican Party took advantage of its new strength to kill not only New Deal agencies which had outlived their usefulness, such as the WPA, the Civilian Conservation Corps, and the National Youth Administration, but the National Resources Planning Board which was developing proposals for post-war, publicly sponsored economic development. Again working with Democratic conservatives, the Republicans reacted to wartime strikes, particularly by the United Mine Workers, by passing over Roosevelt's veto the Smith-Connally Act which restricted the wartime right to strike and forbade political contributions by labor unions. The CIO responded to this law and the unfavorable results of the 1942 elections by organizing a Political Action Committee for the 1944 campaign. CIO-PAC forced Martin Dies to withdraw from the Democratic primary in his district and helped defeat two other HUAC members, Joseph Starnes of Alabama and John Costello of California, both Democrats, in the spring primaries. Alarmed by this show of strength and sensing political possibilities in the aggressiveness of the CIO-PAC, an operation of the revived, wartime Popular Front, the Republicans made an issue out of it in the 1944 election. Roosevelt won reelection but by an unimpressive majority despite American victories on all war fronts. The New Deal coalition was conducting a holding operation, which even victory in a world war could barely underwrite. Roosevelt could no longer impose Wallace on his own party and chose to dump him in favor of Senator Harry S Truman as his running mate for 1944. The "Missouri Compromise" was a Border state

Democrat and a product of the Pendergast machine of Kansas City, who held the center between the liberal/labor forces and the conservative Democrats.

After the comeback of 1938, a new alignment within the Republican Party began to emerge more clearly. Senator Taft assumed the leadership of the conservative wing of the party which was defined by its uncompromising opposition not only to "New Deal Socialism" but to "internationalism" in foreign policy by which it meant intervention in European wars and New Dealist schemes to save the world. In 1940, Taft was a candidate for the Republican nomination for President, but was overwhelmed by a sudden campaign for Wendell Willkie, organized just weeks before the convention. In part, Willkie's victory was a triumph of modern organization—public relations techniques and support from the national media backed by waves of volunteers in Willkie for President clubs. Willkie's nomination also demonstrated that the right did not dominate the party. Although he made his reputation as the attorney for Commonwealth and Southern Utilities fighting a rearguard action against the TVA, Willkie was a moderate and until 1936 a registered Democrat.

In the Congress, the right dominated the terrain because Senators and, even more, Representatives were sent to Washington by states and districts with generally Republican majorities, usually conservative. The seniority system conferred political standing on Congressmen from safe, sometimes one-party areas, which were even more conservative. At the conventions, underrepresented Republicans from other regions where the party was not dominant could redress the balance. With the exception of the South, these regions were generally more moderate than the provincial Midwest which set the tone for the Republican contingent in Congress. At a Presidential nominating convention, delegates also had to give consideration to the requirements for victory in a national election. Conventional wisdom had it that victory necessitated a shift toward the center in order to attract some component of the now dominant Democratic Party. The right was reduced to the argument that a vast stay-at-home conservative vote was waiting for a champion to arouse it. It was well into the post-war period before the right developed the counterstrategy of moving *right* by appealing to conservatives of the Democratic Party and before partisan loyalties were sufficiently loose to make this strategy an attractive alternative.

With their national attitude, reserves of money, and control of national media, Eastern Republicans were well equipped to operate in Presidential politics. Their candidates sometimes had a homespun heartland touch designed to appeal to Republican home folks and undercut conservative politicians in their own districts. From a small town in Indiana, Willkie was piquantly described by Harold Ickes as a "simple, barefoot Wall Street lawyer." A native of Kansas, Eisenhower launched his campaign there and conspicuously had his headquarters in Denver. Even the brisk governor of New York, Thomas Dewey, was born in Michigan. As the East continued to dominate the national conventions in the 1940s, the factional split in the party became steadily more bitter. There were three issues outstanding.

The first was the New Deal. Though not for the most part reformers themselves, Eastern Republicans were willing to concede the social reforms of the 1930s and move on to other issues. Since they were no longer running against the Democratic Party of William Jennings Bryan, the Eastern Republicans also had to compete against the New Deal coalition for the metropolitan vote and thus to appeal to at least the upper strata of the working class. As the inner cities of the North filled with blacks, the moderates also found the pro-Negro tradition of the Republican Party a positive asset rather than an obsolescent tradition. As time went on, a "liberal Republican" faction within the more usually moderate to conservative Eastern wing emerged to reflect the New Deal formula exactly with support from trade unions, racial minorities, and educated liberals.

The second issue between the Republican left and right concerned their attitude toward the state. The right insisted on keeping faith with classic Republican dogma. Since the business elements represented within the right usually produced on a local and state, and rarely more than a regional scale, the federal government was not essential to their operations and was usually felt most directly as the Internal Revenue Service. Even when it provided large-scale subsidies, as for agriculture, Washington was a remote presence. These were not the men who staffed upper-level policy making circles in the federal government or had easy access to them. The major industrial corporations, financial institutions, and their professional auxiliaries did not labor under these limitations and had no objection to state intervention, if it were given proper direction. Their operations were national and increasingly international and could often benefit not only from subsidies and tax benefits but from coordinated national policy. The Eastern wing came to endorse a New Hamiltonian policy.

The third question outstanding was foreign policy. The "internationalists" in the East had a friendly attitude toward Europe and Great Britain and supported intervention in both world wars. This posture reflected the polyglot populations and cosmopolitanism of the Eastern cities, the financial ties between London and New York, and after World War II, immense capital investments in Europe and a strategic doctrine built around the Western Alliance. The Republican right shared none of these cultural and business ties and insisted on a strict nationalism based on continuity with traditional Republican foreign policy. The disagreement over foreign policy tended to revive the older sectional division between East and West. The agrarian West had long regarded the metropolitan East as exploitative and Anglophile. In fact, British capital played an important role in the development of the American West in the 19th century. Before World War I, the British had $3.5 billion invested in the United States, double its investment in India, the linchpin of its empire. Some of the old resentment of Wall Street financial control lived on in the factional dispute within the party. The right also viewed with suspicion the cosmopolitanism of city Republicans and their occasional interest in winning over the foreign masses of the urban areas.

Within the right wing of the party itself, there existed a delicate reactionary/conservative balance. There was more freedom to roam to the right when the Democratic Party was in power. A Republican Administration could help to close the wounds of the 1930s if it shared power with the conservative faction of the party. Things would never be quite the same again because there was, even during Republican Administrations, a faction which would not be reconciled and insisted upon the rigid implementation of its ideological position. Much also depended upon the concrete political situation and whether it tended to mobilize right-wing or conservative perspectives. The relationship between conservatism and reaction within the right wing of the party was constantly shifting. The same political leaders and constituency could move from one to the other, depending upon circumstances. Events could give the initiative to the reactionary forces at one moment, the conservative forces at another.

The Republican right was almost purely bourgeois in its leadership and doctrine. For the most part, this leadership was not metropolitan in roots and national in attitude, but provincial on both counts. In his study of the opposition to the New Deal by the conservative coalition in Congress, James Patterson found a close relationship between rural and provincial constituencies and a political leadership that was upper middle class and responsive to business and farming interests.[9] The crisis of the 1930s did leave a significant residue of the national upper class maintaining a commitment to the old order. The American Liberty League represented this sentiment, and many right-wing organizations continued to receive the backing of wealthy corporate capitalists in the post-war period. Perhaps the most important was the American Enterprise Association which was founded in 1943 to ensure that peacetime reconversion restored a capitalism uncorrupted by public regulation. Two of its trustees, Ernest T. Weir and Raoul Desvernine, a New York lawyer, were active in the Liberty League before the war.[10] Although other factors were operating, those members of the national upper class who maintained close family control over their companies were more susceptible to right-wing views, which stressed the classical values of individualism and entre-preneurship. The DuPont and Pew families were examples of the persistence of family capitalism.

The right had to mobilize a broad constituency to operate politically. Most enthusiastic were those with a small capitalist outlook—small businessmen, farmers, and self-employed pro-fessionals. Such men constituted a sizeable force. In 1950, there were .6 million corporations in the United States and more than 7.5 million proprietorships and partnerships, even though half of industrial production was accounted for by a few hundred corporations.[11] These undertakings did not always represent the principal livelihood of those in control of them and not all of the proprietors were supporters of the Republi-can right. Still, the Republican right was the principal voice of independent capitalism, and any discount of these numbers is offset in part by the dependents of those who remain. Al-though these elements were the core following of provincial Republicanism and set the tone for its politics, they were insuf-ficient to bring electoral victories. They were shored up by a broad base in the most backward section of the working class, particularly the provincial working class. In *Political Man,* Sey-mour Martin Lipset summarized the factors that survey data indicate are correlated with a more right-leaning vote among workers. In the "democratic class struggle" of electioneering, a less class-conscious vote is associated with some exceptions with "1) smaller towns, country; 2) smaller plants; 3) groups with low unemployment rates; 4) majority ethnic or religious groups; 5) women; 6) economically backward regions; 7) white-collar workers; 8) specific occupations: servants, service work-ers . . . subsistence farmers; 9) more skilled workers."[12]

The Republican right developed out of the crisis in Ameri-can capitalism and the system of Republican political rule dur-ing the 1930s. In the new ruling coalition of the Democratic Party and in the policies of the New Deal, the right perceived social democracy and, more remotely, the spectre of Commu-nism. In the face of these threats, it rededicated itself to the principles of true liberalism and Americanism and girded itself for political struggle. Its first opportunity came when the Roosevelt Administration overreached itself politically while its policies were failing economically. After the resurgence of the right in the elections of 1938, the opening moves of a reactionary offensive were made, but were soon overshadowed by the war in Europe. The right was to carry the conflict into the sphere of foreign policy but was there to discover a reconstructed Democratic coalition. The war imposed a moratorium on politics, but both sides prepared to renew the fight in the post-war period.

4

THE OLD NATIONALISM

During its political reign from the Civil War to the Great Depression, the Republican Party established a record on foreign policy. It was not "isolationist." After the Civil War, the party presided over the consolidation of America's continental expansion and over a drive into Latin America and the Pacific during and after the Spanish-American War. The war against Spain was justified as a campaign against Spanish colonialism on the behalf of the Cuban people. Nonetheless, the United States occupied Cuba, off and on, for more than a decade and conquered the Philippines where it was soon engaged in a counterguerrilla war for several years against a nationalist movement which felt betrayed in its expectations of immediate independence.

In the Western Hemisphere, the Monroe Doctrine, which was first formulated merely to warn European powers off the hemisphere and depended for its efficacy in the 19th century on the support of the British Navy, was converted into a fullblown claim to hegemony under the Roosevelt Corollary. By the Monroe Doctrine, thus amended, President Theodore Roosevelt asserted the right of the United States to "exercise an international police power" whenever the internal development of a Latin American state was not to its satisfaction. It made good this claim by chronic intervention, particularly in the Caribbean, and close control over Haiti, Santo Domingo, Panama, Cuba, and Nicaragua. The heavy hand of this policy was lifted somewhat only when Germany, which had pretensions in Latin America, was defeated in the First World War.

In the Pacific, the United States was forced to maneuver more carefully among competing powers including the British, French, Germans, Dutch, Russians, and Japanese. The key to the American position was its control of the Philippines where William Howard Taft, father of Senator Robert A. Taft, served as the first Governor General while General Arthur MacArthur, father of General Douglas MacArthur, supervised the suppression of the rebellion of Aguinaldo. There was, nonetheless, substantial sentiment in the United States in favor of independence, which came to a head in the late 1920s and early 1930s. The movement for Philippine independence was complicated, including, among other forces, not only anti-imperialist idealists but New York banks, heavily invested in Cuban sugar, which wished to eliminate duty-free Philippine competition. Reasoning that not only had America an obligation to the Philippine people to rule them but Japan might absorb the islands if left unprotected, Secretary of State Henry Stimson and Secretary of War Patrick Hurley opposed the Hawes-Cutting bill, which would have granted independence after an interregnum of fifteen years as a commonwealth. When Congress passed the bill, President Herbert Hoover vetoed it. Although Congress passed the bill over Hoover's veto, the Philippine legislature was unsatisfied with the measure and a program for Philippine independence was not worked out until the New Deal under the terms of the Tydings-McDuffie Act in 1934.

With the Philippines secured as a base in the Far East, the American government hoped to increase its influence in China and its share of Chinese trade. In 1899–1900, John Hay, Secretary of State in the McKinley Administration, circulated the "open door notes" which declared America's support for China's territorial and administrative integrity and attempted to obtain the agreement of the other Great Powers to the "principle of equal and impartial trade with all parts of the Chinese Empire." Since these powers had already forced the Chinese government to concede special trading and investment privileges and had divided China into spheres of influence, they correctly regarded the open door proposals of the American government as a lever against them. The open door policy duplicated a proposal of the British Foreign Office in 1898. Wishing to remain independent in its foreign policy and still engaged in war with Spain, the United States refused to cooperate with Britain in maintaining an open door policy in China.

Having once enjoyed 80 per cent of the Chinese trade, Great Britain was under strong pressure at the turn of the century from other powers. In 1894–95, Japan defeated China in war and attempted to extract territorial concessions. France, Germany, and Russia blocked Japanese demands and took economic concessions for themselves. Great Britain was thrown on the defensive and the United States, newly arrived in the Far East, was both unwilling to cooperate with Britain and unable to force its policy unilaterally on the other Great Powers. Nonetheless, the United States established itself as a factor in the balance of forces in Asia. The American desire to prevent the domination of China by other powers would ultimately help to lead it into war with Imperial Japan.

"Isolationism," then, did not describe the foreign policies, considered as a whole, pursued by Republican Administrations, but it was relevant to the Republican attitude on certain issues. The traditional American foreign policy was an independent, or unilateral, policy; it specifically avoided "entangling" alliances and multilateral arrangements. It was jealous of American sovereignty. In particular, intervention in Europe and alliances with Britain were unwelcome as amounting to a strain on American resources without any compensating advantage. American destiny was seen as lying in the Western Hemisphere and the Pacific. Europe was not only the "old world" from which America stood apart on principle; it was a dangerous

arena of Great Power strife from which America was unlikely
to profit. An alliance with Britain could only be a device to
enlist American resources on behalf of British interests.

On balance, isolationism was a form of American nationalism
or "America first." Isolation with regard to Europe was consistent with expansion elsewhere. The first departure from this
general policy was America's intervention in World War I
which was undertaken by the Democratic Administration of
Woodrow Wilson. The net effect of the experience was to confirm in the minds of many Americans, particularly provincial
Republicans, the wisdom of the traditional policy. It was far
from clear that American interests were directly engaged in the
European struggle. American shipping was subject to German
attack when that country inaugurated a policy of unrestricted
submarine warfare. On the other hand, Germany was under
blockade by the British Navy and American trade was re-
dounding only to the advantage of Britain. The American
economy was booming from Allied war orders and New York
banks were floating huge loans to Allied governments to make
possible these orders. American policy was hardly neutral in its
real effects. After the advent of unrestricted submarine warfare, it was the United States that first declared war.

The moral issue in the First World War was hard to discern.
After the February Revolution in Russia led to the downfall of
Czarism in 1917 and the creation of a Provisional government
guided by democratic principles, American liberals persuaded
themselves that the war was an epic struggle between the Western "democracies" and the Central European "autocracies."
Disillusionment with the crusade set in with the Treaty of Ver-
sailles. Wilson formulated his Fourteen Points as the basis for a
settlement providing for a nonpunitive peace and the implementation of the principle of national self-determination. But
the European powers, particularly France, insisted on the im-
position of a punitive peace on Germany, and there was much
wrangling over territorial and material advantage.

The outcome of the war greatly strengthened the world position of the United States. In order to finance the war, Great

Britain and France liquidated foreign investments, many of which came into American hands. They incurred huge debts with the United States, which became a creditor country. America emerged as unquestionably the world's leading economic power and as dominant in the Western Hemisphere. But the American people did not see the war in this light. American losses of 50,000 dead—slight by comparison to the other combatants—did not seem to be redeemed by obvious material advantages or by the realization of the idealistic war aims. The peace conference appeared to be a shabby affair. Far from making the world safe for democracy, the war brought Bolshevism to power in Russia, and a wave of Communist uprisings swept through Central and Eastern Europe. Fascist, authoritarian, and militarist reactions were under way in response.

The League of Nations was initially popular with the American people, who sympathized with its objective of preventing war through international cooperation. But there were several streams of opposition, all based in the Republican Party which controlled Congress. Progressive isolationists, led by Senator William Borah of Idaho and Senator Hiram Johnson of California, were bitterly opposed to the League as a surrender of American sovereignty and as a scheme of world domination engineered by the Great Powers. Another group, based in the East and led by Senator Henry Cabot Lodge, Sr., of Massachusetts and Theodore Roosevelt before his death, reasoned in opposite fashion that the League was an idealistic absurdity and envisioned an arrangement which was openly an Anglo-American entente. A third element, led by William Howard Taft, generally endorsed the League but had questions about Article X of the Covenant which seemed to commit the United States to use its military forces to ensure peace at the direction of the League. Wilson might have secured American participation in the League, had he been willing to cooperate with this last group, but chose to take a position which prevented the ratification by the Senate by the necessary two thirds.

The Republican victory in the Presidential election of 1920 disposed of the League issue and encouraged a return to the traditional tenets of American foreign policy. Wilsonian foreign policy with its stress on Europe, international organizations, reduction of trade barriers, and the principle of national self-determination was viewed as an unfortunate interregnum in the longer sweep of Republican foreign policy based on the doctrines of isolationism (with regard to Europe), unilateralism, protectionism, and regional imperialism. This restoration, however, had to be ersatz in view of the basic changes in the world balance of power induced by World War I and the immense increase in relative American influence. In the 1920s, the United States participated actively in disarmament conferences and efforts to stabilize the world economy.

Still, there was a popular reaction against the war and against the internationalism represented by the League. Though not confined to Republicans, this feeling was most conspicuous among them, particularly those from the hinterland. Developments in the 1930s seemed to confirm the futility of the earlier war aims. In Europe, democracy was on the defensive and the rise of Fascism, an objective of which was to undo the World War I settlement, presaged another war. In the United States, the depression gave domestic questions first priority, and the Roosevelt Administration at first pursued a policy of economic nationalism which discouraged international involvements.

The results of these political trends in the 1930s were the Senate investigation of the munitions industry by the Nye Committee in 1934–35 and the Neutrality Acts of 1935–37. Both were oriented to the experience of World War I. The Nye Committee attributed American participation in the war to the influence of the armaments industry and the New York banks. The Neutrality Acts attempted to foreclose any repetition of the pattern of gradual American involvement in World War I by forbidding American loans to belligerents and imposing an arms embargo on trade with warring states. Again, support for this "isolationist" stance was widespread but strongest in the Republican Party. More than three quarters of the Republican representation in the House and Senate voted for the neutrality legislation, while a large Democratic minority, more than 40 per cent, concurred.

The negative stance of the Republican contingent in Congress toward the pro-British policies of the Roosevelt Administration prior to American intervention in World War II reinforced the stereotype of the Republican Party, particularly its right wing, as "isolationist." In this light, the militancy of the right wing of the party on China and Far Eastern questions in the post-war period became a mystery. In fact, the right wing of the party was isolationist only in regard to its attitude toward intervention in another European war; this sentiment was magnified by a general popular reaction against World War I during the interwar period.

A strict and consistent isolationism was evident only in the Progressive left wing of the Republican Party and geographically only in the sparsely populated states of the Great Plains and, to a much lesser degree, of the Midwest around the Great Lakes. Progressive isolationists often took an explicitly anti-imperialist position and were reinforced in their opposition to European intervention by the large German-American population in the region. Progressives in the East did not usually share this perspective on foreign policy. Theodore Roosevelt and his followers, strongly represented among the cosmopolitan middle class, were among the most jingoistic and pro-imperialist elements in American politics. Outside of the Plains states and the Progressive movement, the Midwest was not inclined to a purist isolationism. Senator Albert Beveridge, arch-imperialist before World War I, had represented Indiana. The voice of Midwestern conservatism, the Chicago *Tribune*, endorsed a strong navy and an active policy in the Western Hemisphere and the Pacific during the 1920s. The newspaper maintained this basic position in the 1930s, although its blind opposition to the policies of the Roosevelt Administration gradually led it into advocacy of an appeasement policy in the Pacific toward Japan, including an abandonment of China and even the defense of the Philippines. Throughout both periods, the *Tribune* regarded Europe as decadent and opposed intervention in another war on that continent. The Anglophile East was hardly better in the eyes of the "World's Greatest Newspaper." New York and the Eastern seaports were the "port of entry of foreign capital and foreign citizens, foreign philosophy, and foreign political doctrines."[1] Midwestern conservatives were phobic about Europe; otherwise, they were not isolationist.

The Republican Party vacillated in its support for "internationalist" programs in the 1920s and 1930s. As they were in control of both Congress and the White House in the 1920s, Republicans in all regions tended to support the foreign policy initiatives of Republican Administrations, such as participation in international conferences and foreign loans and grants, which they were strongly disposed to vote against in the 1930s. Aside from sectional variations, there were also large differences in the support for such programs from representatives from metropolitan and nonmetropolitan districts. Metropolitan Republicans from all sections, but particularly from the East and West Coasts, tended to stray from a nationalist foreign policy in the direction of more support for internationalist measures—namely, Europe-oriented policies, foreign loans and grants, and participation in international agreements. Republican representatives from nonmetropolitan districts, on the other hand, were more likely to depart from a nationalist foreign policy in the direction of a real isolationism.[2] Ethnic factors also played a role within the Republican Party. In 1940, more than 5 per cent of the American people were either of first or second-generation German or German-speaking descent.[3] Most of these were Protestants and supporters of the nationalist wing of the Republican Party in which they represented several times their percentage in the general population. They were naturally opposed to the two world wars against Germany.

The nationalist foreign policy favored by the Republican Party, particularly outside the Eastern seaboard, involved opposition to intervention in European affairs, to alliances with Great Powers including Britain, and to the encroachments on sovereignty which participation in international organizations might represent. Foreign aid and loans were suspect as muddle-headed altruism, while the nationalists continued to support protectionist economic policies which had been necessary in the early phases of American industrialization. Nationalist policy entailed hegemony over the Western Hemisphere and an active role in the Pacific. It required a strong navy, and Republicans regularly voted for increases in naval appropriations. As long as wars with major powers were avoided, a large army was less necessary and Republican support for army appropriations was more qualified. Conscription was opposed as unnecessary to the implementation of this policy and as an aggrandizement of the state.

During the first term of Roosevelt, both parties were preoccupied with domestic policy and the Administration pursued a low-profile foreign policy. Gradually, it became plain that the Administration's foreign policy was a continuation of Wilsonian internationalism in 1) its support for international peace-keeping organizations such as the World Court; 2) its promotion of freer trade through the Reciprocal Trade Agreements Act; and 3) its readiness to enter into an alliance with Great Britain and fight another European war. The Administration lost the fight to secure American participation in the World Court in 1935 due to Republican opposition reinforced by the Hearst press and Father Charles E. Coughlin's National Union for Social Justice. However, Roosevelt and his Secretary of State, Cordell Hull, won from Congress in 1934 the right to negotiate tariff reductions of up to 50 per cent with other nations.

Certain features of Roosevelt's foreign policy went beyond Wilsonian internationalism. The first was a positive policy toward the Soviet Union. This policy began with the diplomatic recognition of the Soviet Union in 1933 and continued with the wartime alliance and effort to work out a post-war *modus vivendi*. These initiatives departed from the decidedly anti-Bolshevik policy of Woodrow Wilson. All of them were strongly opposed by conservative Republicans. The second original feature of Roosevelt's foreign policy was its anti-colonialism. This policy could be considered consistent with Wilson's stress on the principle of self-determination, but Wilson's incautious and abstract liberalism led him into a bungling intervention in Mexico in his first term. By contrast, Roosevelt's policy established a better claim to authenticity by first being applied in the American sphere of influence. The Philippines were granted commonwealth status and a phased plan of independence. The [Theodore] Roosevelt Corollary was renounced in Latin America and troops withdrawn from Haiti and Santo Domingo. Several reciprocal trade agreements were signed. A canal treaty more favorable to Panama was negotiated and transit rights across the Isthmus of Tehuantepec in Mexico abrogated. The Republicans did not strongly oppose these policies, although they certainly did not instigate them. In some cases, Republicans verbally endorsed them. Roosevelt made his anti-colonial policy a basic feature of his wartime "Grand Design" which actively promoted the dissolution of the British and French colonial empires. This anti-colonialism did not become a key issue with the Republicans until it appeared to acquiesce in Communist revolution in Asia.

5

THE STRUGGLE
AGAINST INTERNATIONALISM

The "Great Debate" on intervention in World War II began
with the German invasion of Poland in September 1939, and
the ensuing declarations of war on Germany by Britain and
France. The reaction of the U.S. government was immediate;
Congress repealed the arms embargo by votes of 63 to 30 in
the Senate and 245 to 179 in the House. Nations were allowed
to purchase arms in the United States on a "cash-and-carry"
basis, that is, cash payment for arms transported by their own
ships. In practice, this meant Britain and France. The pattern
of the debate was set. Public opinion, as indicated by the polls,
shifted toward active support of Britain and France, at first
"short of war" but increasingly "even at the risk of war," with
each crisis in the war's development. As the political balance
progressively shifted in its favor, the Roosevelt Administration
sought and obtained from Congress additional measures pre-
paratory to war. Throughout, public opinion opposed direct
entry into the war but supported steps that eventually led to an
undeclared state of war in the Atlantic and to the promulgation
of war aims in the Atlantic Charter in August 1941 before war
was even formally declared. By proceeding step by step, the
Administration was able to hold not only public opinion but the
Democratic Party and a minority of Anglophile Republicans

behind its policy. On the key votes, an average of 85 per cent of the Republicans voted *against* these measures.

After the invasion of Poland, the next decisive event was the Fall of France in June 1940, which was the turning point in the American attitude toward intervention in the war. It was no longer possible to hope that the war would follow the pattern of World War I of a stalemate of forces on the Western front, which might lead to a negotiated settlement and allow the United States to stay out. A $12 billion level of military expenditures received bipartisan support in 1941, and conscription was introduced. However, the term of service was limited to one year and the deployment of troops outside the Western Hemisphere was forbidden.

Nationalist Republicans continued to oppose intervention in the war even after the Fall of France. Keeping in mind Randolph Bourne's axiom of World War I vintage, that war is the health of the state, they maintained that war would mean the institution of some form of "national socialism" at home and thus the destruction of "Liberty." War would destroy the aims for which it supposedly would be fought. From the standpoint of national security, the nationalists argued that the expansion of Nazi Germany posed no threat to the Western Hemisphere or to the world economic position of the United States. The Germans could not overcome the logistical problems of mounting an invasion of the Western Hemisphere, particularly if the Americans and British maintained air and naval superiority. In the eyes of the right-wing Republicans, the German failure to invade England proved this point. It was evident, furthermore, that German expansionist objectives lay in Eastern, not in Western Europe, much less in the Western Hemisphere. Hitler was clearly interested in a settlement with Great Britain. Nazi dominance of the continent of Europe would not be an economic threat to the United States, since economic realities would require a continuation of basic trade relationships.

The nationalists favored the cause of Britain in principle and supported measures of military preparedness. "And in a dangerous world," Herbert Hoover stated in a speech in Lincoln,

Nebraska, "we are determined to be armed to the teeth to defend ourselves and the Western Hemisphere."[1] But their analysis of American interests led them to support concessions to Germany. In *America's Second Crusade,* published in 1950, William Henry Chamberlin still argued that it was a mistake for Britain and France to have guaranteed Poland, and endorsed a free hand for Germany in the East:

> So there was an alternative to the policy which the British and French governments followed after March 1939. This alternative would have been to write off Eastern Europe as geographically indefensible, to let Hitler move eastward, with the strong probability that he would come into conflict with Stalin. Especially in the light of the Soviet aggressive expansion that has followed the war, this surely seems the sanest and most promising course Western diplomacy could have followed.
>
> Critics of this realistic policy of letting the totalitarian rulers fight it out to their hearts' content object that Hitler might have won a quick victory in the East and then turned against the West. But both these assumptions are very hypothetical. The Nazi war machine might just as probably have bogged down indefinitely in Russia and there is no convincing evidence that the conquest of western Europe, much less of overseas territory, was an essential part of Hitler's design.[2]

Chamberlin's argument was basically a restatement of the policy of "appeasement," which, contrary to legend, was devised not by pacifists but by *Realpolitik* conservatives in Britain and France. In America as well, the conservative view was that the regimes of Hitler and Stalin were at least equally obnoxious and that it was a serious blunder to fight a war on either side. War against Hitler on the side of Stalin could only contribute to the expansion of Communism. It was nonsense to believe that a second world war would advance the cause of democracy any more than had the first. In fact, World War I created chaos and unleashed the forces of Communism and Fascism. Another war would do the same. The American right argued that one could not do any worse by sitting out the war, and felt itself vindicated by the war's ultimate results. Its willingness to allow

Hitler to hold sway on the continent of Europe suggests that the Republican right regarded him as much the lesser of the two totalitarian evils.

Like the rest of the country, the Republican nationalists were preoccupied with Europe. They did not oppose, and indeed many supported as consistent with nationalist policy, Roosevelt's hard line toward Japan in the Pacific. There was no uproar when the Administration froze Japanese assets in the United States in July 1941 and thus effectively severed trade relations. But there was some tendency for partisan opposition to Roosevelt's policy in the Atlantic to spill over into opposition to his policy in the Pacific, even though it was consistent with past Republican policy. We have seen that the Chicago *Tribune* retreated from a pro-China position in the direction of an appeasement policy toward Japan. To some, the outcome of the war and the victory of Communist revolution in China demonstrated the bankruptcy of the traditional American policy of maintaining a free and independent China. From a post-war perspective, the China policy was sometimes seen as just as futile as the effort of Britain and France to support the East European states. William Henry Chamberlin frankly declared:

> The cooping up of Japan's growing population of almost eighty million people within an area smaller than the state of California and their exclusion from the mainland of Asia have not worked out happily from the standpoint of American and British interests, especially in the light of what has happened in China.[3]

The nationalists dominated the Republican representation in Congress, but they could not control the Presidential nomination in 1940. The issue of "nationalism" versus "internationalism" within the party became a basic question in that year and the foreign policy foundation for the development of a new right-wing Republican tendency in subsequent years. The nationalist contenders for the Presidential nomination were Senator Robert Taft of Ohio and Senator Arthur Vandenberg of Michigan. The "Eastern internationalist" candidate was at first Thomas E. Dewey who had lost a close election for gover-

nor of New York to Herbert Lehman in 1938 and while serving
as District Attorney in New York City, had won a national reputation as a scourge of organized crime and the urban Democratic machine, which in Republican eyes were two halves of
the same walnut. Dewey finished off Vandenberg by defeating
him in the Wisconsin primary. But Dewey lost credibility as the
war crisis seemed to demand an older candidate with more executive experience. Barely two months before the convention,
Wendell Willkie suddenly stepped forward as a Presidential
possibility with an article, "We the People," in *Fortune* Magazine, a Luce publication. A Wall Street lawyer and a man of
considerable charm, Willkie had the backing of Russell Daven-
port, editor of *Fortune* and Mrs. Helen Ogden Reid, publisher
of the New York *Herald Tribune,* which was the voice of Eastern
Republicanism. He also had the support of a group of Republican politicians and New York financiers. In the spring of 1940,
Willkie strongly advocated American aid to Britain and France
in the face of the German offensive. The crisis activated latent
sympathy for the Allies, which was strong in the moderate,
metropolitan wing of the Republican Party, and brought Willkie's candidacy to life.

With a good press, the Willkie for President Clubs, galleries
packed with his supporters, more than ample funds, and a
public relations blitz, Willkie made a good showing in the early
ballots at the Republican National Convention. He inherited
Dewey's support, while the nationalists and party professionals
lined up behind Taft. On the sixth ballot, Willkie was nominated. Willkie made some conciliatory moves toward the Congressional nationalists. Representative Charles Halleck of Indiana, Republican whip in the House, gave his nominating
speech, while Joe Martin of Massachusetts, the Republican
leader in the House, was designated his campaign manager. In
the early opinion polls, Willkie appeared to be a strong candidate against Roosevelt, but in August the Battle of Britain
began. The crisis put Roosevelt well out in front until October
when a prolonged pause in the air battle indicated that the
British had probably surmounted the challenge. Though

strongly in favor of aid to Britain and France, Willkie at this point began to charge that Roosevelt's policies would lead to war. The sentiment among the American people to remain out of the war if possible redounded to Willkie's benefit and, though he lost the election, he made a respectable showing.

During the Great Debate, internationalist Republicans were active in the Committee To Defend America by Aiding the Allies, which endorsed all aid to Britain and France short of war. The committee was led by William Allen White, well-known editor of the Emporia, Kansas, *Gazette*, although its moving spirit was its executive director, Clark Eichelberger, also director of the League of Nations Association. Representative of the internationalist Republicans active in its affairs were Henry Stimson, former Secretary of War in the Taft Administration and Secretary of State in the Hoover Administration; Nicholas Murray Butler, president of Columbia University; Colonel Frank Knox, publisher of the Chicago *Daily News* and Vice Presidential nominee in 1936; Frederick Coudert, a New York lawyer; and Thomas W. Lamont, a Morgan banker.

Republican internationalists also participated in the "Century Club group," a more informal but more militant group than the White Committee, which sometimes met at the Century Club in New York. Organized by Francis P. Miller, an author associated with the Council on Foreign Relations, this group first made an appearance with a June 10, 1940, statement, signed by thirty persons, which called for an immediate declaration of war. Among the signers were Walter Millis, editorial writer for the New York *Herald Tribune,* and Whitney J. Shepardson, treasurer and director of the Council on Foreign Relations. Among the Republican participants in later activities which took a more muted but still militant line were Ernest M. Hopkins, president of Dartmouth College, Henry R. Luce, founder of *Time* and *Life,* and Geoffrey Parsons, chief editorial writer for the *Herald Tribune.* Out of the Century Club group developed the Fight for Freedom Committee which also took a more aggressive posture than the White Committee. The Right Reverend Henry W. Hobson, Episcopal Bishop of Southern

Ohio, was its chairman and Francis P. Miller its vice-chairman. Its Chicago chapter organized an aggressive campaign against the Chicago *Tribune* including a rally on the theme of "What's Wrong with the Chicago *Tribune?*" Later, the committee circulated petitions advocating the establishment of a new morning newspaper in competition with the McCormick entry. Some months later, Marshall Field, a sponsor of the committee, launched the *Sun.*[4]

The Republican form of internationalism differed from the Wilsonian. Like the foreign policy of Wilson, it was Anglophile and interventionist, but less motivated by the dream of world peace and international cooperation. Its orientation was more toward *Realpolitik* and economic predominance. One of its more notable formulations in this period was made by Henry Luce in "The American Century" in the February 17, 1941, issue of *Life*. Luce began by establishing his Republican orthodoxy on domestic questions:

> We start into this war with huge Government debt, a vast bureaucracy and a whole generation of young people trained to look to the Government as the source of all life. The Party in power is the one which for long years has been most sympathetic to all manner of socialist doctrines and collectivist trends. The President of the United States has continually reached for more and more power, and he owes his continuation in office today largely to the coming of war. Thus, the fear that the United States will be driven to a national socialism as a result of cataclysmic circumstances and contrary to the free will of the American people is an entirely justifiable fear.[5]

Nonetheless, America was already "in the war," even though there had been no formal declaration. This was right, Luce believed, but it was important for the United States to establish its war aims and prepare to assume the international responsibilities of its position. Since the U.S. was the world's leading power in terms of industrial output and the development of its political institutions, this meant an "American Century," or rather the "first American century." The problem in Luce's judgment was that the American people and thus the political direction of the country had lagged behind the real situation. Thus the United States had not stepped into a position of world leadership after World War I but had retreated into isolation. This failure of Americans had "disastrous consequences for themselves and for all mankind" because the failure to provide economic leadership contributed to the world depression and the failure to provide political leadership to another world war.

Luce's vision was not entirely lacking in conventional idealism. He proposed that America act as the "Good Samaritan of the World" and "feed all the people of the world who as a result of this worldwide collapse of civilization are hungry and destitute." Since Hoover's direction of the Food Administration in Europe after World War I, feeding the hungry had become a Republican issue. Luce summarized the American Century in these terms:

> America as the dynamic center of ever-widening spheres of enterprise, America as the training center of the skillful servants of mankind, America as the Good Samaritan, really believing again that it is more blessed to give than to receive, and America as the powerhouse of the ideals of Freedom and Justice—out of these elements surely can be fashioned a vision of the 20th century to which we can and will devote ourselves in joy and gladness and vigor and enthusiasm.[6]

Still, Luce's economic realism was striking: "It is for America and America alone to determine whether a system of free economic enterprise—an economic order compatible with freedom and progress—shall or shall not prevail in this century."[7] He advised his readers to think big, particularly in Asia:

> Our thinking of world trade today is on ridiculously small terms. For example, we think of Asia as being worth only a few hundred millions a year to us. Actually, in the decades to come, Asia will be worth to us exactly zero—or else it will be worth to us four, five, ten billions of dollars a year. And the latter are the terms we must think in, or else confess a pitiful impotence.[8]

Luce's views were contrary to those of Senator Taft, leader of the nationalist and anti-interventionist wing of the Republican Party. According to Taft, the Republican Party "should be opposed to risking the lives of five million American boys in an imperialistic war for the domination of Europe, Asia, and Africa, and the supposed 'manifest destiny' of America."[9] In a sharp reply to an article in *The Nation* by Arthur Schlesinger, Jr., who suggested that the Republican Party was about to break up over the war issue, that conservatism was identified with isolation, and that business was soft-on-Fascism and thus anti-war, Taft noted:

> The more conservative members of the party—the Wall Street bankers, the society group, nine-tenths of the plutocratic newspapers, and most of the party's financial contributors—are the ones who favor intervention in Europe. Mr. Schlesinger's statement that the business community in general has tended to favor appeasing Hitler is simply untrue. I have received thousands of letters on both sides of the question, and I should say without question that it is the average man and woman—the farmer, the workman, except for a few pro-British labor leaders, and the small business men—who are opposed to war. The war party is made up of the business community of the cities, the newspaper and magazine writers, the radio and movie commentators, the Communists, and the university intelligentsia.[10]

In the summer of 1940, nationalist Republicans organized the America First Committee as an anti-war counterweight to the committees that engaged in lobbying and propaganda for the interventionist cause. Officially, America First was nonpartisan. It had the support of Progessive isolationists, such as former governor of Wisconsin Philip LaFollette, who was in transit to the political right, and anti-Administration Democrats such as Senator Burton K. Wheeler of Montana and Senator Bennett Champ Clark of Missouri. It also had the backing of a few liberals, often associated with the University of Chicago, such as Robert Hutchins and William Benton. Chester Bowles, a cofounder with Benton of the advertising agency of Benton and Bowles, was a member. The committee was founded by several Yale Law students, including Kingman Brewster, Jr., later president of Yale and ambassador to England, and R. Douglas Stuart, the son of a vice president of the Quaker Oats Company based in Chicago. Stuart, who became executive director of the committee, was influenced by the University of Chicago liberals.[11]

But the national chairman of the America First Committee was General Robert E. Wood, chairman of the board of Sears, Roebuck and Company in Chicago. Wood and William H. Regnery, president of the Western Shade Cloth Company, provided the initial financing which launched the committee. Both were Republicans and strong nationalists, although Wood showed an unusual tolerance for domestic reform by voting for Roosevelt in 1932 and 1936. The vice chairmen of the committee were Janet Ayer Fairbank, an anti-Administration Democrat, and Hanford MacNider, a Republican political figure, Iowa manufacturer, and former national commander of the American Legion. The organization's executive committee was dominated by Republicans. Before starting the committee, Stuart traveled to the Republican National Convention in June and conferred with Republican political leaders. Senator Taft indicated his sympathy for the project.

In its existence of little more than a year, the America First Committee organized chapters throughout the country, with the exception of the South, and enrolled a membership of more than 800,000, two thirds of which was in a 300-mile radius of Chicago. Its main activity was to mount a public relations campaign against intervention in the European war, which it did through rallies, literature, and lobbying. Its star speaker was Colonel Charles A. Lindbergh, first man to fly solo and nonstop across the Atlantic, who was accused of anti-Semitism when he stated in a speech in Des Moines, Iowa, that the primary forces behind intervention were "the British, the Jewish, and the Roosevelt Administration." The committee attempted to build a broad-based opposition to intervention based on four principles:

1. The United States must build an impregnable defense for America.
2. No foreign power, nor group of powers, can successfully attack a *prepared* America.
3. American democracy can be preserved only by keeping out of the European war.
4. "Aid short of war" weakens national defense at home and threatens to involve America in war abroad.[12]

Thus the America First Committee placed a strong emphasis on military preparedness. Because of developments in military technology, the traditional nationalist emphasis on naval power was increasingly being supplemented by a stress on air power. The nationalists did not desire a mass army, but a limited force of perhaps 500,000 men which would be professional, mechanized, and highly mobile.

Despite the resistance of Republicans in Congress and in the America First Committee, the Roosevelt Administration continued to carry the "battle against isolation." After the Battle of Britain and his reelection in the fall, President Roosevelt was successful in securing the enactment of Lend-Lease legislation in March 1941, which provided for the supply of enormous quantities of war material to Britain. In June 1941, Nazi Germany repudiated the Hitler-Stalin Pact and invaded Soviet Russia. This event gave the anti-intervention forces new impetus.

American nationalists believed that the Nazi invasion of Russia had removed the pressure on Britain and eliminated any reason for American intervention. They also believed that the entrance of the Soviet Union into the war against Nazi Germany had given the lie to the idea of the war as a moral crusade against totalitarianism. Henceforth, participation in the war would benefit the Communists. A much better alternative in their judgment would be to let the two dictatorships mete out to each other their just deserts. "Collaboration between Britain and Russia," Herbert Hoover said in Chicago on June 29, "will bring them military values, but it makes the whole argument of our joining the war to bring the four freedoms to mankind a gargantuan jest."[13] The anti-interventionists strongly opposed the extension of lend-lease aid to Russia. In a statement of June 23, the American First executive committee declared:

> The entry of Communist Russia into the war certainly should settle once and for all the intervention issue here at home. The war party can hardly ask the people of America to take up arms behind the red flag of Stalin. With the ruthless forces of dictatorship and aggression clearly aligned on both sides the proper course for the United States becomes even clearer. We must continue to build our own defenses and take no part in this incongruous European conflict. . . . In the name of the four freedoms are we now to undertake a program of all-out aid to Russia?[14]

On August 5, a group of Republican leaders including Hoover, Landon, Hanford MacNider, former Vice President Charles G. Dawes, former governor of Illinois Frank O. Lowden, former Republican National Committee chairman Henry P. Fletcher, and conservative writer Felix Morley, among others, issued a statement criticizing "unauthorized aid to Russia." With the endorsement of John L. Lewis and Robert Hutchins, the predominantly Republican group took this view of lend-lease and the new developments in the war:

> The representatives of the people, in passing the lease-lend bill, expressed the national conviction that preservation of the British Empire and China is desirable for us and for civilization.
> We hold that view, but the intent of Congress was that lease-lend material should be transferred to belligerent ownership in the United States and utilized only to protect the independence of democracies.
> We hold that in giving generous aid to these democracies at our seaboard we have gone as far as is consistent either with law, with sentiment or with security. Recent events raise doubts that this war is a clear-cut issue of liberty and democracy. It is not purely a world conflict between tyranny and freedom. The Anglo-Russian alliance has dispelled that illusion.[15]

The willingness of American nationalists to give Hitler a right of way in Eastern Europe gave rise to the charge of pro-Fascism. This was not strictly correct. The nationalists favored the cause of Britain in the Atlantic and China in the Pacific but were unwilling to go to war and ready to consider measures of appeasement of Germany and Japan. This position did present political opportunities for elements which were positively pro-Fascist. Pro-Nazi organizations, such as the German-American Bund and the Christian Front of Father Coughlin, supported the America First Committee, and their members often participated in the committee's local chapters. America First repudiated the Bund, but not the Christian Front which had many Irish Catholic supporters in Eastern cities. John T. Flynn, chairman of the committee's New York chapter, rigorously excluded pro-Fascist groups, but other chapters were lax or openly sympathetic toward pro-Fascists. Laura Ingalls, who spoke at some America First gatherings, was later convicted for failure to register as a German agent. Ralph Townsend, who sometimes spoke at local chapter meetings on the West Coast, was later convicted for failure to register as a Japanese agent.[16]

The German Embassy played a clandestine role in the antiwar cause. Hans Thomsen, the German chargé d'affaires, informed his superiors that a "well-camouflaged lightning propaganda campaign" might be useful at the Republican National Convention in 1940.[17] The Embassy financed the publication of full-page advertisements against intervention in major newspapers and paid the expenses for a group of two dozen Congressmen, under the leadership of Representative Hamilton Fish of New York, to travel to the Republican Convention in Philadelphia in order to testify in favor of anti-war planks in the Republican platform before the Resolutions Committee. George Hill, an assistant to Congressman Fish, allowed George Sylvester Viereck, an agent of the German government, to have materials inserted into the *Congressional Record*. These anti-interventionist articles could then be reprinted by the hundreds of thousands by the U.S. Government Printing Office and mailed out free under Congressional franking privileges. Hill and Viereck were later sent to jail as a result of these activities and their sworn testimony regarding them.

Anti-interventionist Republicans in Congress attempted to

block lend-lease aid to Russia in the fall, but failed. They did come close to defeating the bill for extension of Selective Service which passed by only one vote in the House, 203 to 202. The Tripartite Pact, a defense treaty signed a year earlier by Germany, Italy, and Japan, also gave the "war party" pause because it meant that war with Germany would involve the United States in a two-front war on the opposite ends of the earth. The transportation and logistical requirements of such a war would be immense. By the fall of 1941, the interventionists seemed to have pressed their policy to its limit and still Hitler would not declare war. The impasse was broken by the Japanese attack on Pearl Harbor in December and ensuing declarations of war on the United States by Germany and Italy.

The success of the Japanese in sinking half of the American Pacific Fleet at Pearl Harbor created a political scandal, since the American government had broken the Japanese code and was tuned into Japanese communications through a decoding system known as MAGIC. There were no explicit Japanese messages indicating an attack on Hawaii, however, and U.S. strategists believed that the Japanese would inevitably strike south toward the Philippines, Malaya, and Borneo. They therefore alerted their navy and army commanders in Hawaii, Admiral Husband Kimmel and General Walter Short, of the imminence of war and the necessity of preparations for it, but did not indicate the possibility of a direct attack on Pearl Harbor by ordering an all-out alert.

There later grew up a right-wing revisionist interpretation of the origins of American entrance into the war which claimed that the Roosevelt Administration had maneuvered the United States through a "back door to war" in the Pacific while anti-interventionists were preoccupied with blocking the front door to war in the Atlantic. The strong implication was that the Administration had deliberately set up Pearl Harbor as a means of eliciting a Japanese attack which would bring the United States into the war on the basis of popular unity. The U.S. had putatively provoked Japan by refusing to negotiate on any reasonable basis and then baited Pearl Harbor with the Pacific Fleet.

In *Pearl Harbor: The Story of the Secret War,* George Morgenstern, an editorial writer for the Chicago *Tribune,* wrote:

> They [President Roosevelt and his advisors] failed—with calculation—to keep the United States out of war and to avoid a clash with Japan. They reckoned with cold detachment the risk of manipulating a delegated enemy into firing the first shot, and they forced 3,000 unsuspecting men at Pearl Harbor to accept that risk. The "warnings" they sent to Hawaii failed—and were so phrased and so handled as to insure failure.[18]

What was more likely was that the United States had been strategically outmaneuvered by Japan, and this fact was still a political problem for the Administration. Roosevelt established a special commission, headed by Supreme Court Justice Owen Roberts, to investigate the issue, while the War and Navy departments instituted several inquiries of their own. The tendency of the Democratic Administration was to scapegoat Kimmel and Short who were forced to resign from their services and were under threat of court martial for several years. In the election year of 1944, there was considerable political maneuvering over the establishment of a Joint Congressional Committee, which would give the Republicans an opportunity to participate in an investigation of the issue. The Democrats succeeded in getting the investigation put off until after the election. Senator Owen Brewster of Maine and Senator Homer Ferguson of Michigan, right-wing Republicans, dissented from the final report of this committee which was issued in 1946. In their minority report, they did not go so far as to maintain that Roosevelt had organized a conspiracy to involve America in war but were content to place the main burden of responsibility for the Pearl Harbor defeat in Washington rather than in Hawaii.[19]

The "back door to war" thesis was most popular with disillusioned Progressives who did not necessarily share the basic foreign policy perspective of right-wing nationalism. The historian Harry Elmer Barnes was one of its chief exponents. The concepts of a Pearl Harbor conspiracy and an appeasement policy toward Japan had only an ephemeral popularity on the right because they did not accord with its essential viewpoint on Asia. They grew out of partisan fanaticism and were taken up in the middle of a political struggle. On the whole, the Republican right did not oppose Roosevelt's strong posture toward Japan before the war and continued to regard China as the foundation of any policy in the Pacific.

Once the war was under way, the fundamental perspective of the Republican right began to reemerge. Although under the restrictions of wartime unity, the Republican nationalists discreetly agitated for a "Pacific First" strategy. Under the war plan, RAINBOW-5, the General Staff of the U.S. military planned to place priority on the war against Nazi Germany on the grounds that it was the larger and more formidable enemy and that the European theatre was only half as far away as the Pacific theatres and thus would allow a greater application of force as against logistical allocations. This plan accorded with the foreign policy of the Roosevelt Administration which aimed at keeping its Allies, Great Britain and Soviet Russia, in the war rather than risk their piecemeal defeat by Nazi Germany while the United States was occupied elsewhere.

The Republican right questioned the logic of this "Europe First" strategy. It failed to see that America's fundamental foreign policy interests were engaged in the European war and believed that the United States was simply fighting Britain's war for it, as well as irrationally supporting the struggle of its ideological enemy, the Soviet Union. Militarily, the right took the view that the weaker enemy should be defeated first in the theatre where the international position of the United States would stand to gain most.

As it happened, the military command structure reflected this dispute. In July 1941 General Douglas MacArthur was recalled to active duty and designated commander of the United States Army Forces in the Far East. MacArthur was personally committed to the world view of the Republican right. He had served as Army Chief of Staff under Hoover and was a personal friend of the former President, whose early treatise, *American Individualism*, he admired. His Deputy Chief of Staff in that period was Major General George Van Horn Moseley who attracted notice when he resigned from the Army in 1938 with a blast at the New Deal. An anti-Semite, Moseley later advocated vigilante action to defend the Republic and associated with native Fascists such as Gerald L. K. Smith and William Dudley Pelley. MacArthur was a close and lifelong friend of Moseley, although his views were not as extreme. MacArthur's biographer, D. Clayton James, describes MacArthur's philosophy at the beginning of the war as a "curious mixture of Hoover's individualism and Moseley's nativism."[20] This was the curious mixture typical of the Republican right as a whole.

An important formative experience for MacArthur was the Bonus March in 1932, when 20,000 veterans marched on Washington during the depression to demand the early payment of a bonus which they were scheduled to receive at a much later date. Hoover and MacArthur were convinced that the march was controlled by Communists. Two years earlier, after a series of Communist-led hunger demonstrations in Northern cities, Moseley had presented a proposal, not accepted, to round up left-wing aliens and hold them on an island in the Hawaiian group pending deportation. By most accounts, including Army intelligence reports, the Bonus March was far from a Communist operation, although there were some Communists on hand. Nonetheless, the Hoover Administration proceeded on that assumption, and the Army under MacArthur's personal direction dispersed the veterans' encampment. MacArthur came under fire from liberal quarters for his role in the affair and become convinced that he was a marked man. In his *Reminiscences,* MacArthur later claimed:

During the Bonus March communist threats continued to be made against responsible officials. I was to be publicly hanged on the steps of the Capitol. It was the beginning of a definite and ceaseless campaign that set me apart as a man to be destroyed, no matter how long the Communists and their friends and admirers had to wait, and no matter what means they might have to use. But it was to be nineteen years before the bells of Moscow pealed out their glee at my eclipse.[21]

After continuing to serve for two years as Chief of Staff under Roosevelt, for whom he had a grudging respect, MacArthur departed Washington in 1935 to become military advisor to the new Philippine Commonwealth which was beginning to develop its own army. MacArthur took Major Dwight D. Eisenhower with him as his chief of staff and, after retirement from the U.S. Army, was appointed Field Marshal of the Philippine Army. MacArthur was comfortable in this quasi-colonial role as he was later as the post-war "pro-consul" of Japan. MacArthur became a symbol of America's imperial mission in the Pacific. Despite occasional expressions of provincial suspicion of the imperium from men such as Senator Taft, MacArthur was a hero to the Republican right because of this symbolism and because of the continuity he represented with bygone days of Republican greatness. He came to be regarded by the right as its man of destiny.

Nine hours after Pearl Harbor, the Japanese destroyed half of MacArthur's air force in the Philippines on the ground because, as nearly as can be determined, of command confusion and lack of adequate dispersal fields, fighter protection, radar, and anti-aircraft. Unlike Pearl Harbor, no official investigation was ever made of the fiascos at Clark and Iba Fields. MacArthur could, and did, blame Washington for his lack of material but had to bear ultimate responsibility for the failure of his air force either to attack Japanese air fields on Formosa immediately or to move south to the island of Mindanao out of range of Japanese assault. In any case, this was a tactical episode in what was understood to be a holding operation against superior Japanese forces. Under the war plan, ORANGE-3, American and Philippine forces were to hold out for six months until they could be relieved by the Pacific Fleet. The Japanese success at Pearl Harbor disrupted this plan because the American fleet was so depleted that North America itself was exposed to attack, and the fleet could not be used to relieve the Philippines. The Philippines campaign therefore became a desperate fight to the finish. According to plan, MacArthur moved his forces on the island of Luzon to the Bataan peninsula and the island redoubt of Corregidor to set up defensive positions.

In the forbidding year of 1942 with Axis forces victorious throughout the world, the last stand of American forces on Bataan, which were gradually reduced to starvation, became a symbol of American fortitude and a rallying point for the American people. In the spring, MacArthur and his immediate staff, the fanatically devoted "Bataan gang," were ordered to repair to Australia to take control of a Southwest Pacific Theatre. MacArthur successfully broke through the Japanese naval blockade in several PT boats and arrived in Australia with the declaration: "I have come through and I shall return." He was awarded the Congressional Medal of Honor and became not only the favorite general of the Republican right but a genuine national hero.

MacArthur believed that Washington could have made a greater effort to relieve his forces on the Philippines, which eventually surrendered, and was upset at the low priority assigned to his theatre. He was constantly skirmishing with his Washington superior, Army Chief of Staff George C. Marshall, a principal architect of Europe First and an advocate of an early second front there, and with the Navy, which controlled the Central Pacific Theatre and wished to make it the main route of American advance in the Pacific. Republican nationalists generally supported MacArthur in his views. Long before the notorious attack on General Marshall by Senator McCarthy, Marshall was regarded with suspicion by the Republican right as a New Deal general. When organizing the Civilian Conservation Corps in 1933, the Roosevelt Administration wanted to absorb 300,000 young men immediately but found it a prohibitive administrative task for any agency of government. It proposed to have the Army undertake the initial mobilization. Army Chief of Staff MacArthur was unenthusiastic about the project, but many officers in the Army appreciated the assignment as a means of forestalling reductions in the officer corps, contemplated by Congress as an austerity measure due to the reduction of government revenues during the depression. Lieutenant Colonel George Marshall, who oversaw the mobilization of the Civilian Conservation Corps in South Carolina, was enthusiastic about the CCC, and in a public speech called it the "greatest social experiment outside Russia."[22] In the 1930s he was in sympathy with the activist policies of the New Deal.

The right claimed that Marshall was merely a staff officer, failed in his first attempt to command troops and rose to Chief of Staff as a protégé of Harry Hopkins, Roosevelt's intimate advisor and New Deal plenipotentiary. However, Marshall's biographer, Forrest Pogue, cites the supposedly damning report of the Inspector General on Marshall's command of Fort Screven, Georgia, as actually including a special commendation for the "efficient and economical administration of his duties and the high morale of his command."[23] When Marshall became Deputy Chief of Staff, Hopkins was impressed with him and supported his elevation to Chief of Staff. The common observation that Marshall was jumped over thirty-three senior officers was misleading. The Army required that its Chief of Staff be able to serve a full four-year term before reaching retirement age, which disqualified all but five officers when Marshall was under consideration in 1939. Only one of these, Lieutenant General Hugh Drum, was a serious alternative. Marshall benefited from the support of Hopkins, but he also benefited from the sponsorship of Assistant Secretary of War Louis Johnson, his status as a protégé of General John J. Pershing, commander of the American Expeditionary Force in World War I, and from his own substantial talents as an officer.

The apparently meteoric rise of Marshall and Eisenhower was suspect to the right because both men became identified with Europe First and wanted a second front there no later than 1943. Stalin was, of course, demanding such a front in order to relieve the pressure of the Nazi invasion on the Eastern front. Marshall and Eisenhower favored it because it was good military doctrine to concentrate forces at the decisive point, the source of the enemy's war-making capacity, rather than to be drawn into indecisive and marginal operations in the

Mediterranean. The rapidity of the rise of these two men was somewhat deceptive and not necessarily due to political favoritism or accident. The peacetime army was small, less than 200,000 men, and a Chief of Staff could be chosen from the ranks of major general or brigadier general. A colonel could seem to move to high command in relatively short order. Neither Marshall nor Eisenhower were obscure figures within the Army but were regarded as promising officers destined for high position. Marshall had acquired a special influence over many officers as an instructor at Fort Leavenworth and as assistant commandant in charge of the Infantry School at Fort Benning. At the latter, he revolutionized infantry training by taking tactical instruction out of the classroom into field exercises where officers could learn to adjust to realistic battlefield conditions which could be fluid and obscure. Omar Bradley, Walter Bedell Smith, and others were sometimes regarded as "Marshall men," associated with Europe First and Democratic Administrations, in competition with a Republican and Asia-oriented MacArthur faction. It is arguable whether there were organized factions in the Army led by Marshall and MacArthur. In any case, MacArthur's personal attitude was clear, and as a senior general who had been Chief of Staff when his superiors were light colonels and as a theatre commander with the support of a political party, or part of one, he was extremely difficult to control.

In 1943, Republican nationalists, disturbed not only by the low priority of MacArthur's theatre but by the even lower priority of the China, Burma, India (CBI) Theatre, began to organize a MacArthur candidacy for the Republican Presidential nomination. The leader of this effort was Senator Arthur Vandenberg. Vandenberg's "cabinet" consisted of General Robert E. Wood, who "offered to underwrite any necessary expenses"; John D. Hamilton, former chairman of the Republican National Committee, who acted as campaign manager; Kyle Palmer, a reporter for the Los Angeles *Times,* at this time a right-oriented paper, who was the "key man on the Pacific coast"; Joseph N. Pew, leader of the Republican right in Pennsylvania;

Colonel Robert R. McCormick, publisher of the Chicago *Tribune* and a personal friend of MacArthur; Frank Gannett, publisher of a newspaper chain in the Northeast; and Roy Howard, director of the Scripps-Howard chain. In addition to this array of support from press lords within the "cabinet," the Draft MacArthur movement also had the endorsement of the Hearst chain and the other papers owned by the Chicago Tribune Company—the New York *Daily News* and the Washington *Times-Herald*.[24]

In April 1943, Secretary of War Henry Stimson publicly noted that regulations prohibited a regular Army officer from candidacy for public office. After Vandenberg in the Senate and Hamilton Fish in the House attacked this statement as a move to prevent a MacArthur candidacy, Stimson backed down and said that MacArthur would not be excluded from candidacy by the regulations. The strategy of the Vandenberg group was to hold MacArthur aloof from vulgar politics and present him by proxy as a selfless military hero who would heed the call of his country. They dealt with MacArthur, for the most part, through staff intermediaries.

According to opinion polls, MacArthur was favored by 15 to 20 per cent of Republicans for the nomination. His strength was in the farm belt of the Midwest and on the West Coast and diminished as one moved eastward. The front runner for the nomination was Dewey, now governor of New York, who was the choice of something under 40 per cent of Republicans for the nomination. His main competitor was Willkie who was supported by close to 30 per cent of the party rank and file. MacArthur's prospects depended upon Willkie's continuing to keep up the pressure on Dewey, particularly in the East. They also depended upon a draft movement that kept MacArthur out of the primaries and political disputes that would place him in strong competition too soon and destroy his non-political aura. Nevertheless, MacArthur supporters not subject to Vandenberg's control entered his name in the Wisconsin primary. Dewey defeated not only MacArthur but also Willkie decisively, thus destroying the possibility of a deadlocked convention which the Vandenberg strategy required. In April 1944 the MacArthur movement dissolved into farce when Representative A. L. Miller, Nebraska Republican, published without authorization his correspondence with MacArthur. In his letter, the General did "unreservedly agree with the complete wisdom and statesmanship of your comments"—namely, Miller's observation that "unless this New Deal can be stopped our American way of life is forever doomed."[25] This exchange removed the illusion that MacArthur was above politics, while Miller continued to carry on an extended and passionate affair with the press. MacArthur soon issued a statement removing himself from Presidential consideration.

6

THE NEW NATIONALISM

After the 1938 elections, the Republican Party had appeared to be on the way to returning to power. On the issues posed by the crisis of the New Deal—the Constitution, labor conflict, and economic policy, the party maintained a high degree of internal unity, while the Democrats were seriously divided. The coming of the Second World War changed this political alignment. The Southern Democracy supported the Roosevelt Administration on the issue of intervention, while the Republican Party divided into interventionist and anti-interventionist factions. From the anticipation of an early return to power, the Republican right found itself contained as a minority of one third in the Congress and, roughly, in the country as well. Thrown on the defensive in the late 1930s, Franklin D. Roosevelt exercised unparalleled personal authority during the war, which he closely directed with the assistance of Harry Hopkins and the Joint Chiefs of Staff. The post-war settlement was worked out with the heads of state of the wartime "United Nations" coalition through high-level conferences which issued in executive agreements, not treaties which required the ratification of the Senate.

At odds with the internationalist wing of the Republican Party and shut out of national power as never before, the Republican nationalists attempted to strike at the heart of the

problem by capturing the Republican nomination and removing Roosevelt from the Presidency. Considering the exigencies
of wartime unity and patriotism, the Draft MacArthur movement was a bold maneuver, but still a failure. The internationalists nominated Dewey, who appeased the right by choosing Governor John Bricker of Ohio as his running mate.

As a victorious conclusion of the war came into view, it also
appeared that Wilsonian internationalism was triumphant and
that interwar neutralism, not Wilson's League of Nations and
Fourteen Points, was the real interregnum. The idea of a post-
war "United Nations" organization was extremely popular with
the American people. During the war, Willkie kept up the internationalist pressure on the right within the party. After his
brief advocacy of an anti-war position at the end of the 1940
Presidential campaign, Willkie soon overtook Roosevelt's position by advocating the complete repeal, rather than piecemeal
revocation, of Neutrality legislation. Once the war had begun,
Willkie undertook special missions for Roosevelt and there was
even an overture from Roosevelt concerning the formation of a
new political party which would incorporate the liberal internationalists of both parties. In 1943, Willkie published a book
based on his wartime travels, *One World,* which sold two million
copies.

Republican nationalists, particularly in Congress, were suspicious of Willkie and repudiated his leadership by installing a
Taft supporter as chairman of the Republican National Committee. The popular enthusiasm for a new international organization was a force which the nationalists could not for the moment resist. In 1943, the party chairman established a
Republican Postwar Advisory Council consisting of party
leaders who held elective office, thus excluding Willkie, and
convened a conference to work out a policy declaration at
Mackinac Island in Michigan. Under pressure from state governors, the subcommittee on international relations, chaired by
Senator Vandenberg, was forced to take a more advanced position on international organization than it had originally desired. The Mackinac Charter declared in favor of American

participation in "post-war cooperative organization among sovereign nations."[1] The mention of sovereignty provided an escape clause for the nationalists, but in the end there were only seven votes against the United Nations Participation Act. Among them were Senator Kenneth Wherry of Nebraska, the Republican whip and later floor leader, and Senator Taft, who actually directed the party in the Senate, later as chairman of the Republican Policy Committee.

Although it rendered lukewarm support for the concept of a United Nations, the right was far from reconciled to a neo-Wilsonian program, which included as its most basic feature an "open world" of free trade and investment, which the United States, as incomparably the world's strongest economy, would naturally dominate. The "open door" policy in China had been devised with a limited application; it did not require a revision in the tariff policy of the United States. An open door for the world was something else again. The Republican Party's protectionist traditions were under challenge, not to mention highly specific business interests. Although the party's Eastern internationalist wing could live with a revision of this policy, the provincial nationalists were adamantly opposed. In 1945, the Republican contingent in the House voted 140 to 33 against the extension of the Reciprocal Trade Agreements Act of 1934. Three years later, the party including its Eastern faction united behind a "peril points" position which required that the Tariff Commission determine the point at which a reduction in the tariff for any item would threaten a domestic industry. Reduction below that point would require Congressional approval. The Republicans who by this time controlled Congress extended the act for only one year. On their return to power after the 1948 election, the Democrats repealed these provisions.

Neither were Republican nationalists enthusiastic about the new system of international banking and currency arrangements, which was devised at the Bretton Woods conference in 1944. The International Bank for Reconstruction and Development, or World Bank, and the International Monetary Fund were justified as the means necessary to the restoration of world trade and sustained Western prosperity. The nationalists were unimpressed. Although Republicans in the Senate voted for the Bretton Woods agreements in 1945 by a majority of 19 to 14, Senator Taft led a spirited attack on the program: "I see no reason why we should make improvident loans or scatter our assets recklessly throughout the world."[2] Taft noted the defaults on American loans made after World War I and rejected the argument that an increased level of foreign investment and trade would promote peace—a classic 19th-century liberal formula. Given the example of Great Britain in the 19th century, Taft remarked: "We cannot in any way duplicate the British experience under present world conditions, and could never have done so without establishing an economic imperialism contrary to our whole philosophy."[3]

Although they were justified as instruments to finance the expansion of American export trade and to create new markets, economic aid and loans were particularly suspect. The Republican right tended to view these measures as welfare programs and thus a form of world New Dealism. After the 1948 elections, much of the nationalist hostility toward international organizations also revived. The United Nations Organization grew out of the wartime coalition formed by the "Declaration by the United Nations" on January 1, 1942, and incorporated the major Allies in a dominant Security Council with a veto system. It was thus an unpleasant reminder of the wartime alliance with the Soviet Union. The right came to regard the U.N. as the international expression of the old Popular Front and looked askance at its activist social philosophy, embodied in such agencies as the United Nations Educational, Scientific and Cultural Organization (UNESCO). It also viewed the U.N. as a threat to national sovereignty.

Anti-Communism and hostility to the Soviet Union posed a problem for the nationalist right in the post-war period. Although they had warned before the war that an alliance with the Soviet Union would deliver Europe to Communism and felt themselves justified by events, the right-wing Republicans had nonetheless to deal with the consequences. Here anti-Communism came into conflict with the tradition of isolation with respect to Europe. It was clear that the right would have to support an American commitment to Europe if it wished to minimize Russian influence. Ultimately, a section of the right did revise its attitude toward Europe and break with its pre-war position. This shift in policy did not come without a struggle, and it did not represent a conversion to "internationalism" but the abandonment of an old nationalism for a new nationalism. The internal crisis exacted a high political price. After the death of Roosevelt and the end of the war, the political tides were clearly running toward the Republican Party, particularly its right wing. President Truman bungled his reconversion policy and alienated his own support within the labor movement by taking a hard attitude toward the post-war wave of strikes. In the 1946 off-year election, the Republicans gained fifty-six seats in the House and thirteen in the Senate and took control of Congress for the first time since 1932. The "class of '46" strengthened the right-wing forces, particularly in the Senate, which was augmented by John Bricker of Ohio, William Jenner of Indiana, William Knowland of California, George Malone of Nevada, and Joseph McCarthy of Wisconsin, among others.

The moment was apparently right for a reckoning with the New Deal. The right pressed for a tax reduction program of 20 per cent and an equivalent budget reduction, part of which it achieved, thus curbing social expenditures. The 80th Congress also passed the Taft-Hartley Act which reined in the trade unions. The central question of the day, however, was policy toward Europe and the Cold War with the Soviet Union. The right split over the issue and thus lost the political initiative to the Truman Administration.

The moderate wing of the party, consistent with its prewar and wartime positions, followed the Administration on European policy. John Foster Dulles, a New York corporation lawyer and Governor Dewey's chief foreign policy advisor, was a U.S. representative at a number of important international conferences and generally backed Truman's interventionist policy in Europe. More importantly, Senator Vandenberg, the new chairman of the Foreign Relations Committee, defected to the Administration position. In a famous speech on January 10, 1945, Vandenberg signaled his new attitude by proposing a four-power treaty to guarantee the disarmament of Germany. He was immediately embraced by the Administration and sent as an American representative to United Nations and Council of Foreign Ministers conferences. Vandenberg became an advocate of the Truman Doctrine, the Marshall Plan, and the North Atlantic Treaty Organization. He was followed by a right-oriented group in the Senate which included Knowland of California and Styles Bridges of New Hampshire (the leaders of the "China bloc"), Owen Brewster of Maine, Homer Ferguson of Michigan, Eugene Millikin of Colorado, Zales Ecton of Montana, Harry Cain of Washington, and McCarthy of Wisconsin. Taft and Wherry led the old nationalist opposition to these programs and had the support of John Williams of Delaware, Henry Dworshak of Idaho, Wayland Brooks of Illinois, James Kem of Missouri, Hugh Butler of Nebraska, Malone of Nevada, Bricker of Ohio, and others.

The import of this split was first evident in the vote for a $3.75 billion loan to Britain in 1946. More than ever, the British were anathema to the right because they had a Labor government which was nationalizing industry. The Republican nationalists were not persuaded by Administration arguments that the program was necessary for the reconstruction of the European economy and the revival of American exports. The Executive Branch accordingly began to shift its emphasis to the necessity of economic reconstruction as a means to stop Communism. Although Republicans in the House voted 2 to 1 against the loan, Republicans in the Senate opposed it by only 18 to 17. The turning point was Truman's request for a $400 million appropriation in economic and military aid to Greece and Turkey in 1947. Turkey was under direct pressure from the Soviet Union over control of the Dardanelles, while Greece was divided by a civil war involving a Communist insurgency. The bill provided for military appropriations which eventually led to American military advisors down to the regimental level in Greece. Here was a situation that the right could understand. With the support of Vandenberg, the President clothed his request for aid in a "Truman Doctrine," which proclaimed the intention of the United States to resist Communism throughout the world. A majority of the Republicans in the House endorsed the measure, while Senate Republicans voted for it by 35 to 16.

The old nationalist group in Congress was steadily reduced. By themselves, the Eastern internationalists had not more than a quarter of the Republicans in the Senate, while the right consisted of more than half of the Republican contingent and the remainder moved between the two groups. These proportions varied somewhat from election to election. In the House, the right's dominance of the party was even more pronounced.[4] But the split within the right reduced the old nationalist strength to less than a third of the Republicans voting. On the European Recovery Program in 1948, the "Marshall Plan," the old nationalists could muster only 13 negative votes in the Senate and 61 in the House against 31 and 171 favorable Republican votes in the Senate and House respectively. From the beginning, the old nationalists had to pursue a "revisionist" strategy which aimed at the reduction of the appropriations rather than the outright defeat of the plan. In January, a revisionist group of twenty Senators met to organize the opposition. Wherry, an undertaker by profession, led this group because Taft, as a Presidential candidate, was afraid to take an active role. Although not actively pursuing the nomination, Vandenberg was holding himself available for a draft in the hope that Dewey and Harold Stassen, president of the University of Pennsylvania and former governor of Minnesota, would neutralize each other in the primaries. Taft was reluctant to alienate the forces backing Vandenberg, which strengthened the latter's position in the Senate, already formidable because of his committee chairmanship and an informal division of leadership of the two men between domestic and foreign policy.

Still, Taft did eventually emerge to offer an amendment that would cut the authorization from $5.3 billion to $4 billion for 12 months. The Taft Amendment received a bare one-vote majority of the Republican representation and was rejected by the Senate by a vote of 56 to 31. Once authorized, funds would also have to be appropriated. John Taber, Republican of New York, small-town banker, and chairman of the House Appropriations Committee, attempted to reduce the appropriation to the level proposed by Taft. In the Senate, Vandenberg went all out to restore the appropriations cut by the House committee and secured the support of Bridges, chairman of the Senate Appropriations Committee. Dewey and Stassen made public statements in favor of Vandenberg's position, while Taft remained silent. Vandenberg then forced a record vote in the Senate on the issue, and even Taft and Wherry voted on his side. In conference between the Senate and the House, the Vandenberg appropriation was endorsed. Taft, who had called the Marshall Plan a "European TVA," was forced to back down. The "war scare" of 1948 advanced the cause of ERP by mobilizing anti-Communist sentiment. In the wake of a Communist coup in Czechoslovakia, General Lucius Clay, military governor of the American occupation zone in Germany, cabled Washington in March that war could "come with dramatic suddenness." Germany also stood to benefit from the Marshall Plan, and Republicans with large German-American constituencies were well represented on the appropriations committees in Congress.

Senator Vandenberg also cooperated actively with the Truman Administration in the development of the North Atlantic Treaty Organization. In early 1948, the West European countries set the stage for NATO by signing a five-power defense treaty. Working with Administration officials, Senator Vandenberg formulated the Vandenberg Resolution which advocated regional defense organizations under Article 51 of the United Nations Charter. In June, this resolution was passed by the Senate almost without opposition. The next year, the Senate ratified the North Atlantic Treaty 82 to 13, with only eleven Republicans in opposition. The Marshall Plan and NATO represented the high point of "bipartisan" foreign policy. The Republican right split over the issue of an American commitment to Europe. In so doing, one group was led by Senator Vandenberg into a posture of active cooperation with the Administration on foreign policy. Support for a U.S. commitment in Europe and support for bipartisanship in general were not identical, but as long as the focus of American foreign policy was on Europe, the distinction was very fine. A section of the right had modified its position in respect to Europe; it had not abandoned its nationalist orientation. This continuity became clear when the focus of policy shifted to Asia.

In some respects, the Democratic Administration moved toward the right's foreign policy perspective. The reconstruction and rearmament of Germany and Japan were consistent with the prewar nationalist view of the necessity of maintaining a balance of power directed against the Soviet Union. In the post-war period, such a policy had, of course, a different flavor because of the change of regime in those countries. Nonetheless, the right continued to support this position and was in harmony with the Truman Administration's policy. It was strongly opposed to the punitive aspects of policy toward Germany, such as the abortive Morgenthau Plan to "pastoralize" Germany and the Nuremberg War Crimes Tribunals. In any event, punitive measures were a remnant of the Roosevelt Administration and were abandoned within a few years after the close of the war.

Though continuing to profess a paramount concern for "Liberty," the Republican right was a force for a positive policy toward the surviving Fascist states. Senator Vandenberg called for a normalization of relations with the Peron regime in Argentina. Senator Owen Brewster of Maine and Senator Patrick McCarran, an Irish Catholic and right-wing Democrat of Nevada, introduced an amendment to the Economic Cooperation Administration bill in 1950 to have Spain included in the Marshall Plan. This measure had the endorsement of Taft and Bridges, as well as that of the Pentagon which wished to utilize Spain as a site for military bases. The Senate rejected the amendment, although the Republicans favored it by 21 to 14. McCarran succeeded, however, in obtaining authorization for a $62.5 million loan to Spain in the same year.

The strategic doctrine of the nationalists evolved, but within traditional parameters. Increasingly, the right perceived nuclear weapons and air power as the military means to continue the old foreign policy in a new form. In 1948, the President's Commission on Air Policy, headed by Thomas K. Finletter, advocated the expansion of the Air Force to seventy groups. This proposal was endorsed by the Congressional Air Policy Board led by Senator Brewster. The Administration opposed the idea and preferred the concept of "balanced forces," which would limit the Air Force to fifty-five groups. John Taber, the normally parsimonious chairman of the House Appropriations Committee, offered an amendment which added $822 million to the Air Force appropriation, initially enough to fund seventy groups. The amendment was passed by the House and Senate, although Truman had no interest in spending the money. On foreign aid, the right had a marked preference for military rather than economic aid, although it liked no aid at all. The nationalists acquiesced in economic aid only when they could be persuaded that there was a clear and present danger of Communist revolution; otherwise, they saw in foreign aid the spectre of Henry Wallace's "Century of the Common Man" and a quart of milk for everyone in the world, financed out of the American treasury. In 1950, the Truman Administration's Point Four program for technical assistance to underdeveloped countries received a cold reception from all but the Eastern faction of Congressional Republicans. Senate Republicans voted 25 to 8 against it, while House Republicans voted 118 to 29 to recommit the bill incorporating the Point Four program.

The political test of bipartisan foreign policy came in the Presidential election of 1948. Though the right was dominant within the party in Congress and fortified by the 1946 election, Dewey was renominated without difficulty and was not even required to make any concession to the right in the composition of the ticket. Consideration was given to Charles Halleck, who swung Indiana's delegation to Dewey in expectation of the Vice Presidential nomination, but Dewey decided on Earl Warren, liberal governor of California, as his running mate. The moderates continued to control Republican conventions and expected to lead the party into the White House. In early 1948, only 36 per cent of the American people approved of Truman's performance as President. His policies had provoked two new party movements. On the left, the Progressive Party, with the support of the Communists, nominated Henry Wallace to challenge Truman's anti-Soviet foreign policy. On the right, the States Rights Party nominated Governor Strom Thurmond of South Carolina to oppose Truman's civil rights program.

Truman had some subterranean strengths. The Great Depression was still a central issue in American politics. The American people for several years after the end of the war expected an economic collapse at any moment. Truman capitalized on this sentiment by running a militant campaign denouncing the "special interests" and the "do-nothing" 80th Congress. In his State of the Union address of 1948, he also presented a program of social legislation including public housing, health insurance, and tax reduction. By these means, he was able to recoup his position with organized labor. Truman's foreign policies were generally popular. The coup in Czechoslovakia in March 1948 undercut the Progressive Party, which was then destroyed as a serious force by the Soviet Union's attempt to prevent the creation of a West German state by making an issue of Western access to Berlin. The Berlin blockade and the American airlift in response lasted for a full year and constituted the second serious war scare of 1948. The crisis generated a mood of patriotic unity beneficial to President Truman.

Dewey conducted his campaign as if he were the incumbent. Substantive issues were avoided on the principle that controversy could only create possibilities for Truman who was running well behind in the polls. After his nomination, Dewey indicated that he would attack the Democratic record on foreign policy, except for the United Nations and the Marshall Plan in the formulation of which the Republicans had played a supporting role. Wartime cooperation with the Soviet Union and policy toward China would be open to criticism. But the Berlin crisis changed Dewey's attitude. On grounds of national unity, he avoided making an issue of foreign policy. In November, he lost the election.

What was striking about the 1948 election was the success not of Truman who ran behind the ticket, but of the Democratic Party. For the first time since 1936, the Democrats won a major Congressional victory, gaining nine seats in the Senate and seventy-five in the House. The election confirmed the rise of the Democratic Party as the ruling party in the country. Truman's personal strength was not completely parallel to the party's. Even setting aside the states whose outcome was determined by the vote for Wallace, Truman did poorly against Dewey in the Northeast and lost Connecticut, Delaware, New Jersey, and Pennsylvania, which Roosevelt carried in 1944 and, after the Eisenhower deluge, John F. Kennedy would carry again in 1960. On the other hand, Truman was effective in the West and even Midwest, and carried the perennial Republican states of Iowa and Ohio. He ran well not only among farmers but in small towns and cities which were normal Republican strongholds. Not only Truman's foreign policy but domestic policies such as his early confrontations with organized labor and his loyalty and security program for federal employees were political assets in these areas. Against a symbol of Eastern Republicanism, such as Governor Dewey, Truman with his provincial manner ran more like a Wilsonian than a Rooseveltian Democrat.

The election results, which not only arrested but reversed the steady progress toward a return to power which the Republicans had been making since 1938, provoked a crisis within the party. The right was further embittered; the internal struggle between the factions intensified; and bipartisanship in foreign policy was called into question. Attributing electoral defeat to the obstructionist image of the 80th Congress, moderate Republicans attempted to remove Taft from the chairmanship of the Republican Policy Committee in the Senate. The move failed, but alienated Taft with important consequences for his future political leadership. William S. White, Washington correspondent for the New York *Times* and a friend of Taft, noted in his biography of the Ohio Senator:

> All this—the debacle of 1948 and the Eastern challenge to him again in early 1949—stirred him in most unfortunate ways. It seemed even to some of his friends and admirers that he began, if unconsciously, to adopt the notion that almost *any* way to defeat or discredit the Truman plans was acceptable. There was, in the intellectual sense, a blood-in-the-nostrils approach; and no mistake about it.[5]

Far from regarding the 80th Congress as too unyielding in its opposition to Truman's programs, the right believed that cooperation with Truman's foreign policy, duplicated by Dewey's campaign, was the source of defeat. The political appeal of New Deal social legislation in election campaigns, now confirmed by the Fair Deal, had been demonstrated even to its satisfaction. The efficacy of economic and class appeals to the majority only made more imperative the discovery of new avenues of political advance. Bipartisanship in foreign policy was a luxury the right could not afford and which, except for Europe, it had no desire to indulge. In his account of the effect of bipartisan foreign policy on the political fortunes of the Republicans, George H. E. Smith, who had served as staff director of the Republican Policy Committee in the Senate and collaborated with Charles Beard on *The Idea of National Interest* and *The Open Door at Home,* noted that the Republican faction opposed to bipartisanship "looked upon bipartisan policy merely as a device to tie Republican hands on the most dramatic issues of the day while Democrats beat them over the heads on domestic matters."[6] Bipartisanship had unpleasant overtones of Roosevelt's employment of Stimson and Knox to neutralize Republican opposition to his foreign policy in 1940 and his later use of Willkie in a similar capacity.

In 1949, events also began to work to the advantage of the right-wing nationalists and to unite the old and new nationalist groups. Bipartisanship was weakened by the decline of its leadership. Vandenberg was in bad health and unable to lead effectively. Appointed to the U.S. Senate to fill a vacancy, John Foster Dulles lost status when he failed to win an election to determine its regular occupant. Most importantly, the foreign policy of "containment" of the Soviet Union, the basis for bipartisan cooperation and Republican discomfiture, fell on evil days. In September 1949, Truman announced that the Soviet Union had exploded an atomic bomb several years in advance of expectations. This development shook the foundations of American foreign policy, which was premised on nuclear superiority. Since the United States had rapidly demobilized after the war, reducing its armed forces from 12 million to approximately 2 million men, it depended upon its air and nuclear supremacy to underwrite its position in Europe and counter the Red Army. If the Russians achieved nuclear parity, the military balance would shift in their favor. Within a year, Truman ordered the implementation of a program for the development of an hydrogen bomb of much more destructive power than the atomic bomb. The Administration also began discussions of a program for general rearmament outlined in a National Security Council memorandum. NSC-68 postulated that the United States could afford to spend $50 billion on the military establishment, four times the current rate.

Since the Republican right had supported a strategic doctrine built around nuclear weapons and its new nationalist group had endorsed the Administration's European policy, the Soviet acquisition of nuclear weapons did not in itself offer a partisan opportunity. But it did create a generalized vulnerability, which could be exploited when evidence of nuclear espionage on the part of the Soviet Union increased popular sensitivity to security issues and breathed new life into the old "Communists-in-government" issue.

7

CHINA

The second international development which offered an opportunity for the Republican right was the collapse of the Nationalist regime in China. The Chinese Communist Party under the leadership of Mao Tse-tung came to power in the most populous country in the world. In a speech in July 1949, Mao enunciated a foreign policy of "leaning to one side," namely the side of the Soviet Union. In early 1950, the Sino-Soviet Treaty confirmed the new alignment. These developments were the greatest defeat for American policy in the post-war period. They occurred in an area where the Republican Party had never committed itself to the Truman Administration, an area which was also of special concern in the traditional scheme of Republican foreign policy. In a famous remark, General MacArthur had dismissed Europe as a "dying system" destined to become a dependency of the Soviet Union while Asia would determine the course of human history for the "next ten thousand years."

Over the China question, the divided Republican right closed ranks. The leaders of the "China bloc" in the Senate were Knowland and Bridges, who had followed the lead of Vandenberg on European policy. But Wherry and Taft, leaders of the old nationalist opposition to European commitments, also placed a high value on China, consistent with Republican foreign policy traditions. Vandenberg, the architect of bipartisanship on European policy, had carefully excluded China from the sphere of cooperation and, though cautious in his opposition, criticized the Administration's policy. The moderate wing of the party also disassociated itself from Democratic policy in Asia. Governor Dewey attacked the Administration's China policy in late 1947 and refrained from making an issue of it in the 1948 campaign only because of the Berlin crisis. The Eastern-oriented Luce publications took a militant line on China. Henry R. Luce was the son of a missionary to China, while his wife, Clare Boothe Luce, worked in close consort with the right on Asian questions. By 1951, General MacArthur and Chiang Kai-shek were the leading features on the cover of *Time* Magazine, each having appeared seven times.

The China issue created a new political balance within the Republican Party and within American politics as a whole. The right had been unable to capitalize on its new strength in the post-war period because of the internal split over European policy. It was now united and in a position to set the tone within the party, particularly in Congress. Though more circumspect, the moderate wing was also opposed to Truman's policy toward China. The Democratic Party meanwhile was in disarray over Asia. The noninterventionist policy toward China was in surface contradiction with the universal anti-Communism of the Truman Doctrine. The policy could not command the full support of the conservative wing of the party.

The policy of the Roosevelt and Truman Administrations had its origins in the world wars. The defeat of Germany, the collapse of Czarist Russia, and the weakening of Great Britain and France in World War I had made the United States and Japan dominant in Asia. After the two countries went to war, American policy-makers anticipated that the "unconditional surrender" of Japan would create a power vacuum that the United States alone would not be able to fill. American policy, therefore, was to make China a Great Power as a means to ensure stability in Asia. Although not really able to contribute to the war effort on the scale of the United States, Great Britain, and Soviet Russia and not included by them in most of the major wartime policy-making conferences, Nationalist China was accorded by courtesy a role as a fourth Allied Great Power. It was one of the four leading signatories of the Declaration by the United Nations stating Allied war aims on January 1, 1942, and of the Moscow Declaration committing the Great Powers to a post-war international organization based on Wilsonian principles. Later, at Dumbarton Oaks, China was assured of a permanent seat on the Security Council of the United Nations. In order to affirm China's dignity for the performance of this role, the United States and the United Kingdom renounced their extraterritorial rights and special privileges in China, and the U.S. Congress repealed the Chinese Exclusion Act which prohibited Chinese immigration to America. In 1943, the Cairo Declaration promised the return to China of all territories lost to Japan since 1895.

The Roosevelt Administration also valued an alliance with China as a natural extension of the open door policy and as the anchor of an anti-colonial policy in Asia, which envisioned the exclusion of the British, French, and Dutch from their colonial territories through a system of trusteeships under a post-war United Nations Organization. The Chinese alliance was a counterweight to the wartime "Asia for the Asiatics" propaganda of Japan. Finally, China was important as a cobelligerent in the war against Japan. At a minimum, China's belligerency was valuable as a means of tying down large Japanese forces in the occupation of the coastal regions of China. More ambitiously, U.S. strategists hoped to use Chinese forces against Japan in a role analogous to that of the Red Army against Nazi Germany. The huge manpower reserves of China might bear the brunt of the ground fighting while the Western powers supplied the industrial base and the naval and air forces for the war. The Kwantung Army in Manchuria was a one million man force, supplemented by another million Japanese in other parts of China, Korea, and Formosa, which American strategists regarded as so formidable that it might be made the base for a resistance even if the home islands of Japan were occupied. Its defeat was a central military objective of the war in the Pacific. As late as the Washington Conference of May 1943, the Joint Chiefs of Staff submitted a "Strategic Plan for the Defeat of Japan," approved by the Combined Chiefs of Staff and by Roosevelt and Churchill, which designated China the main theatre of the Pacific War. According to this plan, the United States would undertake to recapture the Philippines, while the British and Chinese would conduct a campaign in Burma in order to reopen the overland supply routes to China. A converging offensive against Hong Kong would then be undertaken by the Chinese Armies from the hinterland, the British through the Malacca Straits, and the Americans via an amphibious operation. From Hong Kong, the Allies would conduct a drive into North China which would be made into a base for air attacks on Japan and eventually for invasion.

There were many flaws in this plan. The Nationalist government had no desire to make China into the main front and instead preferred to let the Allies defeat Japan, while it prepared for internal civil war with the Communists. The American plan required the modernization of the ramshackle and half-starved Chinese Army of 300 divisions. The reduction of forces and the elimination of inefficient commanders in order to create an effective and well-equipped, but smaller, force would upset the balance of power within the Nationalist government which was, in essence, a military dictatorship. One of Generalissimo Chiang Kai-shek's sources of power was his leadership of the "Whampoa clique" of military officers, a group originating in the Whampoa Military Academy when Chiang was superintendent. Chiang was afraid that the American conception would disrupt his political machine within the Army. Chiang resisted the plan and was in constant conflict with Lieutenant General Joseph Stilwell, Commanding General of U.S. Forces in the China, Burma, India Theatre, and honorific Chief of Staff of the Chinese Army, who was charged with implementing it. To counter Stilwell, Chiang supported Brigadier General Claire Chennault, commander of the American Volunteer Group within the Chinese Air Force. As a civilian advisor to the

Chinese government, Chennault had developed fighter tactics effective against the Japanese Air Force. The success of his "Flying Tigers" in the inauspicious early days of the war made him a romantic figure rather like MacArthur. A fanatic advocate of air power, Chennault developed a plan in 1942, expounded in a letter which Wendell Willkie presented to President Roosevelt, which claimed that he could "accomplish the downfall of Japan" with 105 fighter aircraft, 30 medium bombers, and 12 heavy bombers. The Chennault plan called for an attack on military objectives in areas of China under Japanese occupation, the destruction of the Japanese Air Force in China when it attempted to defend these objectives, followed by the bombing of Japanese shipping lanes and of Japan proper. While the industrial base of Japan was destroyed and the links to its empire and sources of raw materials severed, an American offensive in the Southwest Pacific Theatre could be pressed forward. Chennault noted that he, not Stilwell, would have to have "full authority." Chennault's plan ignored the vulnerability of his air bases to ground attack and overestimated the efficacy of bombing. In 1945, 800 planes would bomb Japan in a single raid. Marshall referred to Chennault's views as "not bad strategy, just nonsense."[1] However, Chiang embraced the Chennault plan as a defense against the political threat represented by the mission given to Stilwell.

The American strategic plan was too ambitious, not only for the Nationalist Chinese, but for the other Allies as well. Occupied with military operations in the Mediterranean and the defense of India, which also represented their political priorities, the British were unwilling to make the resource commitments necessary for offensive operations in Burma. The United States was also pursuing a "Europe First" strategy and beginning to have success with relatively cheap naval operations in the Central Pacific. Though not formally abandoned until late 1943, the China-oriented plan fell into desuetude.

American policy was also weak in its grasp of internal Chinese political reality. Since the United States government wanted to maximize the Chinese contribution to the war effort and prepare China for a post-war role as a Great Power, it desired to bring about a "united and democratic China by peaceful means." An unobtrusive pursuit of this goal would be consistent with the American effort to renounce an imperial role. Since China had been divided in a civil war between the Nationalists and the Communists since the Revolution of 1924–27, the goal of a "united and democratic" China was far-fetched. Neither the Kuomintang nor the Communists were democratic. Though arrayed together in a "united front" against Japan, the principles and constituencies of the KMT and the CCP were too antagonistic for unity to be more than formal. Chiang had concluded the first united front between the two parties in the 1920s with a bloody purge of the Communists and during the second, had executed a surprise attack on the New Fourth Army of the Communists.

For their part, the Communists did not dissemble their revolutionary objectives. During the united front period, however, Mao Tse-tung formulated the doctrine of the "new democracy" which called for an anti-imperialist and anti-feudal alliance of all the "progressive forces," namely, the modernizing bourgeoisie as well as the peasants and workers. In its base areas during this period, the CCP did not expropriate the landlords and rich peasants but simply enforced reductions of interest rates, rent, and taxes. It was common for American officials and journalists to regard the Communists as a reform movement and to refer to them as "so-called Communists." In a memorandum entitled "How Red Are the Communists?" John Paton Davies, a foreign service officer serving as a political advisor to Stilwell, called the Chinese Communists "backsliders" and compared them to the British Labor Party under the leadership of Ramsay Mac-Donald. Likewise, John Stewart Service, also a foreign service officer attached to Stilwell, regarded the CCP as a "party seeking orderly democratic growth toward socialism, as is being attempted for instance in a country like England, rather than a party fomenting immediate and violent revolution."[2] Such views were not eccentric, but representative of informed wartime opinion. They were encouraged by Stalin's references in the presence of American visitors to the Chinese Communists as "margarine Communists" and "radish Communists"—red outside, white inside. The optimism promoted by the wartime alliance with the Soviet Union and Mao's Marxist conception of an historical transition to Communism in which the New Democracy would be one phase led some American observers to believe that the Chinese Communist Party was not necessarily unfriendly to the United States or beyond the reach of a policy of effecting a united and democratic China by peaceful means.

American policy was thus based on contradictions: the assumption that China was a Great Power when it was not, the formulation of a grandiose war plan which none of the Allies would actually support with resources, the unification of revolution and counterrevolution. Aware of the problems, the War Department hoped to solve them by building up the military potential of the Nationalist government and forcing it to assume a modernizing role. Secretary of War Stimson and Army Chief of Staff Marshall gave full support to Stilwell and advocated the use of American lend-lease aid and military forces as bargaining counters to extract political concessions from the Generalissimo. With the loss of major cities to the Japanese, the Nationalist government had lost touch with the modern forces in China and lapsed into dependence on the landlords and the provincial military commanders. The Kuomintang Party was dominated by Chiang and his immediate family and by the reactionary "C.C. clique" of the Chen brothers, while the Political Science Group, the liberal element led by Sun Fo, and the industrialists, whose base was in the cities, had lost influence. The Nationalist government had become scarcely distinguishable from the warlord and imperial regimes it had superseded. Stimson and Marshall hoped to use American economic aid and military assistance to force Chiang to modernize his armed forces and open his government to the left wing of the Kuomintang and to liberal elements outside of the KMT, such as the Democratic League and the Young China Party. Thus fortified, the theory went, the Nationalist government would be in a position to pursue more progressive social policies, negotiate its differences with the Communists, and effectively lead a united nation in war against the Japanese.

Curiously, the New Deal forces in the American government did *not* support this reformist policy. Alfred Kohlberg, a right-wing leader of the post-war "China Lobby," attempted to argue a more symmetrical thesis:

> The crux of the whole Stilwell story lies in his connection with the plot developed in May 1943 when he returned to Washington. A small group including Alger Hiss, Owen Lattimore, Lauchlin Currie, Edgar Snow and later John Carter Vincent, planned to slowly choke to death and destroy the government of the Republic of China and build up the Chinese Communists for post-war success.
>
> Into this plot were brought Henry Wallace (then Vice-President) and Dean Acheson, Assistant Secretary of State, though both were probably confused tools and unaware of the sinister forces they were aiding.[3]

Actually, Lauchlin Currie, Lend-Lease Administrator of China, supported the recall of Stilwell, which the Nationalist government attempted to obtain in 1942 in favor of his replacement by Chennault. On his mission to China in late 1943, Vice President Wallace also advocated the recall of Stilwell, this time in favor of Major General Albert C. Wedemeyer, an alternative acceptable to the Nationalist government.

President Roosevelt did not endorse the Stimson/Marshall policy because it required more intervention in Chinese internal affairs than he was willing to countenance. The thrust of his policy, indicated by the renunciation of extraterritoriality and the repeal of the exclusion act, was to reject an imperial mission in China, reformist or not. In a letter to Marshall, he noted that Chiang, as the leader of a great nation, could not be treated like the "Sultan of Morocco." He also doubted that the United States could make the resource allocations required by a large-scale China campaign and was intrigued by the possibilities of a cheaper air campaign from China against Japanese shipping. Joseph Alsop, a Washington political columnist and social lion serving during the war as an aide to Chennault, had the ear of Harry Hopkins, Roosevelt's closest advisor, who became an advocate of Chennault's conceptions. The actual result of the return of Stilwell and Chennault to Washington in May 1943 was the reaffirmation of a policy giving priority to supply of the recently created 14th Air Force, commanded by Chennault, over Stilwell's reorganization of Chinese divisions and Burma campaign. In 1943, Roosevelt also endorsed the Matterhorn Project of Major General George Stratemeyer to bomb Japan via Chengtu, which received even higher priority than Chennault's air force.

By the end of 1943, however, Roosevelt had begun to tire of Chinese demands for aid and unwillingness to engage the Japanese. The Operations Division of the War Department had produced an alternative plan for the defeat of Japan via the Central Pacific, a conception which was endorsed at the Cairo Conference in November. The Kwantung Army of the Japanese was an unsolved problem, but at the Teheran Conference the following month Stalin indicated his willingness to enter the Pacific War and eliminate the Japanese position in China. In February 1945, this assurance was formalized in the Yalta Agreement which provided that the Soviet Union enter the war against Japan by an invasion of Manchuria within three months of the defeat of Nazi Germany. In 1944, Roosevelt dealt more firmly with the Nationalist government, refusing a request for a $1 billion loan and demanding a Chinese offensive in Burma. The change in the war plan against Japan weakened China's position.

The Japanese offensive in China beginning in April 1944 advanced this development in Roosevelt's policy. As predicted by Marshall and Stilwell, the Japanese Army rolled forward to capture American air bases when it became necessary. The air power strategy was discredited, while the Chinese Army was still unable to cope with the Japanese. The Operations Division now pressed for the use of Communist forces against the Japanese and the allocation of lend-lease aid to them with the same logic that justified U.S. aid to the Soviet war effort against the Germans. In September, Roosevelt proposed that Stilwell be made Chief of Staff of the Chinese Army in fact as well as

name and have complete authority over commanders and dis-
position of forces. Chiang refused the proposal and replied
with a demand for the recall of Stilwell. Still unwilling to impose a solution on China, Roosevelt complied.

Chiang recovered from the debacle of the "East China" offensive by the Japanese by securing not only the recall of Stilwell but the appointment of an acceptable Special Representative of the President in China—Major General Patrick J.
Hurley, formerly Hoover's Secretary of War. Soon after, Hurley became U.S. Ambassador to China. As a result of the Japanese offensive, however, U.S. policy now required that Chiang
form a coalition government with the Communists in order to
prosecute the war more effectively. Hurley attempted to imple-
ment this policy in a manner favorable to the Nationalist government. The basic issue was the autonomy of the Communist
armed forces, which the Nationalist government wanted eliminated in return for Communist participation in the government and guarantees of democratic freedoms.

Hurley counted on shoring up the Nationalist government
by going over the heads of the Chinese Communists to make a
deal with the Soviet Union. At the Yalta Conference, the Soviet
Union agreed to enter the war against Japan on condition that
the "status quo in Outer Mongolia," a client state of the Soviet
Union, be preserved and that the "former rights of Russia violated by the treacherous attack of Japan in 1904 shall be restored." These "former rights" involved the return of the
southern part of Sakhalin and adjacent islands, the interna-
tionalization of the port of Dairen, and the operation of
railroads in Manchuria by a joint Soviet-Chinese company. The
"preeminent interests" of the Soviet Union, to which the Kurile
Islands were also ceded, in these last two were recognized, but
the agreement stipulated that "China shall retain full sovereignty in Manchuria." The Soviet Union was to obtain the concurrence of Chiang Kai-shek to these provisions and conclude a
"pact of friendship and alliance" between the two countries.[4] In
the Yalta Agreement, the terms of which the Chinese government learned only after four months, Roosevelt compromised

the principles of the open door. Justifiably, the Nationalist government could regard the agreement as a violation of its territorial and administrative integrity. The Soviet Union now hovered over Manchuria and in the negotiations of the Sino-Soviet Treaty, concluded in August, Stalin pressed his claims under the Yalta Agreement to the limit. However, Yalta and the Sino-Soviet Treaty were calculated risks. Ultimately, Chiang proved willing to trade a part of China's sovereignty in return for Soviet diplomatic support of his government, which would have the effect of undercutting the Chinese Communist Party. The terms of the Yalta Agreement on the Far East were not publicly disclosed until a year after the conference.

While Roosevelt had shifted to a new policy in which the Soviet Union would handle the Japanese forces in China, foreign service officers continued to develop the implications of the old Stimson/Marshall/Stilwell policy of the War Department. While Hurley was in Washington for consultation in February 1945, George Atcheson, chargé d'affaires in Chungking, forwarded a collectively drafted policy recommendation to Washington which argued that military necessity required that the United States supply and arm Communist forces. The foreign service officers maintained that this step would put pressure on Chiang to broaden his government and establish a coalition mechanism for the joint control of Communist forces. It would be the most effective means for the peaceful unification of China and the prosecution of the war. Hurley was outraged by this communication, which contradicted his own policy, and which he regarded as an effort to undercut him. He demanded and received the reassignment of the foreign service officers involved.

By the end of 1945, Hurley's own program had failed. The Chinese Communists had not been brought into a coalition government on Nationalist terms through the pressure of the Sino-Soviet Treaty. Their relative position in China was stronger. When the Russian Army invaded Manchuria in August, six days before the surrender of Japan, it allowed the Chinese Communists to flow into areas of its control and capture Japanese arms and supplies. To strengthen the Nationalist position in areas formerly under Japanese control, the United States air-lifted Nationalist troops into North China and occupied key ports and communications lines with U.S. Marines. Though supporting the Nationalist government, the United States still wished to prevent civil war and achieve a peaceful unification of China. The new Truman Administration decided that Hurley's policy of working for a coalition government on Nationalist terms had failed and determined to make American military and economic assistance contingent on a more reasonable negotiating position by Chiang. With this decision, Hurley resigned. In his letter to Truman, Hurley blamed the failure of his mission on the career diplomats in the American Embassy at Chungking and in the China and Far Eastern divisions of the State Department:

> The professional foreign service men sided with the Chinese Communists armed party and the imperialist bloc of nations whose policy it was to keep China divided against herself. Our professional diplomats continuously advised the Communists that my efforts in preventing the collapse of the Nationalist Government did not represent the policy of the United States. These same professionals openly advised the Communist armed party to decline unification of the Chinese Communist Army with the National Army unless the Chinese Communists were given control.[5]

Hurley thus launched the right-wing theory that the fall of Nationalist China was engineered by a pro-Communist clique in the State Department. An incident earlier in the year became organic to this theory. In June 1945, John Stewart Service and Emmanuel Larsen, two foreign service officers, were arrested by the FBI in the offices of *Amerasia,* a left-wing publication specializing in the Far East, along with its editors, Philip Jaffe and Kate Mitchell; a Naval intelligence officer, Lt. Andrew Roth; and a free-lance journalist, Mark Gayn. The FBI discovered many classified documents relating to the Far East on the magazine's premises. At first, the group was charged with conspiracy to violate the Espionage Act but, as no evidence of transfer of the documents to agents of a foreign government was uncovered, the charge was changed to conspiracy to steal government documents. Only Jaffe, Larsen, and Roth were indicted. When it emerged that the FBI had conducted illegal searches, Jaffe and Larsen agreed to plead guilty and *nolo contendere* in return for light fines. The defendants argued that the aura of cloak-and-dagger was bogus and that they were simply acting as journalists trying to maintain good sources. The Republican right, on the contrary, believed that the government had engaged in a cover-up. In 1946, George Dondero of Michigan and other Republicans in the House received authorization for an investigation under the chairmanship of Samuel F. Hobbs, an Alabama Democrat. The Hobbs Committee found no justification for Republican suspicions. Nonetheless, the *Amerasia* case passed into legend as one of the foundations of a conspiracy theory of the Chinese Revolution. The Hearst and Scripps-Howard press kept the incident alive in the late 1940s, and in 1950 Senator McCarthy brandished the case in his attack on the State Department.

After the resignation of Hurley, General Marshall was dispatched to China as the Special Representative of the President. Although the war was over and military factors no longer controlling, Marshall pursued basically the policy he had advocated during the war, although for some new reasons. American policy was still to promote a coalition government between the Nationalists and Communists because Chiang's policy of eliminating the Communists by force had no chance of success. In Marshall's view, the government was too weak and corrupt, and the Communists relatively too strong to be annihilated. The possibilities for guerrilla warfare open to the Chinese Communists were legion in a country of vast extent and population. Marshall also intended to pressure the Nationalist government to reform its policies and broaden its base. As the governments of France and Italy were entering into post-war coalitions with the Communists and later successfully eliminated them at an auspicious moment, so might Nationalist China. The purpose of American policy was still to advance the fortunes of the Nationalist government to the maximum de-

gree possible and to render aid and assistance if its requirements were met. Under no circumstances, however, would the
United States take steps that would lead it into armed intervention in the Chinese civil war. In testimony before an executive
session of the Senate Foreign Relations and the House Foreign
Affairs committees in 1948, Marshall explained the grounds
for this policy:

> We must be prepared to face the possibility that the present Chi-
> nese Government may not be successful in maintaining itself
> against the Communist forces or other opposition that may arise
> in China. Yet, from the foregoing, it can only be concluded that
> the present Government evidently cannot reduce the Chinese
> Communists to a completely negligible factor in China. To
> achieve that objective in the immediate future it would be neces-
> sary for the United States to underwrite the Chinese Govern-
> ment's military effort, on a wide and probably constantly increas-
> ing scale, as well as the Chinese economy. The U.S. would have to
> be prepared virtually to take over the Chinese Government and
> administer its economic, military and governmental affairs.
>
> Strong Chinese sensibilities regarding infringement of China's
> sovereignty, the intense feeling of nationalism among all Chinese
> and the unavailability of qualified American personnel in the
> large numbers required argue strongly against attempting any
> such solution. It would be impossible to estimate the final cost of a
> course of action of this magnitude. It certainly would be a con-
> tinuing operation for a long time to come. It would involve this
> Government in a continuing commitment from which it would be
> practically impossible to withdraw, and it would very probably in-
> volve grave consequences to this nation by making of China an
> arena of international conflict. An attempt to underwrite the
> Chinese economy and the Chinese Government's military effort
> represents a burden on the U.S. economy and a military responsi-
> bility which I cannot recommend as a course of action for this
> Government.[6]

Certainly, Marshall well understood the implications of an intervention on behalf of a weak government in a country of 450
million against an enemy controlling at least 100 million people
and disposing of armed forces of one million men. In addition,
he did not believe that China represented a strategic interest of

the first magnitude. Europe was a gigantic industrial complex, until recently the largest in the world, where the United States and the Soviet Union were in direct competition. With its armed forces being rapidly demobilized, the United States would be foolish to commit its reduced forces to a peripheral area and invite a Soviet counterintervention in China, or worse, in Europe. As Marshall put the case,

> China does not itself possess the raw material and industrial resources which would enable it to become a first-class military power within the foreseeable future. The country is at present in the midst of a social and political revolution. Until this revolution is completed—and it will take a long time—there is no prospect that sufficient stability and order can be established to permit China's early development into a strong state. Furthermore, on the side of American interests, we cannot afford, economically or militarily, to take over the continued failures of the present Chinese Government to the dissipation of our strength in more vital regions where we now have a reasonable opportunity of successfully meeting or thwarting the Communist threat, that is, in the vital industrial area of Western Europe with its traditions of free institutions.[7]

Marshall's policy was, again, Europe First. In China in 1946, he was able to negotiate a cease-fire and the beginning of a settlement through the Political Consultative Conference. These agreements did not last. When the Communists violated the ceasefire by capturing Changchun, the Nationalists launched a military offensive in Manchuria which was at first successful. In August, Marshall imposed an embargo on the export of American arms and ammunition in an effort to force a return to negotiations. By the end of the year, he gave up on his mission and asked to be recalled. As Marshall predicted, the Nationalist offensive left their armies over-extended and vulnerable to counterattack. As the military position of the Nationalists deteriorated in 1947 and 1948, the Truman Administration reaffirmed its policy of not undertaking a military intervention and wrote China off.

Throughout the war and during the post-war period of the

Marshall mission, official policy was to back the Nationalist government. Disagreements within the U.S. government turned on strategy. Roosevelt and Hopkins generally were in favor of dealing gently with Chiang Kai-shek, while Stimson and Marshall desired to put pressure on Chiang in order to improve the efficiency of his war effort. The War Department was also willing to entertain the possibility of arming the Chinese Communists in order to force the Nationalists into line and mount more effective military operations against Japanese forces in China. The possibility that the Chinese Communist Party might be the wave of the future in China and that the United States should maintain good relations with it for independent reasons was raised by junior officials; it was never government policy. American policy toward the Chinese Communists was always governed by the objective of strengthening the long-run prospects of the Nationalist government in the light of what American policy-makers considered a realistic assessment of the situation. Only after 1947 when the Truman Administration began to give up on the Nationalists did disengagement from Chiang for the purpose of preparing for future relations with Mao Tse-tung become a real option. During this period, a "Titoist" solution for China was given consideration, but never became official policy. The first priority of the Administration was containment of the Soviet Union in Europe. In order to purchase nationalist Republican support for its European policy, the Administration maintained its commitment to Chiang Kai-shek long after it abandoned hope for his government. On the merits, the Administration was also ambivalent about a Titoist policy toward China—friendly American relations with a Communist state which out of consideration for its national independence would be hostile to the Soviet Union. An alternative possibility was the pursuit of a containment policy toward China on the model of policy toward the Soviet Union.

The attitude of the Republican right toward China was in close accord with the posture of Chiang Kai-shek and Major General Chennault. Its benchmark was that the United States should uncompromisingly support the Nationalist government and oppose the Chinese Communist Party. The complications of the Stimson/Marshall policy were thus anathema to it. The low priority of the CBI Theatre during the war and reluctance of the Democrats to unlock the American treasury for Chiang Kai-shek were also objects of right-wing Republican criticism. The basic attitude of the right was summarized in a letter submitted to Secretary of State James Byrnes on July 25, 1946, at the time of the Marshall mission by Representative Clare Boothe Luce, Republican of Connecticut:

> We believe that the United States is bound both by its pledges to China and its own interests to help China to unify its territories under the National Government, and to restore to the Chinese Republic full sovereignty in Manchuria as pledged by Russia, England, and ourselves. We believe that we should give no further aid or support to the Chinese Communists and make no further compromises with them. We consider it improper to exert American pressure on the Government of China to make terms with the Chinese Communists. We fear that the present American policy of pressure for a coalition government, if successful, will result (as did our pressure for a coalition government in Poland and Yugoslavia) in making China a satellite of Russia. We will have exchanged the open door for the iron curtain.[8]

This letter was cosigned by a group of right-wing intellectuals and prominent Republicans, joined by some strong anti-Communists of other political persuasions. It sounded the basic themes of Republican criticism of China policy—namely, that the United States should give no support to the Chinese Communists for any reason, exert no pressure for a coalition government, and render effective assistance to the Nationalist government. The compromise of Chinese sovereignty at Yalta was made an issue, although both the Chiang government through the Sino-Soviet Treaty and the Republicans through the diplomatic efforts of Hurley, were implicated in the policy. Earlier in 1946, Yalta was also the subject of a "Manchurian Manifesto," issued by sixty people many of whom also signed the Luce letter:

We must stand firm for justice for China. The test for China is Manchuria. We should lend our support to the demands now being voiced by the Chinese people for a complete revision of the Yalta agreements. But certainly the least we can do is to insist on the strict observance of the promises to China contained in the Sino-Russian agreement which we forced on China.[9]

One key element of the rightist view on China which is still missing from these documents is the theory of a conspiracy of pro-Communists in the United States working for the downfall of the Nationalist government. The theory had already surfaced with Hurley's letter of resignation and the *Amerasia* case. In 1944, Alfred Kohlberg, an importer of Chinese textiles, had also begun his assault on the Institute of Pacific Relations, which became one of the foundations of the theory. As a director of the American Bureau for Medical Aid to China, Kohlberg visited China in 1943 to investigate charges of corruption in the use of aid by the medical services of the Chinese Army. Kohlberg became incensed at what he considered the injustice of these charges and embroiled in a dispute with other officials of ABMAC and the larger organization in which it participated, United China Relief. Edward C. Carter, chairman of the Program and Disbursements Committee for UCR, was one of these officials. Carter also happened to be secretary-general of the Institute of Pacific Relations, an international research organization.

Like many businessmen, Kohlberg was a member of IPR and was persuaded by Dr. Maurice William, a New York dentist and former Socialist, that American Communists manufactured the corruption issue through their influence in the Institute. IPR consisted of an international secretariat, the Pacific Council, and the affiliated councils of participating nations, including the United States and the Soviet Union. It was heavily subsidized by the Rockefeller Foundation and the Carnegie Corporation. It also received contributions from America's largest corporations and its trustees consisted of influential figures such as Arthur H. Dean, a partner in the New York law firm of Sullivan and Cromwell, and Gerard Swope, president of General Electric. Most American experts on Asia participated in its conferences or contributed to its journals and books. Right-wing intellectuals became convinced that IPR monopolized all commentary on Asia, that it enforced an official line through control of book reviewing on Asia, and that it was hostile to the Nationalist government in China. Kohlberg developed the thesis that IPR's staff and inner circle had been infiltrated by Communists and the organization turned into an instrument of Communist policy. Among the many tenuous charges, the most substantial evidence for this claim was that Frederick Vanderbilt Field, secretary of the American Council from 1934 to 1940, developed views sympathetic to the Communist Party. In 1940, he left this position to become director of the American Peace Mobilization, an anti-war organization controlled by the Communists. Field also helped to found *Amerasia* as a publishing vehicle for left-wing analysts whose views could not be stated unambiguously in IPR publications. William Lockwood, Owen Lattimore, and T. A. Bisson, Asia scholars with IPR affiliations, were on *Amerasia*'s board. The Republican right later used any IPR connection as one of its indices of Communist affiliation.[10] During the McCarthy period the Institute was subjected to a full-scale investigation by the Senate Internal Security Subcommittee of Senator McCarran. Eventually, the notoriety led to the demise of IPR.

In the post-war period, Kohlberg became one of the organizers of the "China Lobby," which agitated for the Nationalist cause in the United States; he once declared, "I am the China Lobby." The chief organized vehicle was the American China Policy Association which was founded in 1946 with, after a short interval, Kohlberg as chairman of the board. The ACPA's early presidents were successively J. B. Powell, a former correspondent in China, Clare Boothe Luce, and William Loeb, publisher of the Manchester, New Hampshire, *Union Leader*. Kohlberg often published his opinions in *The China Monthly: The Truth About China,* a Catholic-oriented American publication which closely reflected the views of the Nationalist government.

The editor from 1939 to 1944 was the Right Reverend Monsignor Barry O'Toole, formerly rector of the Catholic University in Peking. He was succeeded by Father Mark Tsai until the magazine ceased publication in 1951. Father Tsai later became head of a girls' school on Taiwan. During the war, *The China Monthly* charged that "Red Second Fronters," who were concerned with the fate of the Soviet Union, were responsible for the low priority of the CBI Theatre. Later, the magazine claimed that it was "first to point out" that journalists who criticized the Nationalist government were "either misled-followers of Communistic ideologies or traitors to their country."[11]

The Nationalist government itself was heavily involved in lobbying efforts in the United States, particularly after 1948 when its hopes for a Republican Administration were disappointed. Shortly after the election, Madame Chiang Kai-shek arrived in the United States and conducted weekly strategy meetings of Chinese officials and commercial representatives in order to organize an effort to influence sympathetic elements in America. One of their chief operatives was William J. Goodwin, a former member of Father Coughlin's Christian Front, who registered in 1948 as an agent of the National Resources Commission of China and in 1949 as an agent of the Chinese News Service. Goodwin lobbied for the Nationalist cause with Congressmen, journalists, and businessmen. Chief of the American business firms which served the Nationalists was Allied Syndicates, a public relations firm, which registered in 1950 as an agent of the Bank of China and assisted in the campaign of Representative Richard M. Nixon for the U.S. Senate in California. In a series in *The Reporter*, Charles Wertenbaker asserted that not only was the Nationalist government putting money into American political campaigns but that the Chinese secret police was gathering information for political use by Goodwin.[12] In 1949, Representative Mike Mansfield, Democrat of Montana, demanded an investigation of the China Lobby to "determine whether American money, originally appropriated to aid the Chinese Government and illicitly diverted to private use . . . is actually being used to promote more legislation for

aid to China by which more money would be made available."
Mansfield also wanted the investigating committee to "inquire
into whether American money provided to help China, but
siphoned off for private use, is being used to finance attacks on
our Secretary of State and other officials charged with conducting our relations with China." [13] Mansfield's proposal was not
acted on, and his charges, as well as others concerning the
China Lobby, were never conclusively proved.

After their victory in the 1946 off-year elections, the Republicans began to develop an alternative to the Truman policy.
After the promulgation of the Truman Doctrine in the spring
of 1947, the Chinese government submitted large aid requests
and the Republican right argued that what applied in Greece
and Turkey should also apply in China. The Democratic Administration could only reply that the implications of intervention in a country of eight million were not the same as those in
a country of 450 million. It did, however, make concessions to
the Republican position. The arms embargo was lifted and
when the Marines were later withdrawn, large quantities of
arms and supplies were left for the Nationalists. John Carter
Vincent, Director of the Office of Far Eastern Affairs of the
State Department, whom the Republican right found obnoxious, was transferred to a post in Switzerland. At the behest of
Dr. Walter Judd, Republican Congressman from Minnesota
and a former medical missionary to China who, together with
John Vorys of Ohio, a graduate of Yale-in-China, led the China
Bloc in the House, Lieutenant General Albert Wedemeyer was
sent on a fact-finding mission to China.

Wedemeyer was friendly to the Nationalist government but
had no illusions concerning its weaknesses. In his September
report, suppressed by Marshall with a top-secret classification,
Wedemeyer recommended a far-reaching American intervention, which included 1) 10,000 American officers and noncom-
missioned officers to supervise Nationalist military forces down
to the regimental level; 2) a five-year program of economic assistance which would be prepared by a "high-level planning

and screening agency" with the aid of American advisors who would also serve in the ministry of finance; and 3) a five-power "guardianship" of Manchuria under the United Nations, consisting of the United States, the Soviet Union, Great Britain, France, and China, which would replace the Chinese Communists as the controlling agency in the region.

The Wedemeyer recommendations indicated that the Republican right, in its zeal to assist the Chiang government, was moving toward a neo-imperialist posture toward China, which would relinquish control of its finances and army. Officially, Marshall ordered the report suppressed on the grounds that its publication would offend the Chinese government as an "infringement of Chinese sovereignty." This tendency was also evident in a program put forward by William Bullitt, first ambassador to the Soviet Union in the 1930s who later had a falling-out with Roosevelt, in his "Report on China," which appeared in the October 13, 1947, issue of *Life*. Bullitt proposed a three-year plan for $1.35 billion in both military and economic assistance. Like Wedemeyer, Bullitt wanted American military advisors and, in addition, American control of Chinese supply services in Manchuria, thirty new Chinese divisions, and the dispatch of General MacArthur to China as the personal representative of the President.

In order to protect its European policy, the Administration made concessions to the Republican program. In late 1947, Secretary of State Marshall indicated that the Administration was preparing a 15-month $300 million aid program for China. Early the next year, the Administration actually submitted a fifteen-month $570 million program, which for its duration approximated the Bullitt program in the scale of aid and which, after modifications and reductions, passed as the China Aid Act. In the meantime, the Administration was forced to concede $18 million in aid to China in order to obtain support for "interim aid" to Europe, pending the Marshall Plan. Judd and Vorys forced this concession in the House with the assistance of Bridges, chairman of the Appropriations Committee in the

Senate. The context for the concessions was set in late 1947 by statements by Speaker Joseph Martin and Senator Robert Taft that aid to China was imperative.

By the end of 1948, the situation of the Nationalist government was clearly desperate. On her visit to the United States, Madame Chiang Kai-shek requested $3 billion in aid over three years. Consultants for the Senate Appropriations Committee, Bullitt and D. Worth Clark, former Democratic Senator from Idaho, returned from Asia with estimates in a crisis vein. With the Berlin blockade still in progress, the threat of war in Europe real, and with new strength from its electoral victory, the Truman Administration had no intention of acceding to these deathbed requests. The task of fending off these demands fell to Dean Acheson who was confirmed by the Senate as Secretary of State in January 1949 by a vote of 83–6. In opposition to Acheson's confirmation were the Republican leaders of the China Bloc—Bridges, Knowland, and Wherry.

In February, fifty-one Republican Congressmen sent a letter to President Truman in which they proposed a commission to reassess conditions in China. Not long after, Senator Patrick McCarran, an anti-Administration Democrat from Nevada who was closely allied with right-wing Republicans, submitted a bill for a $1.5 billion loan to China. Significantly, the House letter was signed not only by right-leaning Republicans such as Lawrence H. Smith of Wisconsin, George Dondero of Michigan, Noah Mason of Illinois, and Richard Nixon of California but by moderates such as Thruston Morton of Kentucky, Christian Herter of Massachusetts, and Clifford Case of New Jersey.[14] The China question had the effect of unifying the party, though giving the initiative to its rightist faction. The McCarran bill took neo-colonialism to a new level by giving authority to American officers to direct Chinese troops in the field and pledging the customs revenues of Chinese ports as collateral for the American loan. Acheson rejected the McCarran program outright in a letter to Senator Tom Connally of Texas, chairman of the Foreign Relations Committee in the new Democratic Congress.

By the spring, the Nationalist regime had all but collapsed, making aid proposals superfluous. The political focus now shifted to what American policy should be toward the new regime. In a June 24 letter to Truman, twenty-one Senators expressed their opposition to the diplomatic recognition of the Communist government. The letter was signed not only by new nationalists such as Bridges, Knowland, and Brewster, but by old nationalists such as Taft, Bricker, and Butler of Nebraska. It was also signed by Republican moderates such as Raymond Baldwin of Connecticut and Edward Thye of Minnesota, and by five Democrats.[15]

The Truman Administration was also reviewing its policy. On July 1, Mao made his foreign policy declaration of "leaning to one side." In the same month, Acheson instructed Philip Jessup, ambassador-at-large, to draw up policy options for the containment of Communism in Asia. Jessup was later joined in the project by Everett Case, president of Colgate University, and Raymond Fosdick, former president of the Rockefeller Foundation. Acheson gave no indication that he expected a Titoist solution in China. When the State Department's White Paper on American policy in China was issued in August under the editorship of Jessup, Acheson stated in his letter of transmittal to President Truman: "The Communist leaders have foresworn their Chinese heritage and have publicly announced their subservience to a foreign power, Russia, which during the last 50 years, under czars and Communists alike, has been most assiduous in its efforts to extend its control in the Far East."[16] He only expressed hope that "ultimately the profound civilization and the democratic individualism of China will reassert themselves and she will throw off the foreign yoke."[17]

The publication of the White Paper, which attributed developments in China to the failures of the Nationalist government, elicited a fresh flood of denunciation from Hurley, Judd, McCarran, Bridges, Knowland, and Wherry. Mao Tse-tung was also unimpressed and saw in the 1000-page document a compulsive need for self-justification by the "newly arrived, upstart and neurotic United States imperialist group."[18] The Republi-

cans held up the confirmation of W. Walton Butterworth as Assistant Secretary of State for the Far East on the grounds that
he was implicated in the failure of past policies. When his
nomination did come to a vote in the Senate in September, the
Republicans, including Vandenberg, voted 27 to 5 against,
while the Democrats voted unanimously to confirm. Only the
moderate wing of the Republican Party generated any support
for Butterworth. While the Truman Administration contemplated measures of containment, it also wanted to disengage from the Nationalists who had set up an exile regime on
Taiwan. The Administration also entertained the possibility of
diplomatic recognition and of tolerating Communist Chinese
membership in the United Nations. American policy was thus
in a fluid state on the eve of McCarthyism.

Although the Republican nationalists moved toward a neo-
imperial posture toward China, it would be a mistake to see this
evolution in terms of direct economic interest. The nationalists
opposed the preconditions for an expansionist policy—the
liberalization of trade, the export of capital, international financial institutions. The sources of their foreign policy views
were deeply *traditional.* They supported the Open Door in
China and Pacific First because they were tenets of the traditional Republican foreign policy. The original architects of the
American policy in Asia were Eastern Republicans in a time
when the Chicago *Tribune* and the New York *Herald Tribune*
could agree on some basic foreign policy questions. As the political home of internationalist business, the Eastern wing of the
party was the economically interested group. This is not to say
that American policy in Asia was a simple function of economic
expansion, as American trade and investment in Asia were not
great then or later.

Though cultural in character, the traditionalism of the Republican nationalists did have roots in material interests. The
right's social base was in a provincial America dominated by
small business and the culture of entrepreneurship. In the conquest of the American West, the nabobs of the Republican
small towns profited directly and acquired an outlook which

disposed them to support a forward policy in the Pacific as an extension of Manifest Destiny. The nationalists endorsed a Pacific First foreign policy as a part of a general defense of a lost world—lost in the sense of national dominance but still hegemonic in specific areas of the country. The central issue was to recover national power and to reestablish the folkways of the "American Way of Life" throughout the land. The implementation of a nationalist foreign policy was one aspect of this program.

Ironically, the political fundamentalism of the right made it more royalist than the king and often pitted it against the Eastern internationalists who had designed *both* the foreign policies which the right supported and those which it opposed. This conflict did not characterize China policy on which the party was united. On other issues, the nationalists tended out of their traditionalism to occupy the abandoned positions of the Eastern internationalists. Influenced by Progressive isolationism, Senator Taft and Senator Wherry led the old nationalist opposition. General MacArthur had a larger view which encompassed an active economic role for America in Asia, and he was more popular with the Republican internationalists than Senator Taft. While provincial traditionalism could resist new foreign policy initiatives, it could as easily embrace them if they fell within the basically expansionist schema of nationalism.

The second key to the foreign policy views of the nationalists was anti-Communism. This attribute led the nationalists toward interventionism not only in Asia but eventually throughout the world. Anti-Communism was a natural expression of the culture and practice of small capitalism. Paradoxically, the nationalists were intensely concerned with the expansion of Communism while not especially interested in the expansion of capitalism, as their interests were local in character. The anxiety concerning Communism derived in large part from the identification of it with domestic social forces which threatened them and were certainly experienced as "alien." They were not usually Communist as such but foreign, Southern, metropolitan, trade unionist, and bureaucratic.

Impelled by anti-Communism and by the strategic requirements of its drive for power, the old nationalism with its
various inhibitions gave way to a less scrupulous new nationalism. In the post-war era, the triumph of the new nationalism
was assured by the new constituencies which the right attempted to recruit in its search for the means to return to
power. Among these were Catholic ethnic groups, which were
anti-British or opposed to Soviet domination of their homelands, and a new capitalism in the South and West, which was
always on the look-out for new worlds to conquer. The new
scourges of the Democratic Party—McCarthy, Knowland, Goldwater, Nixon—emerged from the new nationalism and its new
constituencies. The spiritual Godfather of the new nationalism
was a man usually portrayed in the internationalist literature as
the quintessence of responsible statesmanship—Senator Arthur
Vandenberg, architect of "bipartisanship" on Europe and
organizer of the Draft MacArthur movement during wartime.

II

THE McCARTHY ERA

8

JOE McCARTHY

The crisis of the Truman Administration's containment policy opened up a line of advance for the long postponed counteroffensive against the New Deal. Set in motion by the crisis of the New Deal in the second Roosevelt Administration and by the Democratic defeat in the 1938 election, this reaction was delayed first by the world war, which reconstructed the Democratic coalition and forced a policy of patriotic unity on the Republican right, and then by the Cold War, which divided the nationalist forces into factions supporting and opposing European commitments. The China issue reunited the nationalists, and indeed the Republican Party as a whole, while discomfiting the Democrats. The 1948 campaign, controlled by the Republican moderates and conducted on the plane of airy generalities in domestic policy and bipartisanship in foreign policy, was a failure and prepared the way for a shift to the right within the party.

The 1948 election reopened the wounds of the 1930s by confirming that the Republican Party had lost its dominance in the American polity. It also demonstrated, once again, the political potency of social reform beneficial to the majority. The reaction which followed the election was therefore veiled; it was not formulated as a direct attack on New Deal policies and social forces. This did not mean that the issue for the Republican right was not still "liberty against socialism." In a "Statement of Principles," released on February 6, 1950, Republicans in the House and Senate, joined by the members of the Republican National Committee, criticized the

> administration's program for a planned economy modeled on the Socialist governments of Europe, including price and wage controls, rationing, socialized medicine, regional authorities, and the Brannan Plan [for agriculture] with its controls, penalties, fines, and jail sentences. This program is dictated by a small but powerful group of persons who believe in socialism, who have no concept of the true foundation of American progress and whose proposals are wholly out of accord with the true interests and real wishes of the workers, farmers, and businessmen.[1]

The attack on the Truman Administration was made in the name of "hard anti-Communism." On these grounds, many writers have located the sources of "McCarthyism" in the Cold War between the Soviet Union and the United States, and the "revisionist" school of history of the Cold War has in some instances placed the primary share of responsibility for the origins of the Cold War on the policies of the Truman Administration. By extension, the Democratic Administration can be regarded as having created its own McCarthyist monster. True, the Cold War contributed to an anti-Communist climate in which the pursuit of Communists and presumed Communists might be a profitable undertaking. The "Truman Doctrine" was a manifesto for an ideological crusade which some officials regarded as a dangerous overcommitment of American resources. It is a dubious proposition, however, to attribute the confrontation of two great states and two social systems to Harry Truman or even to one or another of the two countries.

The real effect of the Cold War was paradoxical. Its immediate impact was to *weaken* the right by splitting the Republican nationalists into factions led by Taft and Vandenberg, and thus to allow the Truman Administration to maintain the upper hand in its first term. The Cold War *in Europe* insulated the Democratic Administration from attack for foreign policy weakness toward the Soviet Union and Communist states. It also created the occasion for the dismantlement of Popular Front politics under which the Communist Party and the Democratic Party had tolerated each other domestically, just as the United States and the Soviet Union had internationally. The Cold War thus gave the Democrats the opportunity to prepare a defense against charges of "Communism-in-government" and of political alliance with the heathen. In 1947, well before McCarthyism, the Truman Administration put into effect a federal security and loyalty program designed to eliminate Communists from the federal government. In October 1949, several months before McCarthy's speech in Wheeling, West Virginia, the Department of Justice obtained the conviction of the top leadership of the Communist Party under the Smith Act. In 1950, the Congress of Industrial Organizations expelled Communist-led unions. After the war, the left wing of the Democratic Party split into two factions led by the anti-Communist Americans for Democratic Action and the Popular Frontist Progressive Citizens of America. A political struggle issued in the crushing defeat of the Progressive Party in 1948 and an effective purge of Communist influence from the Democratic Party.

The Communist Party was in decline before McCarthy made his charges. Its membership had fallen; its unions were about to be successfully raided; it had no allies. The party's isolation was compounded by its pursuit of an international policy line set by the Communist Party of the Soviet Union. The "popular front" of 1934–1939 was a defensive strategy "against Fascism," the dominant force in Europe, but a minor phenomenon in America. Under the favorable conditions of the depression, the Communist Party in America grew rapidly as a reformist and pseudo-democratic force, but lost the opportunity to present itself as a revolutionary alternative to the Democratic Party. After the war, again responding to Soviet influence, the party pursued a sectarian policy which isolated it at a time when it really needed a "united front" against reaction. In the CIO, the Communists, who led one fourth of the CIO unions, were in a strong position in the 1930s in an alliance with John L. Lewis of the United Mine Workers. This position even survived the Hitler-Stalin Pact, since Lewis opposed entry into the war.

After the Nazi invasion of the Soviet Union, the Communists swung into support of European intervention which, although it put them back into the mainstream of democratic politics, cost them the alliance with Lewis, who was himself declining as a force within the CIO over the war issue. The 1939–41 period of opposition to intervention in the war had already exposed the party to retaliation. There was widespread resentment of Communist-led strikes in defense industries. The "second Popular Front" of the wartime period was somewhat deceptive since the Communists were now isolated and dependent upon wartime good feeling between the Soviet and American governments. In the CIO, the Communists were surrounded by hostile factions—the old-line AFL unions that had founded the congress, the needle trades led by anti-Communist Socialists, and the growing force of Catholic trade unionism. The Association of Catholic Trade Unionists played a key role in the postwar purge of Communists in the cities of New York, Philadelphia, Pittsburgh, Cleveland, and Detroit. The Catholic Church operated 100 labor schools, 24 of which were administered by Jesuits, which produced more than 7500 graduates per year.[2]

An anti-Communist climate of opinion and a foreign policy directed against the Soviet Union did not expose the Truman Administration to attack. The presence of Communists in minor positions in government was not decisive as long as the Truman Administration did not appear to tolerate them. McCarthyism had another dynamic. Fear of *war* with the Soviet Union grew in step with the war crisis of 1948 and the Soviet acquisition of nuclear weapons in 1949. In early 1950, Klaus Fuchs, a physicist who had worked at Los Alamos, was arrested in Britain on charges of espionage. His apprehension led to the arrest in the United States of Julius and Ethel Rosenberg and others on a charge of conspiracy to commit espionage. Treason was now an issue in an unstable political climate. Even this was not enough to make "Communism-in-government" work against the Democrats. There were several additional desiderata: 1) high government officials would have to be implicated in espionage, preferably nuclear espionage; 2) these officials should be New Deal Democrats; 3) convictions were necessary to make the case beyond a reasonable doubt; 4) a China connection was desirable to mobilize the Republican faithful.

These conditions began to be fulfilled during the hearings of the House Un-American Activities Committee (HUAC) during the special session of Congress in 1948. Elizabeth Bentley, a former courier for the Soviet espionage apparatus in the United States, testified that Lauchlin Currie, a White House assistant during the Roosevelt Administration, and Harry Dexter White, formerly Assistant Secretary of the Treasury, had been involved in passing government documents to Soviet agents. Currie had been Lend Lease Administrator for China, while White had been a principal architect of the World Bank, International Monetary Fund, and the Morgenthau Plan for Germany. Much of Bentley's testimony was hearsay, and her statements were far from definitive, particularly in regard to Currie. White died of a heart attack a few days after testifying before the committee. In the same hearings, Whittaker Chambers, also a former courier for Soviet espionage and senior editor of *Time* where he was part of a right-wing coterie which included William S. Schlamm and John Chamberlain, testified that he had known Alger Hiss, president of the Carnegie Endowment for International Peace, to be a Communist in the 1930s. As an official in the State Department, Hiss had played a role in organizing the conferences which created the United Nations. His brother, Donald Hiss, was a partner in Dean Acheson's law firm, Covington and Burling. Hiss denied these charges and sued Chambers for libel when he made them outside Congress.

These cases were inconclusive and did not appear to influence the outcome of the 1948 elections. After the election, Chambers, who was afraid of political retaliation from the victorious Democrats and wanted to strengthen himself in the libel suit against him, charged that Hiss had actually passed State Department documents to him. He produced evidence which he turned over to HUAC and the Justice Department. Ultimately Hiss was indicted, and in January 1950 convicted, for perjury in testifying that he had not given State Department documents to Chambers. The Hiss case met most of the conditions for effective political use of the issue of Communists in government. There was a conviction and an issue of espionage, though not of nuclear espionage. Hiss had moved in the higher circles of the Roosevelt Administration and was in attendance at Yalta. He was a friend of Dean Acheson, the despised Secretary of State who would not save Chiang Kai-shek but refused to "turn my back on Alger Hiss." With Representative Richard Nixon of California pressing home the issue as a member of HUAC, the Hiss case was an *historical* indictment of New Deal Democracy. It was as much directed against the Roosevelt Administration, which Hiss had mainly served, for its acquiescence in the Popular Front as against the anti-Communist Truman Administration.

The Cold War contributed in some measure to the rise of McCarthyism. War crisis, the possibility of nuclear war, and later the reality of limited war generated a hypersensitivity to the activities of a revolutionary party which allied itself with a foreign state. These circumstances were most important in building support for McCarthyism *outside* the Republican right. Within the right, anti-Communism was a fixed principle which owed nothing to the Truman Administration and which predated the Cold War. It emerged immediately with the Bolshevik Revolution of 1917 and the "Red Scare" reaction to the social unrest of 1919, which made a hero of Calvin Coolidge, then governor of Massachusetts. This early anti-Communism was a natural expression of Republican "Americanism." In foreign policy, the Republican right opposed the diplomatic recognition of the Soviet Union and opposed intervention in World War II largely because it would benefit the Soviets.

McCarthyism pressed post-war anti-Communism into the service of the world view and political objectives of the Republican right. The primary goal was overturning New Deal Democracy and restoring Republican "liberalism" to pride of place. In foreign policy, the objective was to revise the "internationalist" policy which put Europe first. Quite consciously, President Truman and Secretary of State Marshall sacrificed the Nationalist regime in China to the higher priority of European security, then under direct threat from the Soviet Union. The triumph of Communist revolution in China could be seen by the Republican right as the foreign policy equivalent of the "Roosevelt revolution" at home. The New Deal swept Republican principles of government aside in the 1930s. The Chinese Revolution, which the Democratic Administration refused to attempt to reverse, represented an historic defeat for the Pacific-oriented foreign policy of the Republican Party. The nationalists understood this development as the logical culmination of the internationalist policies which had led, uselessly in their eyes, to intervention in two European wars. The "loss of China" brought the Republicans onto the barricades. McCarthy's speeches and charges were the standard ideological fare of the Republican right. Something of the apocalyptic character of this world view came through in the address of Carroll Reece, chairman of the Republican National Committee, to the party's national convention in 1948:

In the world today, there are two powerful forces. They are exponents of two systems of government diametrically opposed to one another.

One of these forces is the Republican Party of the United States—the traditional and undeviating defender of the principles of our representative Republic—the most liberal government ever devised by man. The Republican Party—our Party—is the traditional champion of constitutional government and the unswerving defender of the liberties of the individual.

The other force is the Communist Party, which may aptly be described as an international conspiracy—a conspiracy to destroy free government. Its headquarters are in Moscow, but its cells of adherents are in almost every nation on earth, including, unfortunately, our own where Fellow-travelers—the typhoid Marys of Communism—have insinuated themselves into so many important positions, in and out of Government, during the New Deal regime.

So far as this country is concerned, the struggle for mastery is between these two great political forces. The once powerful Democratic Party in America, torn by philosophical and sectional differences, and handicapped by having been in power too long, is incapable of offering an effective resistance to the march of radical aggression. The Democratic Party has become an intellectually sterile hybrid of radicalism and big city "machinism." It cannot exist with both and it cannot exist without both.[3]

During the favorable conjuncture of espionage cases and the fall of the Nationalist government in China, Senator Joseph R. McCarthy of Wisconsin made a standard Republican speech on Lincoln Day in early February 1950 in Wheeling, West Virginia. His speech was a paste-up job which rehearsed Republican charges of Communism in government, using material from a House speech by Richard Nixon, a story by Willard Edwards in the Chicago *Tribune,* an article on John Stewart Service in the Washington *Times-Herald,* and testimony before Congressional committees. McCarthy claimed that there were 205 Communists in the State Department. The number was derived from a statement by Secretary of State James F. Byrnes in 1946 that 285 out of 3000 federal employees transferred to the State Department from wartime agencies had not been recommended for permanent employment.

The Associated Press picked up the McCarthy speech, and although it had no fresh news value and was generally discounted in the metropolitan dailies, it received enough coverage across the country to make McCarthy's charges a serious political issue. On February 20, McCarthy followed up with a speech in the Senate where he presented some eighty cases drawn from the loyalty files of the State Department. These cases were compiled from the "Lee list," prepared in 1947 by Robert E. Lee, an investigator for the House Appropriations Committee and a friend of McCarthy. The "derogatory information" used by McCarthy was raw data from the files and not necessarily substantiated. Of the 108 cases on the original Lee list, 40 had by 1950 been cleared by full field investigations of the Federal Bureau of Investigation. Not all of the cases had to

do with Communist and left-wing activity. For all of these reasons, the cases had to be used with care. Instead, McCarthy
proceeded to embroider on the information he had to charge
on whatever pretext that the person in question was a "known
Communist."

Sensing a political opportunity, the Republicans demanded a
Senate investigation of McCarthy's charges. As minority leader,
Senator Wherry proposed that the investigation be assigned
to the conservatively inclined Appropriations Committee.
Through Senator Scott Lucas of Illinois, the majority leader,
the Democrats countered by proposing an investigation by the
Foreign Relations Committee, which was more reliable from
their point of view. A resolution was passed and a subcommittee of the Foreign Relations Committee under Senator Millard
E. Tydings, Democrat of Maryland, was constituted to investigate the charges pertaining to the loyalty of State Department
employees.

The investigation was an extension of the Republican line of
attack on the State Department which began with the *Amerasia*
case and the resignation of Patrick Hurley. It was also a part of
the continuing struggle over China policy. The Republican
right rallied to McCarthy's side. Reporters for the Hearst and
McCormick press fed him information and ran his political er-
rands. Alfred Kohlberg conferred with McCarthy, and the
publications which he helped to subsidize—*The Freeman* and
Counterattack—gave him aid and comfort. McCarthy could also
count on extensive and favorable coverage from the Gannett
and Scripps-Howard press. Though unenthusiastic, the national magazines and metropolitan press were under pressure
to match this coverage. The Tydings investigation turned into a
major political confrontation and made McCarthy a national
figure who was considered worthy to draw the fire of the highest officials of the Democratic Party and the Truman Administration.

Before the Tydings subcommittee, McCarthy introduced
new cases which were not included in his Wheeling speech or
subsequent Senate speech but were a part of Republican folk-

lore. Available for use was "Appendix Nine," seven volumes listing the names and associations of some 22,000 presumed Communist sympathizers, which was issued by the Dies Committee staff in 1944 but later recalled at the demand of the full committee. McCarthy also employed the prejudices, theories, and files of Alfred Kohlberg, previous investigations by HUAC, and an attack on the State Department in 1947 by Representative Fred Buseby, Republican of Illinois. The Wisconsin Senator made a pass at Ambassador-at-large Philip Jessup, who, as an opponent of intervention in World War II, might have enjoyed the favor of the Republicans but for the fact that he had the misfortune to edit the State Department's White Paper on China.

In March, McCarthy named Owen Lattimore, a Johns Hopkins professor, as the "top Russian espionage agent" in the United States before the Tydings subcommittee, although he was unable to produce evidence to substantiate the charge. Lattimore was in disfavor with the right because of his affiliation with the Institute of Pacific Relations. He had been a political advisor to Chiang Kai-shek and had accompanied Henry Wallace on his trip to China in 1944. Lattimore began as a supporter of Chiang but became through the 1940s steadily more disillusioned with the Nationalists and sympathetic to the Communists in China. Lattimore's apostasy was an *idée fixe* of Alfred Kohlberg. In right-wing circles, there was an aspiration to make Owen Lattimore "another Alger Hiss." Louis Budenz, former managing editor of *The Daily Worker,* the newspaper of the Communist Party, obligingly stepped forward to identify Lattimore as a Communist. Budenz had left the Communist Party in 1945, returned to the Catholic Church under the tutelage of Bishop Fulton J. Sheen, and was considered an essential source by any agency investigating Communism. Unfortunately, he had quite specifically told a State Department security officer in 1947 that he knew nothing to implicate Lattimore with the Communist Party. In the weeks preceding his testimony before the Tydings subcommittee, he had been in contact with Kohlberg, Robert Morris, an assistant counsel of the subcommittee with right-wing sympathies, and Charles J. Kersten, a former Wisconsin Congressman employed on McCarthy's staff.

In the hearings, the right-wing Republicans also dredged up the *Amerasia* incident. Frank Bielaski had been the employee of the Office of Strategic Services who had first noticed that material in *Amerasia* bore a close resemblance to classified documents. Bielaski testified as he had before the Hobbs Committee in 1946 except that he now maintained that one of the documents at the *Amerasia* offices was marked "A-bomb." None of the other OSS officers who had accompanied him on an initial raid of the magazine's offices could verify this recollection. The FBI discovered no such document and in fact the phrase "A-bomb" had not been coined at the time of the OSS raid. During the same period, Robert Morris attempted to pad the security file of John Carter Vincent, formerly director of the State Department's Office of Far Eastern Affairs, by advising Naval Intelligence that he had information that Vincent was a Communist, although he gave no source. When Morris became counsel of the Senate Internal Security Subcommittee, Budenz testified that Naval Intelligence had filed a report stating that Vincent was a Communist.[4]

The Tydings subcommittee, controlled by Democrats, refused to conduct an independent investigation of the State Department but simply investigated McCarthy's charges which they found wild and unsubstantiated. Nonetheless, McCarthy had brought in a political gusher. President Truman emerged from the 1948 election in a strong position, but the Administration was badly weakened in 1949 by events in Asia, the Soviet atomic bomb, and the espionage cases. In the Gallup Poll, Truman's standing fell precipitously, particularly in early 1950. To the question of whether the American people approved or disapproved of the performance of President Truman in office, the poll gave these results in percentages in 1949 and early 1950:[5]

APPROVE	DISAPPROVE	
69	17	January 21, 1949
57	24	March 30
57	26	July 20
51	31	October 21
45	40	February 17, 1950
37	44	April 12

By the time McCarthy made his charges, Truman was an un-popular President, since the interviews for the April 12 poll were conducted in late February and early March. The Administration was in disarray and McCarthy blundered through the breach. The quality of his cases was not decisive since the Democrats could hardly benefit from the public discussion of the fine points between loyalty and security, Communism and fellow-traveling, espionage and bad judgment. Attacks on McCarthy by President Truman, Vice President Alben Barkley, Secretary of State Acheson, Senate Majority Leader Lucas, and Senator Tom Connally of Texas, chairman of the Foreign Relations Committee, succeeded only in converting McCarthy into a recognized leader of right-wing Republicanism.

The saliency of Communism as a political issue was demonstrated even within the Democratic Party when leading liberal Democrats were Red-baited in the spring primaries. Senator Frank Graham was defeated by Willis Smith in North Carolina, and Senator Claude Pepper was defeated by George Smathers in the "Red Pepper" campaign in Florida. These results did not go unnoticed and reinforced McCarthy's position. In the Senate, the Democrats became increasingly anxious to terminate the disastrous hearings. The Republicans would have been content to expand their scope and continue them right up until the fall election, a course of action which was in fact proposed by Senator Henry Cabot Lodge, Jr., Republican of Massachusetts and a member of the subcommittee. Senator Taft criticized the hearings as a "whitewash" in anticipation of the subcommittee's conclusions. Once the Korean War had begun, the Democrats on the subcommittee moved to terminate the hearings over the protests of Lodge and Senator Bourke Hickenlooper, Republican of Iowa. In July, the subcommittee issued a majority report, which Lodge and Hickenlooper refused to sign, that described McCarthy's claims as a "fraud and a hoax."

The Korean War briefly put an end to the McCarthy uproar. In its first stages, the war *strengthened* the position of the Administration. In a Gallup Poll, the interviews for which were conducted in late August, 43 per cent of the American people now approved Truman's performance in office while 32 per cent disapproved. In another poll, 65 per cent of the American people endorsed the Korean intervention against 20 per cent who did not.[6] The interviews were conducted in early September even before the Inchon invasion had apparently won the war for the United Nations. During the final month of the election campaign, Communist Chinese forces were in Korea, but Chinese intentions were still in some doubt. Despite popular support for the war policy of the Administration, the Gallup Poll showed that the election prospects of the Democrats had been in a slight decline since the spring. The factors which had produced "McCarthyism" were apparently still operative. In the event, the Republicans added five seats in the Senate and twenty-eight in the House. These gains were not as great as those in the three previous off-year elections, but with the recovery of Republican fortunes, advances came harder. Moreover, the main beneficiary of the victory was the right wing of the party.

During the campaign, McCarthy gave thirty major speeches in fifteen states and emerged from the election with the political power he was to wield until his censure. At the time, he was given credit for the defeat of several prominent Democrats. This assessment has since been effectively disputed, and it is difficult to weigh McCarthy's influence among the myriad factors which affect the outcome of any given election.[7] The question has also been overrated because McCarthy's power was not personal but derived from his position as a leader of a faction—the right-wing Republicans. This group, and thus McCarthy, emerged from the election with greatly enhanced political strength. Outside the South, the Democrats were able to elect only 126 Representatives and 9 Senators against 196 Representatives and 18 Senators for the Republicans. Four new pro-McCarthy Republicans entered the Senate—Nixon of California, Herman Welker of Idaho, Everett McKinley Dirksen of Illinois, and John Marshall Butler of Maryland. The political message was clear enough.

Two of McCarthy's principal enemies, Senator Lucas and Senator Tydings, were defeated. McCarthy mounted a large effort against Tydings on Butler's behalf in concert with Ruth McCormick Miller, a niece of Colonel McCormick and editor of the Washington *Times-Herald*. Miller brought in Jon M. Jonkel, a public relations man from Chicago, to organize the campaign, and provided Butler with the *Times-Herald*'s printing services at below-market rates. McCarthy mobilized some of his financial backers, such as Texas oil men, for Butler and his staff cooperated with *Times-Herald* employees to produce a campaign tabloid which included a faked photograph of Tydings conversing with Earl Browder. Fulton Lewis, Jr., delivered a series of radio broadcasts attacking Tydings over the Mutual Broadcasting System. As a state with a large Catholic population, Maryland was particularly susceptible to McCarthy's influence. It can still be doubted whether McCarthy actually defeated Tydings, who labored under local political liabilities and who, as a conservative Democrat, was not popular with blacks or labor. Tydings's defeat had great impact, nonetheless, since Roosevelt had tried and failed to purge him in 1938. Not long after the election, Tydings filed a complaint with the Senate's Subcommittee on Privileges and Elections in which he denounced the Republican conduct of the campaign as "scurrilous."

McCarthy rose to power as a right-wing Republican on a standard right-wing issue—treachery in the State Department. He had the good fortune to raise the issue at a favorable moment and to be attacked by men whose stature added to his own. The results of the primaries and the off-year elections then vindicated him. The legend persists that he was somehow a "populist" or a closet Democrat. Its main basis is that Mc-Carthy was an Irish/German Catholic raised in a Democratic family. In 1936, he was elected president of the local Young Democratic Club and ran for district attorney in the same year on a standard New Deal platform. In the 1930s, the Democratic Party in Wisconsin was still extremely weak, and Mc-Carthy was defeated. In 1938, he was elected circuit judge as a Republican.

For all effective purposes, McCarthy's voting record in the Senate reveals him, without the slightest doubt, as a right-wing Republican on domestic issues.[8] On arrival in 1947, he became known as the "Pepsi Cola kid" for his close association with sugar lobbyists in working to defeat a bill extending sugar controls for one year. A Pepsi Cola lobbyist endorsed a note for $20,000 for deposit with McCarthy's bank in Appleton, Wisconsin, when he was in financial difficulties. McCarthy also involved himself in the question of the post-war housing shortage. He worked with real estate and homebuilding interests in opposing the public housing provisions in the omnibus Taft-Ellender-Wagner housing bill which was under consideration. As a member of the Senate Banking and Currency Committee, McCarthy served on the Joint Committee on Housing and blocked Senator Charles W. Tobey, a moderate Republican from New Hampshire who was sympathetic to public housing, from the chairmanship of the Joint Committee. Although the housing bill passed the Senate in 1948, the Republican leadership in the House prevented its passage. Senator Taft, who supported public housing and was a co-sponsor of the bill, acceded to their wishes, and a McCarthy substitute measure, which eliminated the public housing provisions, was passed. During this period, McCarthy accepted $10,000 from the Lustron Corporation, a firm dealing in prefabricated housing, supposedly in return for a promotional brochure.

In 1949, McCarthy took an interest in the Malmedy massacre case. During the Battle of the Bulge in 1944, American prisoners of war and Belgian civilians were murdered in the Belgian village of Malmedy by troops of the German First SS

Panzer Division. After the war, seventy-three SS soldiers were convicted of carrying out the massacre and forty-nine were sentenced to death. In 1948, they petitioned the U.S. Supreme Court, which refused to hear the cases on grounds of lack of jurisdiction. However, inquiries by the office of the Judge Advocate and a panel led by a Texas Supreme Court judge did find that various forms of psychological pressure, including mock trials, had been used in interrogation, although they found no evidence of torture as claimed by the defendants. By this time, the question had been taken up by some Congressmen with large German-American constituencies. Senator William Langer, Republican of North Dakota, introduced a resolution calling for an investigation by the Judiciary Committee of which he was the senior Republican, but the case was referred, instead, to the Armed Services Committee through a resolution introduced by Senator Raymond E. Baldwin, moderate Republican of Connecticut. This referral ensured that the U.S. Army would not be embarrassed, and indeed a member of Baldwin's law firm had been one of the prosecutors of the German soldiers. Representing a state whose population was 30 per cent German-American, McCarthy sat in on the hearings and denounced the proceedings as a whitewash of the Army. He was aided in his efforts by Tom Korb, a lawyer for the Harnischfeger Corporation in Milwaukee, which was interested in prefabricated housing. Walter Harnischfeger, the firm's head, was a McCarthy backer and a man of rightist, pro-German views. In the end, the investigation vindicated the U.S. Army and the full Armed Services Committee passed a resolution critical of McCarthy's conduct during the hearings.

If McCarthy gave any indication of heterodox views, it was in foreign policy where he followed the lead of Senator Vandenberg and voted for Greek-Turkish aid, the Marshall Plan, and NATO, thus identifying himself as a new nationalist. In 1948, he endorsed Harold Stassen, who was regarded as an internationalist, for the Republican Presidential nomination. In that year, Stassen came out for the outlawing of the Communist Party and was defeated in the Oregon primary on the issue by

Thomas Dewey who opposed Stassen's proposal on grounds of inefficacy. Early in his Senate career, McCarthy shared both staff and financial backers with Stassen. Although McCarthy was endorsed for election to the U.S. Senate in 1946 by Colonel McCormick and the Chicago *Tribune,* the McCormick press later indicated some dissatisfaction with the evolution of his foreign policy views.

In the 1946 campaign, McCarthy showed no affinity for Wisconsin Progressivism, and Progressivism none for him. His opponent in the Republican primary was Senator Robert M. La-Follette, Jr., so that the Progressive forces in the state were aligned against him. Previously, LaFollette had been elected on a third-party ticket, the Progressive Party. In 1946, he attempted to take his following into the Republican Party, but a part of his constituency, organized labor in particular, refused to follow his lead and voted in the Democratic primary instead. The failure to mobilize the urban vote insured his defeat in the Republican primary. LaFollette also suffered from overconfidence and overwork in Washington, and campaigned in the primary for exactly one week. In the general election in 1946, and again in 1952, McCarthy proved to be unusually strong in rural areas and unusually weak in the cities. Compared to other conservative Republicans, he therefore ran somewhat better in rural Progressive counties. This was only by comparison to conservative Republicans; these were not his strongest counties. Whereas the Progressives mobilized the poor, Scandinavian farmers, McCarthy's politics of provincial resentment had a certain appeal in all rural areas, rich and poor.[9] McCarthy was the candidate of the Republican Voluntary Committee, the directorship of the regular Republican machine, led by Thomas E. Coleman, president of Madison-Kipp, a firm dealing in oil systems and die castings. The Progressive press in Wisconsin—the *Capital-Times* of Madison, the Superior *Telegram,* and *The Progressive* magazine—opposed McCarthy throughout his career and carried out a kind of guerrilla warfare against him. *The Progressive* published an issue in 1954 devoted to an exposé of McCarthy. The *Capital-Times* instigated an investigation by the State Board of Bar Commissioners of the propriety of McCarthy running for the Senate while holding a judicial office.

Since McCarthy never ran in a national campaign, it is more difficult to figure the components of the national support for him. The Gallup Polls are a beginning: [10]

FAVORABLE OPINION	UNFAVORABLE OPINION	
15	22	August 17, 1951
19	22	April 13, 1953
35	30	June 24
34	42	August 23
50	29	January 15, 1954
46	36	March 15
35	49	May 24
34	45	June 9
34	45	June 27
36	51	August 22
35	46	November 12

For most of his career, Senator McCarthy was a more *unpopular* than popular figure with the American people. He became generally popular only in late 1953 and then declined in early 1954 during the controversy with the Army. Even at the time of his censure, he retained a base of support roughly equivalent to that which he commanded before his rise in late 1953.

The Gallup Polls also indicate that McCarthy's support was closely related to party affiliation: [11]

Democrats		*Republicans*		
FAVORABLE	UNFAVORABLE	FAVORABLE	UNFAVORABLE	
10	21	22	20	Aug. 17, 1951
39	38	62	19	Jan. 15, 1954
36	44	61	25	March 15
25	59	50	37	May 24
26	50	46	37	June 9
26	60	47	42	August 22
30	51	40	40	November 12

For most of his career, Republicans were roughly evenly divided in support and opposition to McCarthy, while the Democrats were opposed to him by a margin of two to one. At the peak of his influence in early 1954, the Democrats were evenly divided, but the Republicans were overwhelmingly favorable.

The Gallup Polls demonstrate that McCarthy was most favorably regarded by the less educated and by manual workers, while the highly educated and executive, professional, and white collar personnel were most disposed to oppose him.[12] Surveys by International Research Associates (INRA), the Roper organization, and the Survey Research Center of the University of Michigan yield similar results.[13] This is a paradox since the Republican Party is generally the party of the managerial element and the Democratic Party representative of the blue-collar workers; yet, the Democrats were much more negative in their view of McCarthy. The paradox can be resolved if it is kept in mind that the Republican Party was divided in its view of McCarthy. The metropolitan wing of the party, which included the bulk of well-educated Republicans, was skeptical of McCarthy, while the provincial wing, based in areas less developed economically, was well disposed toward him. Manual workers in such areas often voted Republican. The Roper survey also found that small businessmen were particularly pro-McCarthy. In a survey of Bennington, Vermont, Martin Trow found that small businessmen, particularly those of low education, were the strongest pro-McCarthy element. Bennington citizens who were opposed to *both* big business and big labor, "19th-century liberals," were more pro-McCarthy than those actually friendly to big business. At its heart, McCarthyism, like right-wing Republicanism, was *petit-bourgeois*. Trow characterized small businessmen as exhibiting a

> generalized hostility toward a complex of symbols and processes bound up with industrial capitalism: the steady growth and concentration of government, labor organizations, and business enterprises; the correlative trend toward greater rationalization of production and distribution; and the men, institutions, and ideas that symbolize these secular trends in society. These trends and

their symbols were, we believe, McCarthy's most persuasive
targets.[14]

While McCarthy's business support was concentrated on
Main Street, he was also regarded favorably by some larger interests. The section of corporate capital which never accepted
the New Deal endorsed him as it endorsed the Republican
right as a whole. The "Big Four" oil independents in Texas—
Hugh Roy Cullen, Clint Murchison, H. L. Hunt, and Sid Richardson—were friendly to him with varying degrees of inten-
sity. Generally, concerns dominated by families and operating
in highly competitive markets were more likely to be attracted
to the Americanist ideology of McCarthy than firms which were
more bureaucratic in form of control and entrenched in oli-
gopolistic or public markets. However, a survey by *Fortune*
Magazine in early 1954 of 253 executives in 30 cities, including
the chief executive officers of the 100 largest industrial corporations, found them well disposed to McCarthy up to the
point of his confrontation with the Army because of his anti-
Communism and uncompromising attitude toward the New
Deal and Fair Deal. Among these men, McCarthy was most
popular in Chicago, capital of the old Republican right, and in
Texas, locale of an economic boom and a new generation of
millionaires.[15]

Beyond his base in provincial Republicanism, McCarthy had
an additional key asset. All the surveys indicate that Catholics
were distinctly more favorable to him than Protestants, while
Jews were overwhelmingly opposed. By ethnic origin, the
Roper and INRA surveys revealed that those of Irish and Italian heritage were particularly friendly to McCarthy. Those of
recent rather than distant German origin were also pro-
McCarthy as reported by the Roper study. In the Gallup Poll,
McCarthy was strong in the Midwest, but actually strongest in
the *East,* and weakest in the South and far West. Of all sections,
he was most popular in an area which had both a large Catholic
population and a tradition of provincial Republicanism—New
England. In a Gallup Poll, New England measured highest in

"intense approval" of McCarthy and lowest in "intense disapproval" while the South and Pacific coast were highest in intense disapproval of him.[16]

With his strength among manual workers, Catholics, Irish and Italian ethnics, and in the East, it is obvious that Senator McCarthy made inroads into the normally Democratic working class. It is possible that his rhetoric of provincial resentment, which, when not showing its anti-labor face, may give the appearance of a class rhetoric, had something to do with this appeal. On arriving in Washington in late 1946, McCarthy's first political act was to call a press conference to propose that coal miners on strike be drafted into the Army. But in his Wheeling speech, he asserted:

> It is not the less fortunate, or members of minority groups who have been selling this nation out, but rather those who have had all the benefits the wealthiest nation on earth has had to offer— the finest homes, the finest college educations, and the finest jobs in the government that we can give.
>
> This is glaringly true of the State Department. There the bright young men who are born with silver spoons in their mouth are the ones who have been worst.[17]

This is the convergence thesis of radicalism and the metropolitan elite, which is a logical expression of the dual resentments of provincial businessmen or even of the urban middle class, who feel pressure from above and below in the social structure. But it *sounds* like working class rhetoric. How important it was to McCarthy's appeal outside the Republican right is problematic. Outside right-wing Republican precincts, McCarthy's appeal to the blue-collar worker was not general but specific to the Catholic and ethnic worker. He may have mobilized Catholic ethnic resentment of the Protestant Anglo-Saxon upper class.

Foreign policy was the decisive factor. In this area, Republican nationalism as a whole had certain political advantages, although McCarthy, as an Irish/German Catholic, was better positioned than most right-wing Republicans to exploit them. The rapprochement between the Republican right and certain normally Democratic ethnic groups had its origins not in the Cold War but in the struggle over intervention in World War II. Not only German Protestants, who were already in the Republican Party, but Irish Catholics, who were bitterly anti-British, and Italian Catholics, who were often pro-Mussolini and naturally opposed to war with their homeland, were in the anti-interventionist camp. These Democratic ethnic groups were susceptible to the nationalist/revisionist interpretation of World War II as a blunder which had facilitated the expansion of Soviet Communism. Irish- and Italian-Americans each constituted approximately 5 per cent of the American population. Although they continued to vote Democratic, the softening of their support for the Democratic Party was an important factor after 1948 when the Republicans began their assault on Democratic foreign policy.

The Cold War created additional possibilities for the Republican nationalists. Polish-Americans were bitter over the results of the Yalta Conference which allowed the Soviet Union to absorb vast sections of eastern Poland. Although they had generally backed intervention in World War II as a means of combating Nazi imperialism in Eastern Europe, Americans of East European origin were responsive to the Republican nationalist interpretation of the wartime conferences as having opened the way to Soviet domination of Eastern Europe. In order for right-wing politicians to capitalize on these sentiments, it was essential for them to embrace the new nationalism and favor economic and military commitments in Europe. The right would still face formidable competition from the Democratic Party, which had taken a strong post-war stand in Europe. In outbidding the Truman Administration, the rhetoric of the "Yalta sell-out" and the foreign policy doctrine of "Liberation" became crucial. Having abandoned at an early date old nationalist inhibitions in regard to Europe, Senator McCarthy was effective in this political milieu. In his Senate campaigns in Wisconsin, he did unusually well with Czech- and Polish-American voters. In part, "McCarthyism" represented the inauguration of one of the right's basic post-war strategies for a return to power—the Catholic/ethnic/blue-collar strategy.

The Catholic Church was a powerful force in this political context. The Church regarded the institution of private property as fundamental to human society and, of course, opposed Communist atheism. In the late 1930s, the Church and the Communist movement had become grudge antagonists in the Spanish Civil War. After World War II, the Church played a key role in the organization of Christian Democratic parties in Western Europe to counter the left-wing parties, and it mobilized a protest movement throughout the West against the persecution of the national churches in Eastern Europe. Although pleased by the affection of the right-wing Republicans for Franco and by their spirit of anti-Communist militancy, the Catholic Church in America was not officially Republican or pro-McCarthy. McCarthy's employment of the Communist issue was first suggested to him by Father Edmund A. Walsh, regent of the School of Foreign Service at Georgetown University, but Walsh later repudiated McCarthy. While Francis Cardinal Spellman of New York gave McCarthy his blessing, Bishop Bernard J. Sheil attacked him. *Commonweal,* a liberal Catholic weekly, and *America,* a Jesuit weekly, were anti-McCarthy.

The Catholic Church hierarchy in America was dominated by Irish Catholics. The Irish Catholic community was of two minds concerning McCarthy. While sympathetic to his attack on the Roosevelt-Truman foreign policy, Irish Catholics could hardly endorse his unqualified indictment of the Democratic Party and its domestic policies. The Irish were the top stratum of the Catholic immigration to America and were prominent in the leadership of key institutions of the Democratic working class in the East, such as the urban political machines and the American Federation of Labor. They had taken the New Deal and the Fair Deal at the flood and risen to national power in the 1930s and 1940s. No matter how anti-British and revisionist their views might be on foreign policy, the Irish political leadership could not countenance the destruction of the Democratic Party. As a rich conservative and a prewar opponent of intervention as ambassador to England, Joseph P. Kennedy had relatively few inhibitions regarding McCarthy. As a Democratic politician, his son, John F. Kennedy, was caught in the Irish Catholic dilemma.

While McCarthy's base in provincial Republicanism was secure and his appeal to Catholic workers significant, his position with moderate Republicans was more doubtful. The well-educated members of higher-status occupations, the foundation of metropolitan Republicanism, were cool to him. In his early Senate career, McCarthy consistently tangled with moderate Republicans—Senator Ralph Flanders of Vermont over sugar controls, Senator Tobey over public housing, and Senator Baldwin in the Malmedy case. One moderate Republican approach to McCarthy, typified by Senator Lodge, was to encourage the Wisconsin Senator in his demolition job on the Democratic Party, while standing well clear of the falling debris. However, other moderate Republicans attacked McCarthy at the beginning. He was repudiated in a "Declaration of Conscience" in June 1950 by seven moderate Republican Senators—Margaret Chase Smith of Maine, George Aiken of Vermont, Wayne Morse of Oregon, Edward J. Thye of Minnesota, Robert C. Hendrickson of New Jersey, Irving Ives of New York, and Tobey of New Hampshire. In the same month, three moderate Republican governors—James H. Duff of Pennsylvania, Alfred E. Driscoll of New Jersey, and Earl Warren of California—criticized McCarthy at the Governor's Conference. Although committed to the cause of Chiang Kai-shek, Time Incorporated realized after a year of McCarthyism that McCarthy's intrigues and inaccuracies could become a liability to the cause of hard anti-Communism and a hard Asian policy. While no intimate of McCarthy, Senator Taft gave him his political endorsement. In an October 1, 1951, editorial, entitled "Taft and McCarthy," *Life* Magazine urged Taft to repudiate him:

> Senator Taft has a special stake in truth and decency. They are popularly associated with his name. There are hundreds of thou-

sands, maybe millions, of Americans who, though disagreeing with Taft on other matters, would willingly and prayerfully vote for Taft and integrity in corrupt times like these. But how will they vote if his name is also associated with McCarthyism? On that issue the truth-and-decency vote will require a stand. The have-it-both ways game is about over. Joe is becoming a liability and a danger, both to the Republicans and the nation.[18]

Several weeks later *Time* did a cover story, "Demagogue McCarthy: Does He Deserve Well of the Republic?" *Time* summarized its *Realpolitik* case against McCarthy as follows:

1. His antics foul up the necessary examination of the past mistakes of the Truman-Acheson foreign policy.
2. His constant imputation of treason distracts attention from the fact that patriotic men can make calamitous mistakes for which they should be held politically accountable.
3. There are never any circumstances which justify the reckless imputation of treason or other moral guilt to individuals in or out of office.
4. McCarthy's success in smearing Tydings and others generates fear of the consequences of dissent. This fear is exaggerated by the "liberals" who welcome McCarthyism as an issue; but the fear exists—and it is poison in a democracy.[19]

Despite the palpable tension between the moderate Republicans and the McCarthyites, the moderate wing of the party ultimately proved too inhibited to stop McCarthy. While the party was out of power, the moderates benefited politically from McCarthy's aspersions upon the Democrats as traitors and friends of traitors. When the Republican Party came to power, it became imperative not to divide the party and endanger the political basis of its rule.

9

THE RETURN OF MacARTHUR

The rise of Joe McCarthy as the right-wing impresario of Communism in government was only one manifestation of the Republican reaction of the early 1950s. The right made its strongest bid since the 1930s to nominate one of its own for President. The nomination and election of Robert A. Taft as President would have been the most effective means of establishing the principles of Americanism, true liberalism, and nationalism as authoritative guides to policy. In the meantime, Republican nationalists supported the effort of General Douglas MacArthur to take control of Asian policy.

In 1950, MacArthur's prestige was at its height. The shadow over his military reputation cast by the defeat in the Philippines in 1942 had been subsequently eliminated by his bypassing and amphibious campaigns, the reconquest of the Philippines, and his acceptance of the surrender of Japan. As Supreme Commander, Allied Powers (SCAP), he had, in effect, ruled 80 million Japanese since the war. In that capacity, he was acknowledged on all sides to have turned in a brilliant performance in the economic reconstruction, demilitarization, and democratization of Japan. Often regarded as the "proconsul" of Japan, MacArthur did bear comparison to the reforming viceroys of the British Empire in its days of glory. He was also Commanding General, United States Army, Far East, and exercised control over the Air Force and Navy in the area as Commander in Chief, Far East. In these multiple roles, MacArthur had unique political and military influence in the Pacific.

In early January 1950, a State Department "policy information paper," which advised U.S. missions abroad that the conquest of Formosa by the Communists was expected and should be taken in stride, leaked through MacArthur's headquarters in Tokyo. The day before, Senator Knowland released a letter from Herbert Hoover which proposed that the United States prevent invasion of Formosa through the use of the Navy and continue to support the claim of the Nationalist government to represent the people of China. Senator Taft immediately endorsed this position. In another letter to Knowland, Hoover suggested that Formosa could still legally be considered to be a possession of Japan and thus within the jurisdiction of MacArthur. This conception had been put forth earlier by Senator H. Alexander Smith, a moderate Republican of New Jersey and, like many Eastern Republicans, pro-Chiang.

The position of the Truman Administration was that Formosa was a part of China in accordance with the wartime Cairo Declaration. The Administration had no desire to maintain a commitment to Chiang Kai-shek, much less to undertake a military defense of Formosa, although the Nationalists continued to receive unexpended funds from the China Aid Act of 1948. In a speech to the National Press Club in January, Secretary of State Acheson reiterated the thesis of his letter transmitting the White Paper the previous year—namely, that the Soviet Union had imperialist designs on China's northern provinces and "We must not undertake to deflect from the Russians to ourselves the righteous anger, and the wrath, and the hatred of the Chinese people which must develop." [1] From the point of view of policy, the speech was ambiguous. Acheson spoke only of the "Chinese people" and held open the possibility that the Communist regime might be regarded as a puppet state of the Soviet Union on the model of Eastern Europe. This was the most natural interpretation of the speech since Acheson considered Communism the "spearhead of Russian imperialism" and referred to those in China "who are allowing themselves to be used as puppets of Moscow." Acheson did not completely foreclose the alternative—that the government of Mao Tse-tung might evolve in a "Titoist" direction of nationalist hostility to the Soviet Union. If the Communists did reduce Formosa and eliminate the Nationalist government, this option would be the most practical way for the Acheson thesis to operate. Essentially, the Truman Administration's policy was to wait "until the dust settled," as Acheson had told a group of Congressmen the previous year, before making any irrevocable policy decisions. It was also determined to disengage from the Chiang regime on grounds of political expediency. At the same time, the detention of American diplomats in China and in February 1950 the Sino-Soviet Treaty had set up a countertendency moving the Administration in the direction of a hard line toward the Chinese Communists.

The Republican nationalists were determined to force the Administration into a permanent commitment to Chiang Kai-shek. If the United States undertook a naval defense of Formosa, it would be all but impossible for it to recognize the People's Republic and to discontinue its recognition of the Nationalist regime as the legitimate government of China. Furthermore, the United States could hardly support the admission to the United Nations of a government it did not recognize. American policy toward China would tend to set the tone for its policy throughout Asia, particularly toward Indo-China where an anti-colonial revolution was in progress under Communist leadership. The question of Formosa thus took on compelling significance.

Formosa was important to the Republican nationalists for another reason. The strategic doctrine of the nationalists was based on air and naval superiority and alliance with island nations. It specifically counseled against land war on the Eurasian land mass against countries with superior manpower reserves. MacArthur's views were typical in this respect. As a perverse means of demonstrating dissatisfaction with the Administration's Formosa policy in 1950, Representative John Vorys organized an effort in the House to defeat a supplemental Korean aid appropriation. The Republicans voted six to one against it, and the bill failed of passage by one vote. Even after leaders of the China bloc in the Senate protested this sabotage, Republicans in the House voted five to two against another bill including the aid program, which, however, passed. This episode demonstrated the equivocal nationalist attitude toward commitments on the Asian continent.

China posed a problem for the traditional nationalist policy. As with Europe, anti-Communism seemed to call for increasing military commitments to the continent of Asia. The special place of China in the Republican scheme of foreign policy accentuated the dilemma. In the last years of Nationalist control of China, Republicans supported the Bullitt and Wedemeyer plans which, with their provision for thousands of American military advisors, almost certainly would have led to a ground war in China. The exile of the Nationalist government to Formosa resolved the central contradiction of nationalist foreign policy by converting the true China into an island. Formosa was an issue around which the Republican nationalists could effectively rally. Later, the Korean War would *not* have the same attraction.

In the spring of 1950, the Truman Administration won the first round over Formosa and China policy. The Hoover proposal carried some risk of war should the Communists undertake to carry out an invasion of Formosa against American opposition. Senator Connally denounced the proposal in these terms, and the Democratic Party united behind him. Public opinion would not support an action that was openly provocative. Positive support for the Administration's policy was much weaker. According to Gallup Polls, the American people opposed the recognition of Communist China by a two to one majority. Although the Administration withheld recognition, it did not rule it out in the future. In May 1950, twenty-one Senators sent President Truman a letter opposing both the diplomatic recognition of Communist China and its admission to the United Nations in lieu of the Nationalists. On the latter question, the Administration attempted to pursue a middle course by voting against admission on "procedural" grounds but not exercising its veto. The Senate letter indicated a high degree of unity in the Republican Party on the issue, as it was signed not only by the leaders of the China bloc but by old nationalists, such as Bricker of Ohio and Wherry of Nebraska, and by Eastern internationalists, such as Leverett Saltonstall of Massachusetts and Ralph Flanders of Vermont. The letter also revealed division in the Democratic Party since it was endorsed by several conservative Democrats, including Harry F. Byrd of Virginia.

On June 25, the army of North Korea invaded the South. Within forty-eight hours, the Truman Administration determined to use American armed forces to repel the invasion and to provide greatly augmented military assistance to the Philippines and to the French in Indo-China. Truman also approved military aid to Nationalist China, a military survey of the requirements of Chiang Kai-shek's forces, and reconnaissance flights along the coast of China. But policy toward China and thus toward Asia was not completely settled by the North Korean invasion. Although the Administration blocked the Formosa Strait with the U.S. Seventh Fleet, it clung to a remnant of its disengagement policy by announcing that it was merely "neutralizing" the strait and preventing aggressive acts by either side. President Truman also announced that the "determination of the future status of Formosa must await the restoration of security in the Pacific, a peace settlement with Japan or consideration by the United Nations." He thus backed away from his statement the previous January that Formosa was a part of China in accordance with the Cairo Declaration, but he still did not fully commit himself to Chiang Kai-shek. The new policy would be to seek a determination by the United Nations on the Formosa question. In a report to Truman later in the summer concerning his meeting with MacArthur, W. Averell Harriman, Special Assistant to the President, referred to the possibility of an "independent government" for Formosa, apparently meaning a government which made no claim to sovereignty in China. This alternative would have achieved the Administration's objective of denying Formosa to a "hostile power" as a potential military base, while still not committing the United States to Chiang Kai-shek as the legitimate ruler of China.

President Truman successfully sought United Nations condemnation of the invasion and U.N. sanction for intervention. General of the Army Douglas MacArthur was designated Commander in Chief, United Nations Command. After the North Korean invasion, Chiang offered Chinese Nationalist troops for use in Korea. The Truman Administration did not accept the offer as it might provide the justification for a counterintervention by the Chinese Communists. MacArthur agreed with another rationale for this rejection, which was that the logistical effort of placing Nationalist troops in combat could be put to better use on more effective American forces. But he did not agree with the neutralization of the Formosa Strait, which in his judgment freed the Communists from the strategic necessity of defending their coastline against possible Nationalist invasion and thus changed the strategic calculus in the Korean War. MacArthur also desired a more definite commitment to the Nationalist government than ambiguous "neutralization" of the strait.

On July 31, MacArthur went in person to Formosa to survey the island's defensive situation and to explain to Chiang the reasons why the United Nations Command could not accept his offer of troops. After the visit, both MacArthur and Chiang issued statements which seemed to imply to the Administration a greater commitment to the Nationalists than had actually been made. Harriman was dispatched to Tokyo to expound Administration policy to MacArthur. Harriman laid great stress on Chiang Kai-shek's interest in a war between the United States and Communist China which could lead to the restoration of his control on the mainland. This was not the policy of the United States and would jeopardize United Nations support for the war. MacArthur seemed to agree that Chiang's goal could not be realized, but he did not change his views on neutralization of the strait and unequivocal economic and military support of the Nationalist regime as the legitimate government of China. He would, however, follow orders. After Harriman's departure, MacArthur issued a denunciatory statement that the purpose of his trip to Formosa had been "maliciously misrepresented to the public by those who invariably in the past have propagandized a policy of defeatism and appeasement in the Pacific."

The Administration replied with a directive from the Secretary of Defense stating that MacArthur was not to authorize a Nationalist attack on the mainland or take any action which would risk general war. MacArthur continued his public campaign with a message to the annual encampment of the Veterans of Foreign Wars. President Truman ordered the message withdrawn but it had already been printed in the *U.S. News and World Report* and other publications. In the message, MacArthur argued the case for the military defense of Formosa. The island was an "unsinkable aircraft carrier and submarine tender" which in the hands of a potential enemy would constitute a major threat to the American line of defense in the Pacific. He probably had little difficulty in convincing himself of this point, since the Philippines had been attacked in 1941 by Japanese planes based on the island. In his message, as in his earlier skirmish with the Administration, MacArthur was arguing a position consistent with the nationalist case originally expounded in Hoover's letter to Knowland, the "Senator from Formosa." Invasion of mainland China was *not* his central concern, but full military and political support for the Nationalist government *on Formosa* and the maintenance of the threat of Nationalist invasion for the effect it would have on the course of the war *in Korea*.

In 1950, the Truman Administration's policy toward Formosa was opposed by Louis Johnson, Secretary of Defense, who favored a military commitment to its defense. A conservative Democrat from West Virginia and a former national commander of the American Legion, Johnson was a close friend of Truman and had rendered financial assistance to the latter's

1948 campaign for reelection when it was at its lowest ebb. Also a believer in fiscal restraint, Johnson had much in common with the Republican nationalists and discussed with them the possibility of removing his nemesis, Secretary of State Acheson, from office. Instead, Johnson himself was removed. The Truman Administration nominated as his successor perhaps the one man in America who had the political and military stature to contain MacArthur—George Catlett Marshall.

The Republican nationalists made a serious fight against the Marshall nomination. They took their principal stand on a bill which would permit Marshall to be exempted from a requirement that the Secretary of Defense be a civilian. Generally, the nationalists occupied the high ground of civilian control of the military as their reason for opposing Marshall. On this occasion, however, Senator William E. Jenner of Indiana made his notorious attack on General Marshall as a "front man for traitors." According to Jenner, a "day of reckoning" had arrived concerning "how the Democratic Party has been captured from within and used to hasten our destruction, both from within and without, during these tragic years." Beginning with the "vicious propaganda of the 'four freedoms,' " Jenner recited the nationalist grievances against Marshall for his personal involvement in 1) the Pearl Harbor debacle and the effort to "trick the American people into a war"; 2) the extension of lend-lease to Russia; 3) the wartime conferences "selling out" East Europe and China; 4) the Marshall mission to China pressing for a coalition government including Communists; 5) the Marshall Plan which made a *pro forma* offer to include Russia. The reappearance of Marshall, who was Acheson's predecessor as Secretary of State, as Secretary of Defense was, according to Jenner, a continuation of the same story:

So, Mr. President, General Marshall has been appointed as Secretary of Defense, not for the purpose of straightening out the mess we are in, not for the purpose of returning to American principles and for at least safeguarding American interests, but for the frightening purpose of providing the front of respectability to the vicious sell-out, not only of Chiang, not only of Formosa, which is vital to our security, but of the American GI's who are fighting and dying even now because of one treachery, and whose valiant suffering will again be auctioned off on the bloody block of power politics.

Secretary Johnson refused to go along with the deal that is in the making to sell China down the river and seat the Communist delegates in the United Nations. [2]

Senator Jenner was extreme even for the Republican right in his willingness to implicate General Marshall in "treason." But his view of the policies with which Marshall was associated was typical. Senator Taft formulated the position, minus the conspiracy:

The appointment of General Marshall is a reaffirmation of the tragic policy of this administration in encouraging Chinese Communism which brought on the Korean War and has made the whole situation so precarious in the Far East. General Marshall in China tried to force the Chinese Communists into the Nationalist Cabinet, a policy which was followed so disastrously by the Benes government in Czechoslovakia. He is a good soldier and undoubtedly he was acting under orders from the President. But he adopted certain policies then which he must now feel the necessity of justifying in future action. If I voted for General Marshall, I should feel that I was confirming and approving the sympathetic attitude toward Communism in the Far East which has dominated the Far Eastern Division of the State Department; and that I would be approving the policies of Secretary Acheson in China, Formosa, and Korea. I believe that a continuation of these policies may easily bring disaster to the people of the United States. [3]

The bill permitting Marshall to be exempted from the requirement that a civilian be Secretary of Defense was passed by the Senate in September 1950 by a 47 to 21 vote. The Republicans voted 20 to 10 against it. Marshall's nomination was then approved by 57 to 11 of which all negative votes were Republican.

If the Republican nationalists felt strong enough to attack Marshall, the architect of victory in the world war, they felt no inhibitions at all in defaming Dean Acheson. In some ways, the Secretary of State was an odd choice. He had been eliminated as Under Secretary of the Treasury in the first Roosevelt Administration because of his opposition to a gold purchase policy and had later put in an appearance at a Liberty League function. His foreign policies in Europe were resolutely anti-Communist. But Acheson had served in several capacities in the State Department since 1941 and was closely identified with Democratic internationalism. His foreign policy put Europe first and attempted to take some cognizance of the Asian revolution. He was also politically vulnerable. He was a stylish embodiment of the Eastern upper class but, as a partisan of Truman serving in a Democratic Administration, he could not count on the support of his own. None of the elements of the Democratic coalition were committed to him. The Republican right felt free to have at him as a symbol of the Anglophile East. Senator Hugh Butler of Nebraska exclaimed: "I watch his smart-aleck manner and his British clothes and that New Dealism, everlasting New Dealism in everything he says and does, and I want to shout, Get out, Get out. You stand for everything that has been wrong with the United States for years."[4]

Acheson was also unlucky enough to be nominated for Secretary of State in early 1949 just as the political position of the Truman Administration began to crumble. He was confirmed by an 83 to 6 vote, but the negative votes included Bridges, Jenner, Knowland, and Wherry. The Republican nationalists made much of testimony by Adolf A. Berle, a former Assistant Secretary of State, before the House Un-American Activities Committee in which Berle claimed that he had lost his job in 1944 for advocating a hard line against the Soviet Union in opposition to a faction led by Acheson which took a "pro-Russian" view. In 1950, the right took advantage of Acheson's statement regarding Alger Hiss to describe American foreign policy as the "Acheson-Hiss policy." Demands for the resignation of Acheson became a basic feature of the debate over Asian policy in 1950. The Secretary of State was accused of "inviting" the North Korean invasion by excluding South Korea from the U.S. defense perimeter, although this was also Pentagon policy. In a speech on the Senate floor in early 1950 under the heading of "Who Is the Master Mind in the Department of State?"

Senator Bridges posed several dozen questions for investigation by the Tydings subcommittee, all of which came to one master question:

> We cannot escape our obligation. We must find out the master spy, the servant of Russia who moves the puppets—the Hisses, the Wadleighs, and others—in and out of office in this Capital of the United States, using them and using our State Department as he wills.
>
> Who is he, Mr. President?[5]

Disingenuously, Bridges concluded his speech with a proposal:

> I suggest that Dean Acheson be thoroughly questioned by the committee. He has been, with the exception of a few months, a top side policy making official of the State Department since February 1941. Longer than any other man he has been a key functionary of the State Department.
>
> Dean Acheson could answer many of the questions I have asked today.[6]

The attack on Acheson culminated in a resolution of the Republican Conference in Congress in December 1950 which demanded his resignation. President Truman brushed aside this demand. Against a background of unfavorable developments in Asia, the Republican campaign against Acheson nonetheless had an effect. At the time of his nomination for Secretary of State in early 1949, 38 per cent of the American people had reacted favorably to Acheson in the Gallup Poll and only 5 per cent unfavorably. By the end of 1950, 30 per cent believed he should be replaced against 21 per cent who disagreed.[7]

In September, MacArthur had all but destroyed the North Korean army by catching it in a pincers between an offensive from the Pusan perimeter and an amphibious landing in the North Korean rear at Inchon. With the approval of the United Nations, the United States was now determined to unify the North and South under one regime. The original policy of containment was abandoned for a war of liberation. In October, Chou En-lai warned that China would intervene if U.N. forces crossed the 38th parallel which separated North and South Korea. Although the U.S. Eighth Army had briefly encountered sizable Chinese forces in Korea earlier in the month and it was known that there were large troop concentrations in Manchuria, MacArthur in late November tested his thesis, with the acquiescence of the Administration, that "it is in the pattern of the Oriental psychology to respect and follow aggressive, resolute and dynamic leadership." Driving quickly to the Yalu River border between North Korea and China with divided forces, he was met by 300,000 Chinese who exploited the gap in his center. MacArthur informed Washington that the U.N. forces were in an "entirely new war" and that "steady attrition leading to final destruction can reasonably be contemplated." In press statements, he also defended his conduct of the campaign and complained of inhibitions placed upon him by Washington in the use of air power against Chinese supply lines in Manchuria. These statements provoked a directive by Washington to all officials, but aimed at MacArthur, that statements to the press regarding foreign and military policy were to be cleared in advance by the State or Defense departments.

During December and January, the Chinese remained on the offensive and forced a 275-mile retreat by the Eighth Army, the longest in U.S. military history. During this period, MacArthur urged upon the Joint Chiefs of Staff a four-point program for reversing the tide of battle: 1) reinforcement of his forces in Korea with Nationalist Chinese troops; 2) a naval blockade of the Chinese coast; 3) air attacks against the Chinese communications and transportation network, industrial facilities, supply depots, and troop assembly points; and 4) "diversionary action possibly leading to counter-invasion" by Nationalist Chinese troops against the mainland. Later, MacArthur would abandon his request for Nationalist Chinese troops in Korea but add a proposal for a strict economic embargo on Communist China by the United States and its allies. The Joint Chiefs rejected MacArthur's program and called upon him instead to defend his forces with existing means and to withdraw in "successive positions" until either the front was stabilized or evacuation became necessary. In the event of evacuation, however, the Joint Chiefs had prepared a contingency plan of sixteen measures, including MacArthur's four points.

Chinese intervention meant not only an entirely new war, but an entirely new political situation. Already fortified by the election results, the Republican right was now vindicated in its hostile attitude toward the regime of Mao Tse-tung. It was in this context that the Republican Conference demanded the resignation of Acheson. The staff of the Republican Policy Committee was giving consideration to the question of the impeachment of Truman. War with China provoked a general crisis in American foreign policy and a renewal of the political struggle between internationalists and nationalists, relatively quiescent since Pearl Harbor, over what America's global posture should be. This struggle took place on three fronts: 1) China policy; 2) troop commitments to Europe; and 3) the theory and practice of "limited war."

Under the pressure of events, the Administration's China policy disintegrated. When President Truman stated at a press conference on November 30 that use of atomic weapons in Korea was within the realm of possibility, Clement Attlee, Prime Minister of Great Britain, flew to Washington to obtain assurances that atomic weapons would not be used without consultation in what was formally a war by the United Nations and that General MacArthur would not be given discretion in their use. Attlee was also concerned that the United States would become committed to a war with China to the degree that the security of its European allies would be exposed to danger from the Soviet Union. Although Britain had endorsed the effort to unify Korea by force, Attlee now advocated that the United States consider withdrawal from Korea and the Formosa Strait and concede Communist China a seat in the United Nations as the price for extrication of U.S. troops from a hopeless position. Acheson rejected this proposal:

> At the next meeting I suggested that Mr. Attlee would be making a serious mistake to believe that the American people would follow a leadership that proposed a vigorous policy of action against

aggression on one ocean front while accepting defeat on the other. The public mind was not subtle enough to understand so ambivalent a policy, which was fortunate because it would be a wrong policy. Discussion of priorities was one thing; wholly different attitudes on the same issue on two sides of the world was another.[8]

Acheson's reply was not inconsistent with previous American policy in a formal logical sense, but it did suggest the coalescence of a concept of world-wide containment of both the Soviet Union and the People's Republic of China which would determine American policy in the Far East. The change in attitude became concrete in early 1951 when the Administration decided to seek $300 million in military aid for Chiang Kai-shek.

Ironically, while the Truman Administration's China policy was moving their way, the Republican nationalists became more suspicious than ever. They believed that the Attlee discussions signified that Acheson was entering into a cabal with the British Socialists to sell out Chiang Kai-shek's Republic of China and Syngman Rhee's Republic of Korea. "Munich" and "appeasement" were the bywords of their rhetoric, despite the fact that these terms might better have been forgotten, given the original support of the nationalists for both Munich and appeasement. Twenty-four Republican Senators endorsed the resolution of Senator James P. Kem, Republican of Missouri, calling for ratification by the Senate of any agreement which might be concluded between Truman and Attlee. The suspicions of the Republican nationalists were further aroused when the United States tolerated efforts first by India in December and then by the Prime Ministers of the British Commonwealth in January to bring about a cease-fire and a conference on the Far East through the United Nations. The American government did not share the view that Formosa and other questions affecting China could be discussed under conditions of a shooting war, but it was also determined not to be diplomatically isolated. The United States therefore endorsed the U.N. resolutions in the knowledge that Peking would reject the overtures because a cease-fire would be militarily disadvantageous to the still advancing Chinese armies. These rejections set the stage for a U.N. resolution which condemned Chinese intervention.

Although successful, this diplomatic maneuver exposed the Administration to criticism at home and obscured its real policy. The nationalists were convinced, correctly only in part, that the Truman Administration shared British attitudes toward Communist China. The British had already extended diplomatic recognition to the Communist government. Attlee wanted American commitments in Korea limited, MacArthur reined in, and the use of nuclear weapons precluded. His government regarded Formosa as a part of China within the authority of the Mao regime as the legitimate government of China. The British were willing to concede the Communists both Formosa and a U.N. seat in order to secure a settlement of the Korean War. The Republican nationalists agreed with none of these positions. They also resented the British trade with Communist China through Hong Kong, although there were restrictions on trade in strategic materials. Anti-British sentiment, traditional within the right, reemerged with full force. Representing a section of Irish Catholic opinion, Joseph P. Kennedy also entered the lists in December with a statement critical of American foreign policy, the Allies, and the United Nations. The Republican nationalists, too, were growing impatient with the U.N., the ultimate symbol of internationalism. In their eyes, the U.N. had become a forum for appeasement when it should have been condemning Chinese aggression.

The Republican nationalists were of two minds in respect to the British. They desired to maintain America's traditional freedom of action and were easily exasperated by "collective security" which in practice often tied American foreign policy to Great Britain. The ethnic composition of their political base gave their politics a distinct pro-German and anti-British bias, as did the old agrarian resentment of the distant influence of British capital. Yet the nationalists were never so British as when they opposed the British. As Taft often noted, nationalist foreign policy concepts were basically an adaptation of classic

British diplomacy which based itself on sea power, the maintenance of a balance of power on the continent of Europe, an aversion to alliances, and the use of surrogates in ground warfare. The Hoover/Taft strategic doctrine called for an alliance with Great Britain as the anchor of America's Atlantic position. On domestic policy, the right in its Americanist mood deplored the backward-looking and effete Anglophilia of the East Coast, while propagandizing the muscular virtues of True Liberalism whose theoretical and practical roots were thoroughly British. General MacArthur and his staff regretted the British influence on American policy to the point of paranoia, but MacArthur gave a good imitation of a British imperial administrator and was regarded by Sir Alan Brooke, Chief of the Imperial General Staff during World War II, as the best strategist of the war. The Republican nationalists had great difficulty in shaking off their own ethnic and cultural ties to Great Britain.

While American forces retreated in Korea, President Truman announced on December 19 the intention of the United States to send additional troops to Europe as the U.S. contribution to NATO forces. What later turned out to be four divisions would supplement the two divisions already in Germany as part of the occupation. Although the general intention had been known since September, it seemed to the nationalists that the "North Atlantic isolationists," as MacArthur called them, could think of nothing better to do, while the Eighth Army was in retreat in Korea, than to send troops to Europe. In a nationwide radio broadcast from New York on December 20, Herbert Hoover proposed an alternative foreign policy and military doctrine. Hoover advocated that the United States base itself in the "Western Hemisphere Gibraltar of Western Civilization" and ally itself with island powers in the Atlantic and Pacific, principally Britain and Japan. To underwrite this policy, "we should arm our air and naval forces to the teeth." Hoover counseled against military commitments which could involve the United States in a land war on the continents of Europe and Asia without the assistance of allies who disposed of adequate ground forces. He therefore proposed:

To warrant our further aid they [the nations of Western Europe] should show that they have the spiritual strength and unity to avail themselves of their own resources. But it must be far more than pacts, conferences, paper promises and declarations. Today it must express itself in organized and equipped combat divisions of such huge numbers as would erect a sure dam against the red flood. And that before we land another man or another dollar on their shores. Otherwise we shall be inviting another Korea. That would be a calamity to Europe as well as to us.

Our policy in this quarter of the world should be confined to a period of watchful waiting before we take on any commitments.[9]

In a major foreign policy speech on January 5, 1951, Senator Taft seconded Hoover's program and stressed, as Hoover did, the necessity to limit military expenditures in order to preserve free enterprise and liberty against the encroachments of big government and militarism. Taft's concrete program, however, called for a military budget of $40 billion and a military establishment of 2.9 million men—not exactly unilateral disarmament. Although placing more stress on the air and naval components of military power, Taft's program was not much smaller than the actual expenditures of the following year of $44 billion for a military establishment of 3.6 million men.

On the Korean War itself, Hoover and Taft were far from militant. Hoover was ready to write Korea off as a lost cause: "It is obvious that the United Nations have been defeated in Korea by the aggression of Communist China. There are no available forces in the world to repel them."[10] Taft took a similar view: "It is far better to fall back on a defensible position in Japan and Formosa than to maintain a Korean position which would surely be indefensible in any third world war."[11] Once the crisis in Korea had passed and the front was stabilized, Taft regained his nerve, but the response showed the grudging character of nationalist support, particularly old nationalist support, for any ground war on the Asian continent. Taft and the other old nationalists swung into support for MacArthur's military program for victory in Korea only with the understanding that it would not involve the commitment of additional American troops.

On January 8, the European issue was joined when Senator Wherry introduced a resolution that it was the sense of the Senate that no American ground forces be sent to Europe "pending the adoption of a policy thereto by Congress." The resolution raised a Constitutional question of Truman's authority to send troops abroad. The Republicans had long been disturbed by the increase in executive power through the route of national security policies which they did not agree with in any case. The Republican opposition believed that Roosevelt had used executive agreements to circumvent the power of the Senate to ratify treaties and was dismayed that Truman did not bother to seek a declaration of war from Congress to justify his intervention in Korea.

Led by Hoover, Taft, and Wherry, the effort to delay a commitment of American troops to Europe was an old nationalist operation. In February, a "Declaration of Policy" consisting of six points was issued by 118 Republicans in the House:

1. Whatever our future military or political policy is to be, it must be determined with the full participation and approval of the Congress.
2. Make this country impregnable to attack.
3. Reduce nonessential civilian expenditures.
4. Build a strong defense system in the Western Hemisphere.
5. Establish a strong defense line in the Atlantic and Pacific. Refuse further aid of any kind to Western Europe unless persuaded that Western Europe is carrying its full share of the burden. In any case invite Britain and the British Commonwealth of Nations to participate fully in this program.
6. Conclude peace treaties with Germany, Japan, and Austria.[12]

Like Hoover's speech, this program bore a family resemblance to the principles of the America First Committee. On the other hand, the Republican internationalists, led by Dewey, Dulles, and Lodge, endorsed the Administration's position on troop commitments to Europe. Equally important, the new nationalists also supported the Administration. In January, Senator Knowland gave a speech in favor of troop commitments. When a resolution emerged from committee, it was in a form calling for Congressional concurrence in such decisions *and* approval of the actual commitment of four divisions to Europe. Most of the old nationalists including Wherry himself therefore voted against it, while the Republican internationalists and the new nationalists, such as Bridges, Knowland, Nixon, and McCarthy, voted for it. The resolution passed, but was not of decisive importance since it did not carry the force of a legal requirement. Truman won the "second Great Debate" just as Roosevelt had won the first.

By the end of January, the immediate crisis in Korea had passed. After the death of his predecessor in a freak accident in December, Lieutenant General Matthew B. Ridgway had taken field command of the Eighth Army and gradually developed tactics effective against the Chinese. These involved "defense in depth" against Chinese tactics of infiltration and envelopment and the concentration of massive firepower in a methodical advance against their armies. As their supply lines progressively lengthened, the Chinese had difficulty in sustaining their offensive. In February and March, the Eighth Army began to push them back toward the 38th parallel. Although the spectre of evacuation had disappeared, MacArthur still advocated his four-point program because he believed that a "theoretical military stalemate" was bound to develop between the two contending forces. As the Chinese retreated, their supply lines would shorten and their offensive potential revive. An "accordion-like" warfare would result. The United States was still in an entirely new war which would require new commitments and a new strategy.

The Truman Administration took a different view. As Ridgway's offensive ejected the Chinese from South Korea, the Administration dropped the objective of uniting Korea and reverted to the original United Nations mandate to preserve the Republic of Korea from aggression. The "Korean incident" had gone on long enough. The political and strategic importance of the Korean peninsula did not deserve the resources being devoted to it. The Soviet Union was the principal enemy, and the Russians were not nearly so committed to the war as the United States. Truman and Acheson regarded Korea as a "trap" that altered the balance of forces in favor of the Soviet Union in other areas, particularly Europe, where the United States and its Allies were just beginning to build up their ground forces to deter the Red Army. The war was creating divisions among the NATO Allies which might endanger the creation of this deterrent in Europe, which was the "major strategic prize" as it was the largest industrial complex outside the U.S. and U.S.S.R. Once the Chinese armies were driven back, the Administration was ready to seek a settlement as it had not been willing to do earlier when its forces were in retreat. In late March, President Truman issued a statement declaring that the United Nations objective had been substantially achieved, calling for a cease-fire, and noting that a "prompt settlement of the Korean problem would greatly reduce international tension in the Far East and open the way for the consideration of other problems in that area by the processes of peaceful settlement envisaged in the Charter of the United Nations." [13]

The Administration was apparently seeking a settlement on a *status quo* basis. It was far from evident that it was willing to settle "other problems in the area" in a manner satisfactory to Communist China; and, it had already gone far toward a positive commitment to Chiang Kai-shek by its new program of military aid for him. MacArthur, however, reacted to Truman's statement in the light of the peace efforts of the British and the United Nations the previous winter. Major General Courtney Whitney, MacArthur's biographer and closest associate, later wrote: "It seems reasonable to assume that in some parts of the U.N. and the U.S. State Department, and in some very high places elsewhere in Washington, men were scheming to change the status of Formosa and the Nationalists' seat in the United Nations." [14] To forestall this possibility, MacArthur issued on March 24 his own statement offering to confer with the enemy commander on a cease-fire "if the issues are resolved on their own merits without being burdened by extraneous matters not directly related to Korea, such as Formosa and China's seat in the United Nations." MacArthur also informed the Chinese that they "must by now be painfully aware that a decision of the United Nations to depart from its tolerant effort to contain the war to the area of Korea, through expansion of our military operations to his coastal areas and interior bases would doom Red China to the risk of imminent military collapse."[15] With this direct challenge to Truman's authority to conduct American foreign policy, MacArthur's days were numbered as Supreme Commander, Allied Powers; Commanding General, United States Army, Far East; Commander in Chief, Far East; and Commander in Chief, United Nations Command.

The final incident was the release by Joseph W. Martin, Jr., minority leader in the House, on April 5 of correspondence in which MacArthur expressed approval of a speech in which Martin had advocated a "second Asiatic front" along the lines proposed by MacArthur. Truman thereupon relieved the General of all his commands. Immediately, the Republican Party leadership in Congress went into conference and emerged with proposals for a Congressional investigation of the Administration's foreign and military policy and for an address to Congress by MacArthur. "In addition," Martin pointedly noted, "the question of possible impeachments was discussed." Meanwhile, MacArthur returned to the United States for the first time in fourteen years. On route, he received tumultuous tributes from hundreds of thousands of people in Tokyo, Honolulu, San Francisco, and Washington. After delivering his "Old Soldiers Never Die, They Just Fade Away" speech to Congress, he was greeted by millions in a ticker-tape parade in New York. Hearings on the "Military Situation in the Far East" were held before the Foreign Relations and Armed Services committees of the Senate in May and June. Afterward, MacArthur embarked on a "crusade" of speech-making throughout the United States which culminated in his delivery of the keynote address to the Republican National Convention in 1952.

When the smoke cleared, the Truman Administration still held the field. The two issues in the MacArthur crisis were China policy and military strategy in the Korean War. The Administration undercut the Republican nationalists on China policy by way of capitulation. In an address to the China Institute on May 18, Dean Rusk, Assistant Secretary of State for the Far East, removed the ambiguity from American policy:

> It is not my purpose, in these few moments this evening, to go into specific elements of our national policy in the present situation. But we can tell our friends in China that the United States will not acquiesce in the degradation which is being forced upon them. We do not recognize the authorities in Peiping for what they pretend to be. The Peiping regime may be a colonial Russian government—a Slavic Manchuko on a larger scale. It is not the Government of China. It does not pass the first test. It is not Chinese.
>
> It is not entitled to speak for China in the community of nations. It is entitled only to the fruits of its own conduct—the fruits of aggression upon which it is now willfully, openly, and senselessly embarked.
>
> We recognize the National Government of the Republic of China, even though the territory under its control is severely restricted. We believe that it more authentically represents the views of the great body of the people of China, particularly their historic demand for independence from foreign control. That government will continue to receive important aid and assistance from the United States.[16]

It is not clear what role the MacArthur crisis played in the development of the policy, enunciated by Rusk, of continuing to support the Nationalist regime as the legitimate government of China. Most likely, it was the final episode completing an evolution, already set in motion by the Sino-Soviet Treaty and the Chinese intervention in the Korean War. At no time did the United States actually follow a policy of actively supporting Communist China against the Soviet Union; this was merely a possibility, which was soon ruled out by the Sino-Soviet treaty. The basic policy was to disengage from Chiang Kai-shek on the grounds that his regime was a political liability. The controlling factor was not political sympathy for the Communists or even a desire to turn Chinese nationalism against the Soviet Union, but an estimate of American resources and national interest which placed the priority elsewhere. At one point, the United

States was willing at least to consider diplomatic recognition of the Communist government, its seating in the United Nations, and control of Formosa as a matter of simple political realism, not necessarily implying approval of the regime. Later, it hoped somehow to keep Formosa out of Communist hands while also disengaging from Chiang Kai-shek. Gradually, the United States was led by events into a policy of active containment of Communist China and of maintaining a commitment to the Nationalists. Its actual political preference was best expressed by Marshall in his 1948 testimony to Congress concerning his mission to China. Marshall recognized that China was undergoing a social revolution that would ultimately undo the Chiang regime as then constituted. But he was not happy with the Communist leadership of this revolution; he would have preferred a new force consisting of the left wing of the Kuomintang, the Third Force liberals, and the moderate elements of the Chinese Communist Party, all under the leadership of Chiang Kai-shek. When this alternative proved utopian, the Truman Administration decided to cut its losses. But its policy of disengagement also collapsed. The consolation for the Truman Administration was that this collapse removed the first issue between it and MacArthur. The dust had settled.

There remained the question of the conduct of the Korean War and the larger issue of the relative priority of Asia in American foreign policy. MacArthur disagreed emphatically with the basic "Europe First" premise of the Truman Administration which underlay its desire to liquidate the war on the basis of an acceptance of a military stalemate. Although it might be true that Western Europe was currently a main center of industrial production and the greatest market for American trade and capital, the future belonged to Asia. In a speech in Seattle in late 1951, MacArthur developed his views:

> To the early pioneer the Pacific Coast marked the end of his courageous westerly advance. To us it should mark but the beginning. To him it delineated our western frontier. To us that frontier has been moved across the Pacific horizon. For we find our western defense geared to an island chain off the coast of continental

Asia, from which with air and sea supremacy we can dominate any predatory move threatening the Pacific Ocean area. Our economic frontier now embraces the trade potentialities of Asia itself; for with the gradual rotation of the epicenter of world trade back to the Far East whence it started many centuries ago, the next thousand years will find the main world problem the raising of sub-normal standards of life of its more than a billion people. The opportunities for international trade then, if pursued with the vision and courage of the early pioneer, will be limitless. . . .

Such possibilities seem, however, beyond the comprehension of some high in our governmental circles, who still feel that the Pacific Coast marks the practical terminus of our advance and the westerly boundary of our immediate national interests—that any opportunity for the expansion of our foreign trade must be found mainly in the area of Europe and the Middle East. Nothing could more surely put a brake upon our growth as a strong and prosperous nation. Intentionally or not, it would yield to industrialized Europe the undisputed dominion over the trade and commerce of the Far East. More than this, it would in time surrender to European nations the moral, if not political, leadership of the Eastern hemisphere. Nothing could more clearly attest a marked recession from that far-sighted vision which animated the pioneer of 100 years ago. . . .[17]

Here is a classical Republican (pre–New Deal) vision of American history. In opposition to Europe, the United States was embarked upon a westward expansion that had taken it to the Pacific Coast and now into East Asia. The economic development of Asia with its hundreds of millions of people would also ensure the economic future of America. Despite the imperial tone of these remarks, MacArthur did not see this Pacific destiny as in conflict with the aspirations of the peoples of Asia. "British imperialism" was as much despised by Republican nationalists as "Communist imperialism" and often, it seemed to them, the two were in league. In his address to Congress, MacArthur proclaimed the rise of Asia:

Mustering half of the earth's population and 60 per cent of its natural resources, these peoples are rapidly consolidating a new force, both moral and material, with which to raise the living standard and erect adaptations of the design of modern progress to their own distinct cultural environments. Whether one adheres to the concept of colonization or not, this is the direction of Asian progress and it may not be stopped. It is a corollary to the shift of the world economic frontiers, as the whole epicenter of world affairs rotates back toward the area whence it started. In this situation it becomes vital that our own country orient its policies in consonance with this basic evolutionary condition rather than pursue a course blind to the reality that the colonial era is now past and the Asian peoples covet the right to shape their own free destiny.[18]

The practical models of MacArthur's vision were the development of the Philippines and Japan to which he had personally contributed. In these countries, a rigorous anti-Communism had been combined with a strategy of capitalist development. MacArthur's administration of Japan ruthlessly swept away the remnants of feudalism and pressed forward political democracy, a Constitution with guarantees of human rights, a program of land reform, and trade unionism. With its close association with the landlord class, its neo-Confucian "New Life Movement," its crypto-fascist Blue Shirts, and its secret police, the Nationalist government in China had failed in its modernizing role and fallen back into dependence on moribund social forces. But MacArthur refused to accept this failure as a fact, and, above all, Communism had to be stopped.

Although MacArthur's military program for the war with Communist China in Korea called for the use of Nationalist Chinese troops, of whom there were 600,000 on Formosa, he did not seriously entertain the thought that Chiang Kai-shek would march in triumph to Peking. In his own way, MacArthur was also interested only in a limited war and containment of Communist China, but a limited war with a conclusive result and a containment program conceived in a Korean victory. According to MacArthur, Communist China was expanding on three fronts—Korea, Formosa, and Southeast Asia. If the Communists were defeated *in Korea,* their whole program of expansion would be undermined. If not defeated, the reverse would be the case. He did not conceive of the Nationalist forces invading China in a "grand amphibious effort," but engaging in a campaign of harassment and maneuver on a larger than guerrilla scale. The main effect of the campaign would be to force the Communist Chinese to divert forces to the south and thus weaken their military position in Korea. In his testimony before the Senate committees, MacArthur explained that even the threat of invasion "would result in relieving the pressure on our front in Korea. I believe that they would have to tend to shift the center of gravity of their military mobilization down further south than they are at the present time."[19] Combined with the full application of American air, naval, and economic power, this two-front strategy could result in a decisive victory in Korea. As far as American ground forces were concerned, that would be the end of it. In his address to Congress, MacArthur emphasized that "no man in his right mind would advocate sending our ground forces into continental China and such was never given a thought."

The alternative was "prolonged indecision." Acceptance of a military stalemate meant acceptance of permanent bloodletting along an immobile front in the style of World War I. The continuation of the war without the objective of a military victory brought "killing Chinese" to the fore as the only military objective or the destruction of China's "trained manpower" as Acheson put it. This was the essence of Ridgway's "meatgrinder" tactics. Said MacArthur, the "very concept shocks me, old soldier that I am." The Truman Administration's more "moderate" approach to limited war was as important a departure from the traditional military ethic as the bombing of civilian population centers during World War II. MacArthur and the Republican nationalists explicitly took issue with this strategy on moral grounds. MacArthur told the Senate:

> . . . I shrink—I shrink with a horror that I cannot express in words—at this continuous slaughter of men in Korea.
> The battle casualties in Korea today probably have passed the million-man mark. Our own casualties, American casualties, have passed 65,000. The Koreans have lost about 140,000. Our losses, on our side, are a quarter of a million men. I am not talking of the civilian populations, who must have lost many, many, many times that.
> The enemy probably has lost 750,000 casualties. There are

145,000 of them that are now in our prison bull pens, prisoners, so they might be excepted from that figure because they live; but a million men in less than 11 months of fighting, in less than 11 months of this conflict, have already gone and it grows more savage every day.

I just cannot brush that off as a Korean skirmish. I believe that is something of such tremendous importance that it must be solved, and it cannot be solved by the nebulous process of saying, "Give us time, and we will be prepared; or we will be in a better shape 2 years from now"—which is argumentative.

I don't know whether we will, or not; and neither do you, because you do not know, and none of us know the capacity of the enemy.

He may build faster than we do. I couldn't tell you.

I don't know that, you are gambling on chances; but I say there is no chance in Korea, because it is a fact—you have lost a million men now. You will lose more than a million if you go on another year; if you go on until 1953, you will lose another million.

What are you trying to protect?

The war in Korea has already almost destroyed that nation of 20,000,000 people.

I have never seen such devastation.

I have seen, I guess, as much blood and disaster as any living man, and it just curdled my stomach, the last time I was there. After I looked at that wreckage and those thousands of women and children and everything, I vomited.

Now, are you going to let that go on, by any sophistry of reasoning, or possibilities? They may be there, but this is a certainty.

What are you going to do? Once more, I repeat the question, What is the policy in Korea?

If you go on indefinitely, you are perpetuating a slaughter such as I have never heard of in the history of mankind.[20]

After the conclusion of the hearings, a group of Republican Senators on the committees—Bridges, Hickenlooper, Knowland, Brewster, Flanders, H. Alexander Smith, Alexander Wiley of Wisconsin, and Harry Cain of Washington—submitted a statement of "Individual Views" which made MacArthur's point formally:

The policy of the United States in Korea, as outlined in the testimony of the Secretary of State and the Secretary of Defense and others, is that of destroying the effective core of the Communist Chinese armies by killing that government's trained soldiers, in the hope that someone would negotiate. We hold that such a policy is essentially immoral, not likely to produce either victory in Korea or an end to aggression. At the same time such a policy tends to destroy the moral stature of the United States as a leader in the family of nations.

War in any form is abhorrent. War means other humane ways of settling disputes have failed. Only a nation without regard for the sanctity of human life could be committed to a policy of prolonged war with no intent at winning a victory. American policy, in every war in which this Nation has engaged, has been designed to win the conflict at the earliest possible moment at the least possible loss of human life—especially American life, but also the lives of those who oppose us.[21]

The Administration had various replies to this accusation. One of them was that it stood ready to negotiate a truce on a *status quo* basis, but that Communist China refused to come to terms, and therefore had to bear its share of responsibility for the bloodshed.

In their testimony during the Senate hearings, the Joint Chiefs of Staff were skeptical of MacArthur's program. An economic blockade in strategic materials was already in effect. A naval blockade of the coast would pose the problem of a direct confrontation with the Soviet Union, particularly since China could be supplied through the two Russian-controlled ports of Dairen and Port Arthur. A blockade would also require the support of America's allies, particularly Britain, who would be opposed to the measure. The effect could be partially offset overland by the Trans-Siberian railroad. The Joint Chiefs had a low opinion of the combat effectiveness of the Nationalist Chinese, and their operations would have to be supported by an American logistical effort, which would be a diversion from America's own war effort. U.S. military advisors would also be required. Air attacks on Manchuria or other parts of China would not be decisive because much of the Chinese war effort was supplied through the Soviet Union. Air Force Chief of Staff Hoyt S. Vandenberg testified that the U.S. did not have sufficient air groups to carry on a massive campaign against China without significantly weakening its strategic deterrent against the Soviet Union. In sum, the Joint Chiefs did not believe MacArthur's strategy would be effective. Its failure would create pressure for the introduction of U.S. ground troops into China. At several points, the strategy carried the risk of a confrontation with the Soviet Union. If World War III broke out, the United States would find itself largely committed in Korea and China, while the Soviet Union would possess 200 uncommitted divisions to use as it pleased. A strategy of doubtful effectiveness hardly seemed to justify such risks.

Despite the Sino-Soviet Treaty, MacArthur doubted that the Soviet Union would intervene unless the "relativity in military or other potential is in its favor on a world-wide basis." He detected a contradiction in the claim of the Administration that the United States possessed ultimate strategic superiority on the basis of its air/atomic capability, at least until 1953–54, and yet acting as if it had to hold troops in readiness for use against the Red Army in Europe, troops which were inadequate to the purpose in any case. It did not matter whether the U.S. rearmament program were complete or how many divisions NATO could put into the field in Europe. If the Red Army occupied Western Europe in a war, the situation would still be that the United States could carry out atomic attacks on the Soviet Union, while the reverse would not be true. Either the U.S. had an effective nuclear deterrent or it did not. This was one of MacArthur's strongest arguments and, indeed, NATO never did generate sufficient divisions to deter the Red Army without nuclear weapons. Vandenberg's testimony was the most effective counterargument. He noted that America's strategic air capability against the Soviet Union would be reduced by 80 per cent if it should lose its air bases in Europe through alienation of its allies or Soviet occupation.

MacArthur also noted that a military stalemate amounted to a political victory for the weaker power: "In war a great nation which does not win must suffer all the consequences of defeat." In fact, the Truman Administration discovered that, although truce negotiations were begun, Communist China was in no hurry to reach an agreement. The issue of repatriation of prisoners of war also intervened. The war dragged on for two more years, as all the while the U.S. international position suffered and the Truman Administration's domestic position disintegrated. Both sides suffered substantial casualties, and the devastation of Korea and its people continued, even though major offensives were not launched. Ground forces were built up to more than 700,000 on each side, and China acquired a formidable air force from the Soviet Union. When a truce was finally signed in 1953, it may have been the result of the cumulative effect of the U.S. meatgrinder and/or of a new attitude in the Communist world after the death of Stalin. It was also true that the Eisenhower Administration informed the People's Republic that it was prepared to use tactical nuclear weapons against military targets in Manchuria. While the United Nations did preserve the integrity of the Republic of Korea, China also won a political victory which was as important to its prestige in Asia as the defeat of Russia in the 1904–05 war was to Japan.

Limited war was a conundrum. If MacArthur's strategy would not work, neither did the Administration's. The Administration could defend South Korea only at the cost of terrible and continuing bloodshed in Korea, a political victory for Communist China, and the decay of its own domestic political position. Even if MacArthur's strategy would work in Korea, he could not guarantee that the war would not continue along the Yalu River. As Senator William Fulbright of Arkansas brought out in questioning, the United States would then be under pressure to follow the precedent of Japan with a ground invasion of China. But the Japanese introduced 2 million troops into China without ultimately eliminating either the Nationalist government or the Communist guerrillas. Since it was also a limited war strategy, MacArthur's program posed the possibility of "prolonged indecision" at a higher level. In the final analysis, limited war was not solely a military question. Marshall advised against American intervention in the Chinese civil war

because he realized that the United States should not have to
guarantee a regime which could not effectively defend itself
against equivalent forces. Alone, Syngman Rhee could not cope
with North Korea. The United States brushed aside the forces
of Kim Il Sung without difficulty and did not have to face a
revolutionary war of unmanageable proportions. But the U.S.
could only achieve a stand-off against Chinese manpower reserves backed by Soviet material on a front near to hand for
the Communist powers. Decisive victory would require a general Asian war. If the U.S. committed itself to a far greater
degree than the Soviet Union, it would endanger its own security. Although Korea was, mercifully, a conventional war, the
United States still found itself overcommitted in a minor
theatre against mere proxies of the Soviet Union.

MacArthur lost the political engagement. The Democratic
Party controlled Congress and thus the hearings. Under the
chairmanship of Senator Richard Russell of Georgia, the hearings were closed, although edited transcripts were released.
The public impact of the hearings was thus minimized. After
the first few days of MacArthur's testimony, Administration officials testified for weeks on end and took his arguments apart.
MacArthur committed a tactical error by arguing initially that
the Joint Chiefs supported his views. He based himself on the
contingency plan of the previous January which incorporated
his four points. The Joint Chiefs rejected this claim and stated
that the plan was to be considered only if U.S. forces were
forced to the point of evacuation. The Chairman of the Joint
Chiefs was General Omar Bradley and the Army Chief of Staff,
General J. Lawton Collins, both of them closely identified with
Marshall. Given the political weakness of the Truman Administration, the principle of civilian control had largely to rely on
the defense of the "Democratic Generals."

In these circumstances, Joe McCarthy sallied forth in June to
denounce Marshall on the Senate floor. Given Marshall's historical importance, this denunciation amounted to a 60,000
word indictment of American foreign policy since 1939. It was
the usual nationalist/revisionist interpretation, following the

lines of the "Georgetown school" led by Charles Callin Tansill and Stefan Possony. The question was how "since World War II the free world has been losing 100 million people per year to international communism." While a more impartial view might have regarded *both* the United States and the Soviet Union as having expanded their influence at the expense of the moribund European empires, McCarthy saw every advance in the Soviet position as a net loss to the "free world." Not only that: "The vast and complicated culture of the west . . . is in manifest decay." Among men of the right, there was a growing tendency toward gloomy Germanic philosophizing on the "decline of the West." Certainly, Republican Americanism and nationalism had been in decline since 1929.

In McCarthy's mind, it was now definitely established that Marshall and Acheson were the leaders of a "conspiracy on a scale so immense as to dwarf any previous such venture in the history of man." President Truman was merely "their captive." The defeat of MacArthur revealed the current strategy of the conspiracy:

> It is to abandon American interests in the Far East, surrendering Formosa to the grasp of a United Nations strewn with our enemies and wanting nothing so much, under the leadership of the temporary Socialist Government of Britain and the Communist-loving present Government of India, as to thrust the United States out of the Far East.
>
> It is because he differed with that policy that General MacArthur was recalled from the Far East. He stood as a barrier to the final fulfillment of the Marshall-Acheson policy for China.[22]

Since McCarthy as a new nationalist upheld troop commitments to Europe, he regarded the "great debate" on European policy as merely a "diversionary trick" engineered by Marshall to distract attention from the issues in Asia. While the speech mainly concerned Marshall, Dean Acheson elicited the most inspired vitriol:

> I have studied Acheson's public utterances sidewise, slantwise, hindwise, and frontwise; I have watched the demeanor of this

glib, supercilious, and guilty man on the witness stand; I have reflected upon his career, and I come to only one conclusion: his primary loyalty in international affairs runs to the British labor government, his secondary allegiance is to the Kremlin, with none left over for the country of his birth. The only trouble Acheson ever encounters is where Socialist-British and Russian-Communist policy diverge, which, in recent months, has been seldom. Then he reluctantly follows the lead from Socialist London.[23]

According to Major General Whitney's account, MacArthur also believed that the British Foreign Office was the source of much of Acheson's policy. Whitney added that the British diplomats and defectors, Burgess and MacLean, who were posted in Washington at the time, probably kept the Communists informed of American military intentions. The British, the Communists, and the Europe First Democrats brought down MacArthur:

> They [the Communists] found a ready, though initially innocent, ally in the "Europe-first" clique in the War and State Departments in Washington at the time of the outbreak of World War II. Together, for their separate reasons, these two groups sought to block acceptance of MacArthur's view that Europe and Asia—the Atlantic and the Pacific—were equally important in the contemplation of our national interest and security. Together they attempted to discredit MacArthur in every way and thwart even his efforts against the enemy in World War II and Korea. Together they fostered the tragic notion that appeasement instead of defiance would win in Asia. Together they were responsible for MacArthur's recall.[24]

Not long after the conclusion of the Senate hearings, Marshall left government. In his speech-making tour, MacArthur denounced, among other things, the "insidious forces working from within." Later, James Rand, of the Committee for the Nation and the Dr. William Wirt incident of the 1930s, brought MacArthur to Remington, Rand as chairman of the board.

10

THE STRUGGLE FOR POWER

The crisis in American foreign policy, precipitated by war first with North Korea and then with Communist China, had mixed results. The Truman Administration carried the day on troop commitments to Europe and limitation of the war to the territory of Korea. On the other side, Chinese intervention in the war led to the China policy that the Republican nationalists had demanded. The crisis also had important consequences for the Republican Party. While the old nationalists had failed to alter European policy, the new nationalists emerged victorious on China policy. Even within the Republican right, the new nationalists were a minority. In the Senate, the most important of them were Bridges, Knowland, Nixon, McCarthy, Brewster, and Millikin. But the heirs of Vandenberg occupied a strategic position. On China policy, they led both the old nationalists and the Eastern internationalists in a unified Republican assault on the Truman Administration. As the Eastern Republicans were the original architects of America's open door policy for China, they were as disturbed, or more disturbed by its collapse in Communist revolution than the old nationalists.

On European policy, the new nationalists favored an American commitment and in so doing discovered a new base for Republicanism among the normally Democratic ethnic groups who had opposed intervention in World War II or whose homelands were under the shadow of the Red Army. They were able to extend the narrow base of provincial Republicanism without making any concessions on domestic policy. On foreign policy, their support for anti-Communist measures in Europe did not necessarily commit them to other parts of the internationalist program such as free flow of international trade and investment, the United Nations, and foreign aid for underdeveloped countries. They were driven, however, to ever more extreme statements of their European views—the doctrine of Liberation—in order to outflank the Democrats on the issue. In many ways, the new nationalists were the most militant rightists and nationalists and yet *at the same time* they could occupy a strategic center position in the Republican Party, and draw the political leverage therefrom, because of the dispute between the old nationalists and the internationalists. Here was the wave of the future within the party.

In his quest for the Republican nomination for President, Robert Taft began to move toward the new nationalist position on foreign policy. In contrast to most of the old nationalists, he voted for the Senate resolution approving the dispatch of four divisions to Europe and drew what comfort he could from its nonbinding provision for Congressional approval of any further troop commitments. Still, the spirit of Taft's Republicanism remained different from that of the new nationalists, who were uncompromising on domestic policy and interventionist in foreign policy. Like his father, President and Supreme Court Chief Justice William Howard Taft, Senator Taft was an organizational regular but animated by some of the old Progressive spirit. He was willing to entertain social reform if he thought that capitalism was not dealing with a problem and if selective reform might shore up the principles of the system by providing equal opportunity in an overall competition based on individual achievement. Thus he endorsed public housing and federal aid to education. On foreign policy, he was suspicious of the interventionism of the Eastern internationalists which he thought verged on imperialism. Like his father, who vigorously enforced the anti-trust laws as President, he looked askance on monopolistic practices and economic concentration, which upset the moral foundations of free enterprise. It also happened that much of this economic power was wielded by his political enemies in the East.

Taft's politics were based on an ideological commitment to capitalism as a system, which he considered endangered by the expansion of the public sector. His desire to reduce federal expenditures while maintaining in the last analysis a large military establishment spelled drastic reductions in social expenditures. His animus against the Eastern Establishment was a common regional attribute not limited to Progressivism. Its basic source was in the economic development of the United States in successive waves from the East Coast financed from New York and London. Resentment of financial dependence on the East did not require a zeal for social reform. It is nonetheless interesting that Taft's closest friend in the Senate was Robert LaFollette, Jr. His lieutenant, Kenneth Wherry, had been a protégé of the Progressive leader, Senator George Norris. But Western Progressivism was a dying force in the Republican Party. The Progressives had either turned to the right in horror at the New Deal, joined the New Deal as Democrats, or lost their political base as poor farmers were driven out of business and into the cities or became prosperous and conservative. Wherry defected to the regulars in Nebraska and defeated Norris in 1940. The last of the Republican Progressive breed in the Senate was William Langer of North Dakota, who was reformist on domestic policy, anti-interventionist on foreign policy.

In 1951, the Republican Party began to gear up to exploit the disenchantment of many Democratic voters of recent European origin with the foreign policy of Roosevelt and Truman. The Republican National Committee established an Ethnic Origins Division and within it a section on Foreign Language Group Activities which was directed by Arthur Bliss Lane, former ambassador to Poland and author of *I Saw Poland Betrayed*. Lane was an early enthusiast for Joseph McCarthy. In Lane's opinion, the key to the ethnic vote was a Republican commitment in the 1952 platform to repudiate the Yalta

Agreements and to declare for the "liberation" of the East European countries under Soviet hegemony. In 1951 and 1952, the doctrine of Liberation gathered momentum. In 1951, Charles Kersten, reelected to the U.S. House of Representatives from Wisconsin after an interlude on Senator McCarthy's staff, introduced an amendment to the Mutual Security Act, which set aside $100 million for the establishment of military units, as part of NATO, of exiles from the Soviet Union, Poland, Czechoslovakia, Hungary, Rumania, Bulgaria, Lithuania, Latvia, Estonia, and the Russian zones of Germany and Austria. The Kersten Amendment passed, but the Administration refused to spend the funds.

In 1951, Senator Taft published a book drawn from his speeches, *A Foreign Policy for Americans,* in which he endorsed liberation, which he conceived mainly as a propaganda offensive on behalf of the concept of Liberty but which might also involve an "underground war of infiltration in Iron Curtain countries." Taft was still some distance from the liberation militants. He had even voted against NATO because he believed it would be provocative of war. His "policy of the free hand" was a version of classic Republican strategic doctrine as formulated by Hoover. It was anti-Communist and pro-German, but designed to avoid land engagements on the continents of Europe and Asia. In 1940, Taft had opposed war with Nazi Germany and in 1951 believed that "Russia is far more a threat to the security of the United States than Hitler in Germany ever was." His conclusion was to let Asians fight Asians or, for that matter, Europeans fight Europeans. The United States should extricate its troops from Europe as soon as it was practical to do so. Taft was still suspicious of the Eastern internationalists and the ideas of Henry Luce: "There are a good many Americans who talk about an American century in which America will dominate the world." In Taft's view, the real implications of such a policy were far from altruistic:

> In their hearts they want to force on these foreign peoples
> through the use of American money and even, perhaps, Ameri
> can arms the policies which moral leadership is able to advance

only through the sound strength of its principles and the force of its persuasion. I do not think this moral leadership ideal justifies our engaging in any preventive war, or going to the defense of one country against another, or getting ourselves into a vulnerable fiscal and economic position at home which may invite war. I do not believe any policy which has behind it the threat of military force is justified as a part of the basic foreign policy of the United States except to defend the liberty of our own people.[1]

In view of this stress on "moral leadership" in lieu of military force, Taft found himself in some strange company on the liberation issue. In *Containment or Liberation,* published in 1952, James Burnham, right-wing intellectual and former Trotskyist-Communist, advocated liberation as a strategy which has "Eastern Europe as its geopolitical focus—Europe from the Iron Curtain to the Urals." In 1948, the United States and the Soviet Union had come close to war over the reconstitution of a German state, which the Soviet Union considered a major threat to its security. It took little imagination to foresee the consequences of a policy with the objective of liberating "Europe from the Iron Curtain to the Urals"—i.e., liberating Moscow—backed by exile military units. Taft, like the policy-makers of the Democratic Administration, came to see liberation in this sense as war-mongering. His own views ran to a "Monroe Doctrine for Europe," with U.S. ground forces held well back of the European front.

Taft's principal competition for the Republican nomination was General Dwight D. Eisenhower, who was closely identified with the European-oriented policies of the Roosevelt and Truman Administrations and whose ultimate political base was the Eastern internationalist wing of the Republican Party. In the 1930s, Eisenhower had served as MacArthur's chief of staff in the Philippines, but his career had languished in that Far East outpost. On his return to the United States, he was assigned, after a time, to the War Plans Division of the War Department, a strategic position as war approached. In 1941, he was the principal architect of the victorious plan of the Third Army in the largest manuevers in Army history in Louisiana. When war came, Eisenhower's experience with MacArthur naturally led to a central role in the Pentagon's response to the Japanese attack on the Philippines. Soon after, Eisenhower became chief of the War Plans Division and after the reorganization of the War Department, assistant chief of staff in charge of the Operations Division. Ultimately, he was designated Commanding General, European Theatre of Operations. Under Army Chief of Staff George Marshall, his career horizons knew no limit.

The invasion of Normandy and the subsequent campaign in Europe were brilliant successes in which the Allies achieved the unity of command that had eluded them during World War I. After the war, Eisenhower was first Military Governor of the American zone of occupation in Germany and then Army Chief of Staff. Short of Marshall himself, no military figure was more closely associated with the Europe First policies of the Democratic Administrations, and there was a certain logic in President Truman's offer of the Democratic nomination to him in 1947 and again in 1951. Both times, Eisenhower refused. During an interlude as president of Columbia University, Eisenhower became friendly with leaders of the Eastern wing of the Republican Party, particularly the Reid family, owners of the New York *Herald Tribune,* and its publisher, William Robinson. By 1951, the leaders of the banking and corporate law establishments of New York and Boston were determined to make Eisenhower their Presidential candidate. President Truman had designated Eisenhower the first Supreme Allied Commander in Europe under NATO, and in a conference with Taft during the "Great Debate" over European troop commitments, Eisenhower was dismayed by Taft's foreign policy views. When Senator Lodge visited him in Europe in September and urged upon him the necessity of making himself available for the nomination as a means of blocking Taft, Eisenhower was receptive. In 1952, Governor Dewey convened an "Initial Advisory Group" in New York to plan the Eisenhower effort and Lodge was made campaign manager.

In the struggle between Eisenhower and Taft, the main issue was foreign policy, particularly European policy. Just as Taft was moving toward the new nationalist position in an attempt to neutralize foreign policy as an issue, so the Eastern internationalists were also moving toward the new nationalism in order to strengthen themselves with the Republican right. In May 1952, John Foster Dulles, presumptive Secretary of State in the shadow government of the Eastern internationalists, published an article in *Life*, "A Policy of Boldness," which formulated a new synthesis. Dulles defended the containment policies which he had previously endorsed—the Western Alliance, NATO, the limited war in Korea, the Berlin airlift, policy toward Japan—and criticized those who "would turn their backs on all the world's problems and wrap the United States in some magically 'impregnable' isolation." But containment was too *ad hoc* and "defensive." It required levels of military expenditure which courted the "twin evils of militarism and bankruptcy." It was too much oriented toward Europe: "Those who think only of Western Europe and of making it 'impregnable'— without regard to the Near, Middle, and Far East and Africa— are just as blind as those who think only of the United States and making it 'impregnable.' Policies that do not defend freedom in Asia are fatally defective."[2] In its military strategy, the United States could not match Soviet forces operating from interior lines along a 20,000 mile frontier through a prohibitively expensive Maginot Line defense. The only solution was the "creation of a community punishing force known to be ready and resolute to retaliate, in the event of any armed aggression, with *weapons* of its choosing against *targets* of its choosing at *times* of its choosing." The United States would have to operate with "atomic energy coupled with strategic air and sea power." Here was the doctrine of "massive retaliation" in embryonic form.

The United States, according to Dulles, also could not afford to remain passive in the face of Communist techniques of political penetration. The United States should take the "political offense": "We should be *dynamic*, we should use *ideas* as weapons, and these ideas should conform to *moral* principles." Dulles's concept of liberation as an ideological offensive was

closer to Taft's view than to the military version embodied in
the Kersten Amendment. Dulles had a concrete program for its
implementation. The United States should take the lead in con-
stituting "political task forces" for each of the "captive nations"
whose purpose would be to design "freedom programs." The
U.S. could expedite the escape from these countries of political
leaders who could help to formulate these programs. The U.S.
should also coordinate its propaganda and intelligence operations with these freedom programs, exert economic pressures,
and if necessary, sever diplomatic relations with any of these
countries. Together with its Allies, the United States could pro-
mulgate a "great new Declaration of Independence" for Eastern Europe.

In a national radio broadcast timed to coincide with Eisenhower's stagey "return to Abilene" in early June of 1952, Taft
greeted Dulles's ideas with enthusiasm. He had already approached Dulles to see if he would be willing to draft the
foreign policy plank of the Republican platform to which
Dulles agreed. Taft clearly believed he had found the means of
neutralizing the foreign policy differences between himself and
Eisenhower and thus of undercutting the *raison d'etre* of the
Eisenhower campaign. In his first press conference on his return to the United States, Eisenhower observed that his domestic political views conformed to the 1950 "Statement of Principles" of the Congressional Republicans and the Republican
National Committee. Taft observed that he had drafted much
of the statement. On domestic policy, indeed, Eisenhower had
less enthusiasm for social reform than Taft, and in his refusal
of the Democratic nomination, Eisenhower told Truman that
he thought his policies were too pro-labor.

The Republican National Committee continued to propagandize the concept of Liberation with a pamphlet, *Republican Policy of Liberation or Democratic Policy of Containment.* Ultimately,
the foreign policy section of the Republican platform, drafted
by Dulles, declared in favor of liberation and repudiating the
Yalta Agreements:

The Government of the United States, under Republican leadership, will repudiate all commitments contained in secret understandings such as those of Yalta which aid Communist enslavements. It will be made clear, on the highest authority of the President and the Congress, that United States policy, as one of its peaceful purposes, looks happily forward to the genuine independence of those captive peoples.

We shall again make liberty into a beacon light of hope that will penetrate the dark places. That program will give the Voice of America a real function. It will mark the end of the negative, futile and immoral policy of "containment" which abandons countless human beings to a despotism and godless terrorism, which in turn enables the rulers to forge the captives into a weapon for our destruction.

The policies we espouse will revive the contagious liberating influences which are inherent in freedom. They will inevitably set up strains and stresses within the captive world which will make the rulers impotent to continue in their monstrous ways and mark the beginning of their end.[3]

The campaign to nominate Eisenhower had much in common with the Willkie effort of 1940. There were the same Eastern money, enthusiasm of the national press, masses of volunteers enlisted in the "crusade," and the "nonpolitical" candidate. With his international renown and prestige with the American people as the victor in the European war, Eisenhower was a much stronger candidate than Willkie. Yet the General prevailed over Taft only with difficulty. Since 1940, the right had grown stronger from the elections of 1942, 1946, and 1950. The basic post-war political environment of prosperity and Cold War was congenial to it. Its special issues—China, espionage—were the questions of the day. Taft was also the favorite of the party regulars, and the Taft forces controlled the convention machinery. The Taft campaign started with an apparently secure base of delegates from the shadow party in the South. In the Midwest, Taft was also effective as a vote-getter. Despite the efforts of the CIO to defeat him, Taft won reelection by a 400,000 vote majority in 1950. In 1952, he won the primaries in Illinois, Ohio, Wisconsin, Nebraska, and South Dakota. But the opinion polls showed Eisenhower the first choice of the Republican rank and file and also a stronger candidate among Democrats. On the East and West Coasts, he won the primaries—New Hampshire, Pennsylvania, New Jersey, Massachusetts, Oregon, and also Minnesota. Going into the convention, Taft was still ahead. The Eisenhower forces prevailed by making a "moral issue" of contested delegations from the Southern states of Texas, Georgia, and Louisiana. When the twenty-three Republican governors at the Governors' Conference issued a statement declaring that contested delegates should not vote on the seating of other delegations, the Eisenhower organization embodied it in a "Fair Play Amendment," which provided the technical means of setting aside part of the Taft vote and winning crucial tests of strength. Soon, the shift to Eisenhower was on. In a subsequent analysis of the results mailed to his political allies including MacArthur, Taft did not attribute his defeat to this tactical maneuver but to other "underlying causes":

> First, it was the power of New York financial interests and a large number of businessmen subject to New York influence, who had selected General Eisenhower as their candidate at least a year ago. There was a strong and substantial minority of Taft supporters among business leaders, but they were a minority, particularly in the East.
>
> Second, four-fifths of the influential newspapers in the country were opposed to me continuously and vociferously and many turned themselves into propaganda sheets for my opponent. Of course, this was not true of the McCormick papers, the *Wall Street Journal, The Omaha World Herald,* and the *Los Angeles Times.* The *Philadelphia Inquirer,* the Hearst papers, and the Knight papers remained neutral. But most other Republican papers were almost campaign sheets for Eisenhower and were supplemented by the violent support of every New Deal and so-called independent paper. Like the editors, the majority of Republican governors were sold on Eisenhower support, although a majority of Senators and Congressmen were in my favor. However, the governors had far more political influence on the delegates.[4]

For some time, Governor Dewey had regarded Senator Richard Nixon of California as the strongest running mate for Eisenhower. As a representative of the right wing of the party from the West Coast, Nixon would provide both political and geographical balance to the ticket, while his views on crucial foreign policy questions were acceptable. Nixon had also demonstrated enthusiasm for Eisenhower. He had visited him at his headquarters in Europe and done what he could to promote the Eisenhower candidacy and undermine the "favorite son" control of the key California delegation by Governor Earl Warren. Young and popular, he had won election to the Senate in 1950 by a huge majority with his "Pink Lady" campaign against the Democratic candidate, Helen Gahagan Douglas. He was also effective. In contrast to McCarthy's wild lunge at Professor Lattimore, Nixon had made the case against Alger Hiss stick. At the meeting to determine the Vice Presidential nominee after the victory of Eisenhower, the Eisenhower leadership agreed on Nixon. Paul Hoffman, director of the volunteer Citizens for Eisenhower, later said, "I told them that everything I had heard about Senator Nixon was good. I looked on him as one of the Republicans who had enlightened views on foreign affairs, and I thought that a man of his views should run with General Eisenhower."[5] Hoffman was president of the Ford Foundation and had been the chief administrator of the Economic Cooperation Administration which channeled Marshall Plan aid into Europe.

The Nixon nomination was another victory for the new nationalism. Although neither the old nationalists nor the Eastern internationalists, who together constituted most of the Republican Party, were enthusiastic about the concept of liberation, the new nationalist doctrine had emerged as accepted policy as a means of unifying the party on foreign policy and making a bid for the East European ethnic vote. In militant anti-Communism, the new nationalist right had no better. Anti-Communism was fundamental to the politics of the Republican right and the new nationalists were the most anti-Communist men of the right—those for whom anti-Communism had prevailed over old foreign policy dogmas and prejudices against Europe. This tendency was already becoming the political

home away from home of reactionary governments and defeated social forces from five continents, forces which had a
strong interest in *revanchist* wars on the regimes ruling their
homelands. This was a paradox, since the *laissez-faire* capitalist
doctrine of the Republican right often had little in common
with the reactionary nationalism of some of these regimes, such
as the Nationalist governments of Chiang Kai-shek on Formosa
and Franco in Spain. The Republican right had thrown the
epithet of "Fascism" at the New Deal in the 1930s. MacArthur's
administration of Japan demonstrated that the right's posture
was still modernizing in some contexts. However, the revolutionary threat of Communism had a transforming effect on the
Republican right. This was not unprecedented. European Fascism itself was largely a romantic retrogression by the Central
European middle class which abandoned its liberal beliefs in
the face of Communist revolution.

In the United States, the Republican right had favored the
appeasement of Nazi Germany before the war because of
German-American influence within the party but also because
of the overriding objective of countering the Soviet Union.
After the war, Republican nationalists had become close allies
of the Nationalist Chinese not only in Asia but in cooperative
political maneuvers *within the United States.* Under the banner of
liberation, they took East European emigrés to their bosom in
the early 1950s. Since East Europe was, indeed, under the heel
of Soviet imperialism, the Republican right in this case could
choose from a broader range of political formations than outright counterrevolution. As the regular pulse of rebellion and
repression within Eastern Europe in the post-war period demonstrated, the nationalist identification of Eastern Europe as a
potential weakness in the Soviet strategic position was not a fic-
tion. There was a real question whether the Red Army could
ever afford to take the offensive into Western Europe with a
rear area ready to erupt into revolution. With the armies of
NATO and the Warsaw Pact facing each other in Europe, however, a serious policy of liberation still posed an immediate
danger of general war.

General Eisenhower had a more lively awareness of this possibility than many of his political friends, but was pressured into support of the liberation doctrine. In August, he met with Representative Kersten and issued a statement criticizing "mere containment" and declaring for the peaceful restoration of the freedom of the "captive nations" of both Europe and Asia. His press secretary was careful to differentiate his views from Kersten's proposals for exile legions. In late August, Dulles made an appeal to the Polish-American vote in Buffalo in which he laid out the tactics of liberation: Voice of America broadcasts to foment resistance, the air-drop of supplies to freedom fighters, followed by the inevitable victory of the heroic resistance with no general war. At this fatuity, Eisenhower rebelled and called Dulles to reprimand him for not stressing that liberation would be pursued only "by peaceful means." In early September, Eisenhower delivered a speech in which he emphasized that liberation was essentially a moral commitment, not a military one, and that the prevention of World War III was paramount.

During the campaign, the Republican National Committee agitated the issue among East European ethnic groups. The Foreign Language Groups section turned out reams of propaganda and seeded the foreign language press. Committees of Crusades To Lift the Iron Curtain organized "Liberation Centers," "Liberation Rallies," and "Liberation Weeks" with appropriate proclamations by Republican governors. In October, Eisenhower gave a Martyrs' Day address, commemorating the end of the Hungarian War of Independence, in which he reaffirmed Republican support of liberation "by peaceful means." On Pulaski Day, Senator Nixon appealed to the Polish-American vote with a call for the repudiation of the Yalta Agreements. On the same day, Eisenhower took note of the pledge in the Republican platform to repudiate Yalta. The Democratic response to all this was to denounce liberation as a cynical political ploy to exploit the East European ethnic vote and to raise false hopes in their homelands. According to Truman and Governor Adlai Stevenson of Illinois, the Presidential nominee, the liberation doctrine could lead to mass slaughter in hopeless revolts in East Europe. The Democrats also pointed out that their platform was committed to the liberalization of the immigration laws on which the Republicans were silent. In 1952, the Congress passed over Truman's veto the Immigration and Naturalization Act (the McCarran-Walter Act), which continued the discriminatory national origins quota system. Actually, the Democrats themselves voted for the act by small majorities. Consistent with their tradition of nativist Americanism, the Republicans in the House and Senate voted for the act by overwhelming margins.

Eisenhower did his best to relegate liberation to a secondary role in the campaign. Liberation was essentially the right's strategy for increasing its political base with minimum compromise of its principles. Eisenhower's base was in the center, and the provocative strategy of liberation could be more of a liability than an asset to him. During the campaign, he declared in favor of the liberalization of the immigration laws, an alternative approach to the East European ethnic vote. Eisenhower still had the problem of keeping the Republican right with him. He endorsed the election of all Republican candidates, including Jenner and McCarthy whom he despised. Although explicitly critical of McCarthy's "methods," Eisenhower dropped a defense of General Marshall from a speech he delivered in Wisconsin.

The compelling political necessity was *détente* with Taft. At a meeting at Morningside Heights in New York City in September, Eisenhower agreed to a statement drafted by Taft which ruled out a purge of the Taft faction within the party and committed Eisenhower to the maintenance of the Taft-Hartley Act, observance of the Constitutional limitations on the power of the Executive Branch, and reduction of federal expenditures to $60 billion by Fiscal Year 1955. According to the Taft statement, there was a central question before the American people:

As I see it, there is and has been one great fundamental issue between the Republican Party and the New Deal or Fair Deal or

Stevenson Deal. It is the issue of liberty against creeping socialization in every domestic field. Liberty was the foundation of our Government, the reason for our happiness, and the hope of our future. The greatest threat to liberty today is internal, from the constant growth of big Government, through the constantly increasing power and spending of the Federal Government. The price of continued liberty, including a free economic system, is the reduction of Federal spending and taxes, the repudiation of arbitrary powers in the Executive claimed to be derived from Heaven and the stand against statutory extension of power by the creation and extension of Federal bureaus.[6]

The press stigmatized Eisenhower's agreement to this statement as the "surrender of Morningside Heights." The fact was that Eisenhower genuinely subscribed to these principles. And on the crucial question of foreign policy, the Taft statement merely noted that there were "differences of degree" between the two men.

In the final analysis, Eisenhower did lead a relatively united Republican Party to victory in the November election. Most of the Republican right lined up behind him. Only MacArthur held himself aloof. The main crisis of the campaign was the revelation by the liberal New York *Post* and other papers that Nixon had benefited from a special fund, provided by wealthy businessmen in California, to defray his expenses as a Senator. Nixon survived the episode by emphasizing that the fund had not been used for personal enrichment and by making an effectively maudlin televised defense, the "Checkers speech." It also emerged that Governor Stevenson had used a similar fund to supplement the public salaries of officials in Illinois. Realizing that the removal of Nixon from the ticket would still undo his "moral crusade," Eisenhower resisted pressure from his internationalist advisors and the Eastern press, particularly the *Herald Tribune*, to dump Nixon. The episode left a residue of bitterness between Nixon and the Eastern Republicans. The removal of Nixon would not have upset the basic political calculations which led to his choice in the first place. If Nixon faltered, Eisenhower's advisors had another new nationalist Senator from California lined up—William Knowland. In the election results, the liberation propaganda appeared to have had some effect. The Polish-American vote, normally 70 per cent Democratic, dropped to 50 per cent. In the main, Eisenhower's victory derived from his great appeal to the political center, not from the rightist tactics of liberation.

In the campaign, McCarthy returned Eisenhower's lack of enthusiasm for him. Taft did not inspire McCarthy either. Although Thomas E. Coleman, Wisconsin party leader, was Taft's floor manager at the convention, McCarthy held out for MacArthur. McCarthy's politics were in a different key than Taft's. He did not share Taft's foreign policy inhibitions and residual Progressivism. McCarthy may also have resented the failure of the Republican leadership in the Senate to secure good committee assignments for him in his first term. Even among his political confraternity, McCarthy was something of an outsider. He was younger than the average Senator and of genuinely humble social origin, a rarity in the millionaires' club.

McCarthy's main contribution to the Presidential campaign was a nationally televised broadcast in October, financed by General Robert E. Wood of Sears, Roebuck and by Clint W. Murchison and other Texas oil men, in which he referred to Governor Stevenson as "Alger" rather than "Adlai" and took him to task for giving a character deposition on behalf of Hiss. The Republican National Committee used McCarthy extensively in support of Republican candidates throughout the country, where McCarthy could bend his efforts for men of his own stripe. In the election, McCarthy appeared to duplicate his 1950 feat of defeating his main enemy among the Senators of the opposition party as well as the majority leader who backed him. Senator William Benton, a liberal Democrat, was defeated in Connecticut by William Purtell, a right-wing Republican, and Ernest McFarland, the Democratic majority leader, was defeated in Arizona by Barry Goldwater, another right-wing nationalist. McCarthy campaigned actively for both of the victors. Benton served as a vice president of the University of Chicago in the 1930s and 1940s, after which he became chairman of the board of *Encyclopaedia Britannica*. In the first years of the Truman Administration, he was an Assistant Secretary of State. These credentials commended him as the natural enemy of Joe McCarthy. In the summer of 1951, Benton brought a resolution calling for McCarthy's expulsion from the Senate, later moderated to censure. The Benton Resolution was timed to coincide with a strong attack on McCarthy by President Truman. Evidently, the Administration felt itself in a position to move against McCarthy after its victory over MacArthur. Twenty-five Republican Senators immediately came to McCarthy's defense with a denunciation of the "smear tactics" of the Administration.

One of the legends of the McCarthy period is that the junior Senator from Wisconsin bestrode Washington like a colossus and that no one dared take him on. On the contrary, McCarthy's entire career consisted of little more than attacking, being attacked, and counterattacking. McCarthyism was a perpetual motion machine of political intrigue and vendetta. Rarely did any substantive policy question intrude. After his defeat in the 1950 election, Senator Tydings filed a complaint against McCarthy with the Subcommittee on Privileges and Elections which led to a critical, though ineffectual, report. The Benton Resolution was referred to the same subcommittee which after a Byzantine series of parliamentary maneuvers and countermaneuvers by the pro- and anti-McCarthy forces issued in early 1953 the Hennings Report which focused on McCarthy's finances. It was the theory of Senator Mike Monroney, Democrat of Oklahoma, that McCarthy's political vulnerability was personal corruption. The Hennings Report cited the deal with the Lustron Corporation, possible diversion of contributions to the anti-Communist crusade for personal use, possible violations of tax laws and corrupt practices acts governing political campaigns, and like matters. During the Eisenhower Administration, the Hennings Report was referred to the Justice Department, the Internal Revenue Service, and the Federal Deposit Insurance Corporation, none of which found any basis for legal action. *The Reporter* magazine took the report to a Wall

Street law firm which confirmed this conclusion on technical and substantive grounds. The report did succeed in raising serious questions about McCarthy's personal probity and became a basic source for anti-McCarthy journalism and rhetoric. *The New Republic* magazine sold 150,000 copies of the report in a condensed version.

After 1948, American politics bent to a wind from the right. The Republican defeat in a New Deal-style campaign in 1948, the shift of the focus of foreign policy from Europe to Asia, the Communist revolution in China, the Korean War and the limited war with China, the Soviet atomic bomb, the espionage cases, the results of the 1950 election, and the discontents of Democratic ethnic groups over the Roosevelt/Truman foreign policy rallied the Republican right and built up the forces of reaction. Serious as they were, these developments did not refer solely to themselves but were the occasion for the release of forces which had been growing since 1938. For the right, the great questions were the fall of the Republican Party from power, the abandonment of "true liberalism" as the foundation of domestic policy, and the reversal of a Western Hemispheric and Pacific First foreign policy—all of which occurred between 1933 and 1945. The ultimate objects of antagonism were the victorious, multi-ethnic Democratic Party, the New Deal policies of social reform and "big government," and the internationalist, Europe First foreign policy. Held in check since 1938, the reaction against this basic shift in the direction of American history was released in a rush between 1948 and 1954.

This general reaction has come to be known as the "McCarthy era." Senator McCarthy himself had a franchise on only a small piece of it—the issue of "Communism-in-government." After the loyalty/security program of the Truman Administration and the internal struggles and purges within the Democratic Party, it is open to question whether McCarthy even had a real issue. Certainly, the Democrats asserted that he did not. The issue of Communism in government was the practical application of the right-wing theory of the Democratic Party as the Trojan horse of Socialism and Communism. The entire

Republican right subscribed to this Trojan horse theory with varying degrees of paranoia and realism. The factual core of the theory was that the Communist Party once played an important role in American politics and during two periods aligned itself with the Democratic Party in a "Popular Front." For some on the right, this was enough to prove Communist control. For others, these alliances of convenience were disturbing evidence of some long-run parallelism in the goals of the Democratic Party and the Communist Party. Even the anti-Communist Democrats often turned out to have Socialist tendencies and, according to Marx, Communism would require two stages, the first of which was described as Socialism. Senator McCarthy's basic political role was to propagandize this theory of the Trojan horse. The expulsion from government of Communists, Popular Frontists, and those suspected of such tendencies was important for the educational effect that such a purge would have on the electorate as to the nature of the Democratic Party. This educational campaign concerning the "twenty years of treason" would translate itself into votes and votes into a shift in political power—the power that larger men such as MacArthur and Taft required to reorient American foreign and domestic policy. Therefore McCarthy was first the investigator, then the political campaigner. By 1950, the issue even for Republicans was less the Communist Party than the Democratic Party. The Senator from Wisconsin was the Republican National Committee's guided missile which, together with the rhetoric of Liberation, was aimed at the Democratic bases among the Catholic blue-collar workers of recent European origin in the great cities of the East and Midwest.

The inauguration of a Republican Administration, while in some measure a result of the reaction, also posed a crisis for it. Ironically, the principal beneficiaries of the reaction were the Republican moderates who had generally stood aloof from it. Most of the constituency of moderate Republicanism was repelled by McCarthyism, but some of its higher-echelon leadership, such as Henry Cabot Lodge, understood its political usefulness. The question was now whether a new political equilibrium had been achieved. While the right and moderate wings of the Republican Party had established a high degree of unity over Asian issues, there was tension between them over the general precepts of internationalist foreign policy, the balance of power within the party and the new Administration, and over McCarthy himself. The central problem of the first years of the Eisenhower Administration was how far the shift to the right would be allowed to progress. The Democratic Party had now been removed from power and could not for very long function as a scapegoat *in absentia*. The potentiality existed that the Republican Party would split apart over the three great issues before it: 1) how the Republican Party could best be restored to the status of a ruling party; 2) what attitude should be taken to New Deal social legislation; and 3) whether American foreign policy should be kept on an internationalist course.

The Eisenhower Administration conceded considerable ground to the right. In its high-level personnel, the new Administration was much less an Eastern operation than the Presidential campaign, which in turn was less Eastern than the nomination drive. Important cabinet portfolios went to Midwestern industrialists—Charles E. Wilson of General Motors in Detroit as Secretary of Defense and George Humphrey of the M. A. Hanna Company in Cleveland as Secretary of the Treasury, although only Ezra Taft Benson, a leader in the Mormon Church who was appointed Secretary of Agriculture, was actually a Taft Republican. The political split in business was not simply regional in character. Taft himself remarked that there were "too many big businessmen" in the cabinet. During the nomination campaign, the slogan, "Wall Street for Eisenhower, Main Street for Taft," was sometimes heard. Although Secretary of the Treasury Humphrey was a man of impeccably conservative fiscal views and known to Taft as a resident of Ohio, Taft objected to the appointment because it was not cleared in advance with the senior Senator from Ohio. Taft also desired the appointment of Senator Byrd of

Virginia to the position as a means of advancing the coalition of the Republican right and Southern Democrats.

Taft's main objection was to the appointment of Martin Durkin of the plumbers' union as Secretary of Labor. Durkin was an outspoken critic of the Taft-Hartley Act and the appointment seemed to indicate that Eisenhower was not going to fulfill his commitment in the Morningside Heights statement to alter the act only in ways acceptable to Taft. Durkin himself was under the impression that the Taft-Hartley Act would be amended to his own satisfaction, but in a few months Durkin was separated from the Administration. For the rest, the Administration steered a conservative course in domestic policy. The end of the Korean War brought the elimination of wage and price controls. Although Taft was unhappy about the size of the budget in the first fiscal year, Eisenhower did bring expenditures down to $64 billion in fiscal year 1955, close to the objective set in the Morningside Heights statement. All in all, Eisenhower and Taft worked together effectively in domestic policy. In the 1952 election, the Republicans won control of Congress by small margins, and Taft assumed formal leadership of the party as majority leader in the Senate. His influence was such that he was sometimes called the "Prime Minister" in the new Administration. The Republican moderates who had actively supported Eisenhower's candidacy were relegated to a secondary role in the Senate, and the right took control of the command positions—Knowland as chairman of the Republican Policy Committee, Bridges and Millikin as chairmen of Appropriations and Finance. The new Administration made no move to tamper with New Deal social legislaton, but neither did it take any reform initiatives in Eisenhower's two terms. This approach was sufficient for Taft, and the right-wing militants found themselves isolated on domestic policy.

In foreign policy, the Administration implemented the synthesis of internationalism and nationalism which had been outlined in *Life* by Dulles, now Secretary of State. The Administration maintained the basic policies of internationalism and collective security but on the basis of a new strategic doctrine resembling the Hoover/Taft proposals. Admiral Arthur W. Radford, Commander in Chief, Pacific, and a partisan of air/sea power and an Asian policy emphasis, was appointed chairman of the Joint Chiefs of Staff. A major objective of the "New Look" was the reduction of military expenditures. As formulated in a National Security Council paper, 162/2, primary reliance was placed on the capability of the Strategic Air Command to deliver nuclear weapons on the Soviet Union. An effort was made to build up anti-Communist ground forces on the periphery of the Soviet Union—Korea, Formosa, West Germany, and elsewhere. U.S. ground forces were to be equipped with tactical nuclear weapons and redeployed in a "strategic mobile reserve" within the United States, while military manpower reserves would be strengthened to enable a rapid expansion of the Army in a crisis. It was hoped that this system would provide "more basic security at less cost."

The new synthesis in foreign policy was not always stable. Old nationalists were attracted by the New Look but not always by the foreign policy which it served. New nationalists were sensitive to signs of lack of militancy in Asia and Europe. In its first year, the Eisenhower Administration found it necessary to sacrifice the rhetoric of Yalta and Liberation. Despite the pledge in the Republican platform to repudiate the Yalta Agreements, the Administration formulated a resolution on Yalta which merely took the Russians to task for not observing the agreements. This had been the Democratic position on Yalta all along. After the death of Stalin in February 1953 created a delicate international situation, even this resolution was dropped. In June, workers in East Berlin, followed by workers in cities throughout East Germany, began strike actions and demonstrations against the regime. When the Soviet army moved to suppress the unrest, the United States stood aloof and the doctrine of liberation failed its first test. The Administration also offended the Republican right by nominating Charles E. Bohlen, an interpreter at the Yalta Conference, as ambassador to the Soviet Union. It required the personal intervention of Taft to save the nomination. The strength of the new nationalism was in its tactical position, not in its popular base. The relative ease with which Eisenhower disposed of the Yalta/Liberation rhetoric demonstrated that the new nationalists could be isolated when the internationalists combined with at least some of the old nationalists.

In 1953, the old nationalists themselves directly challenged the internationalist foreign policy of the Administration with a proposed Constitutional amendment introduced by Senator Bricker and cosponsored by forty-five Republicans and nineteen Democrats. The provisions of the amendment prohibited treaties or executive agreements from contravening the Constitution or having the effect of law internally except through Congressional action. This affirmation of Constitutional government won substantial bipartisan support. The right was particularly concerned that the various treaties and executive agreements with the United Nations would have the effect of implementing the U.N.'s social philosophy within the United States. The right perceived the spectre of "Socialism by treaty." The Administration opposed the amendment, since it limited its power to make executive agreements and might open the treaty-making process to the cumbersome prospect of Constitutional ratification. In 1954, the amendment failed to receive the necessary two-thirds by only one vote in the Senate. In essence, the Bricker Amendment's bipartisan popularity was a function of the dissatisfaction of Congress with the tendency of the Roosevelt and Truman Administrations to bypass it in the making of foreign policy.

The Administration made some concessions to the nationalist conception of foreign policy. Eisenhower "unleashed" Chiang Kai-shek, that is, removed the Seventh Fleet from the Formosa Strait. The practical effect of this action was minimal, since the Truman Administration had for a year previous adopted this plank in the MacArthur platform by allowing Chiang to make raids on the mainland. Early in the Administration, Dulles admonished the West Europeans to accelerate their rearmament. Most importantly, Eisenhower conferred with MacArthur shortly after his election on means to bring the Korean War to an end. MacArthur proposed a nuclear ultimatum, which the Administration actually delivered the following year. Whether it was the decisive factor in ending the war is a moot point because of the new policies initiated in the Communist world after the death of Stalin. In any case, the end of the war seemed to vindicate the national security policies of the new Administration.

The French/Indo-China war posed a more difficult problem for the New Look. In the spring of 1954, the French were on the verge of defeat at Dienbienphu and approached Washington for air strikes to relieve the position. The United States had supported the French war for some years and since 1950 had assumed 75 per cent of the financial burden of the effort. But American armed forces were not directly engaged. The Eisenhower Administration was in a bind. Eisenhower's election and subsequent popularity were closely related to the expectation, which proved justified, that he would bring the Korean War to a conclusion. He could hardly involve the United States in a new Asian war one year after the end of the first. The whole thrust of his security policy was against any new ground war, particularly in Asia. At the same time, the Administration was convinced that the war was stage-managed from Peking in consultation with Moscow and that the development of any new Communist state must be prevented. The Administration was already committed to the French war effort and desired French support for the European Defense Community, a plan for integrated, multi-national armed forces including Germans, which was highly unpopular in France.

An air strike might solve these dilemmas with a minimum additional American commitment. This was the view of Dulles and Radford. But Army Chief of Staff Matthew Ridgway and Eisenhower himself were skeptical that the French garrison at Dienbienphu could be relieved by air strikes when the opposing forces were so closely engaged under thick jungle cover. Nathan Twining, Air Force Chief of Staff, proposed the use of tactical nuclear weapons. These "tactical" weapons were larger than those dropped on Hiroshima and Nagasaki and, as Eisenhower later remarked, it was difficult to employ these weapons against the Viet Minh forces without simultaneously vaporizing the French garrison. In sum, Eisenhower believed that air strikes would only embarrass the United States by extending its commitment to a losing venture.

Inexorably, the Administration was drawn toward the initiation of another ground war. Eisenhower attached certain conditions to the use of American forces, consistent with the basic policies of his Administration. He was disturbed that the United States was in league with naked colonialism in Southeast Asia and required that the French develop a viable plan for the independence of Indochina. He also required that Congress approve any American military operation and that U.S. forces be used only in the context of "united action" by the French and other American Allies. These conditions could hardly be fulfilled. The French were fighting to preserve their colonial position, not abstractly to contain Communism, and did not welcome troops from other countries which would weaken their influence in the area. The British had no intention of involving themselves in the war. Congress was reluctant to approve an American commitment, particularly if it were a unilateral one. When Vice President Nixon in "off-the-record" remarks at the annual meeting of the American Society of Newspaper Editors suggested that American ground forces might have to be used, there was a public uproar. In the end, the Administration acquiesced in, though it did not sign, the Geneva Accords which partitioned Vietnam with the prospect of elections two years after. The Administration came under fire from the right, particularly Senator Knowland, for participating in this conference with the Chinese Communists. In a famous incident at Geneva, Dulles refused the hand of Chou En-lai when it was offered. The U.S. tried to influence the outcome of the Geneva talks by sending aircraft carriers armed with nuclear weapons to the coast of Indochina. The partition of Vietnam was an outcome more acceptable to the United States than the military situation justified, but the political factors in the country pointed to a Communist victory in the forthcoming elections.

The Indochina crisis was a foreign policy problem that the structure of U.S. policy could not handle. It was not possible to follow the principles of collective security, Constitutional process, anti-colonialism, and the New Look, and still achieve a non-Communist Indochina. American foreign policy was also dominated by strategic concepts, such as the "domino theory," and material and operational considerations which failed to grasp the political realities. The United States government was unwilling to admit that it was confronted with a social revolution in the area that might install Communist governments. It preferred to believe that it was dealing with "internal subversion" and "indirect aggression" by alien forces. Dulles hastened to create the Southeast Asia Treaty Organization (SEATO), consisting of the United States, Great Britain, France, Australia, New Zealand, the Philippines, Thailand, and Pakistan. Theoretically modeled on NATO, SEATO was a paper organization which never developed armed forces and which was dominated by Western powers outside Asia. It also threw its net over Indochina. Dulles described SEATO as an "Asiatic Monroe Doctrine." Through a formal structure of collective security, which required unanimous action by the SEATO powers and a formal request for help from the government affected, the United States now claimed hegemony over Southeast Asia.

In its contingency planning, the United States actually contemplated a unilateral ground invasion of North Vietnam in which U.S. forces would march on Hanoi after a landing at Haiphong. Eisenhower overruled this proposal. A team of experts dispatched to Vietnam by General Ridgway had already determined that a war there would offer more military and logistical problems than Korea. Essentially, Korea had been a conventional, not a revolutionary war. The regime of Kim Il Sung had been installed by the Soviet Union after World War II when North Korea was under occupation by the Russian Army. On the Korean peninsula, therefore, the United States did not face the "people's war" which it avoided in China through Marshall's policy but which now awaited it in Indochina.

On internal security issues, the Eisenhower Administration also shifted to the right. Eisenhower implemented a new loyalty/security program which eliminated loyalty review boards and departmental panels and established in their stead security officers and security boards to handle appeals. The criterion for dismissal was not political loyalty alone, but a broadened concept of "security," which included almost any form of personal misconduct or deviance. The burden of proof was placed on the employee, who was expected to demonstrate that his retention was "clearly consistent" with security interests. Under the new regime, J. Robert Oppenheimer, who had overseen the development of the atomic bomb at Los Alamos during World War II, was declared a security risk. Scott McLeod, a former FBI agent and aide to Senator Styles Bridges, was appointed security officer of the State Department and conducted a purge of the "China hands." In 1954, President Eisenhower stated that 2,200 Federal employees had been dismissed under the new security program.

The Administration also obtained new internal security legislation. New laws made peacetime espionage a capital offense, extended the statute of limitations from three to five years, increased the penalties for harboring fugitives, granted immunity to witnesses in order to compel testimony under certain conditions, and in general strengthened the prosecution in cases relating to national security. Congress did not enact other Administration requests to strengthen perjury laws and allow the use of wiretap evidence in federal court in national security cases. It did enact a law providing for the forfeiture of citizenship of persons convicted of advocating the violent overthrow of the government.

The general policy of the Eisenhower Administration did not offer an obvious vulnerability to the right. In all major areas—domestic and foreign policy, internal security—the Administration was well to the right of the Eastern forces which sponsored the Eisenhower candidacy. In the first year of the Administration, the right was reduced to minor challenges over symbolic questions, such as the Yalta resolution and the Bohlen nomination. The Administration's position with the right was shored up by Taft. In the summer of 1953, Taft died of cancer. He was succeeded as majority leader by Knowland, publisher of the Oakland *Tribune* in California, who was both more recalcitrant politically and less influential with his faction of the party.

Knowland himself was challenged from the right for the leadership by Everett Dirksen, chairman of the Republican Senatorial Campaign Committee. Dirksen based his early political career in Illinois on the American Legion. As a member of the House, he demonstrated some tendency toward moderation in domestic policy and new nationalism in foreign policy. In his statewide campaign for the Senate in 1950, however, he was under the gun of the Chicago *Tribune* and developed a harder position of more old nationalist tint. At the 1952 convention, he made himself conspicuous by delivering a personal attack on Governor Dewey. In 1951, he introduced an amendment to the Mutual Security Act to cut military and economic assistance to Europe by $250 million. Knowland was paired against this amendment. Knowland and Dirksen were also on opposite sides of the vote on the Japanese Peace Treaty in 1952. Knowland supported the treaty, which had been negotiated by John Foster Dulles, while Dirksen voted against it and endorsed the reservations, introduced by Senator Jenner, which embodied nationalist views on American sovereignty, the United Nations, Yalta, and Nationalist China. Dirksen's candidacy for the party leadership in the Senate was supported by a combination of new nationalists, for whom the Administration's foreign policy was insufficiently militant, and old nationalists, for whom its foreign policy was too internationalist. Bridges and McCarthy were in the first group and Jenner, Bricker, Malone, and Welker in the second.

For all his notoriety, Joe McCarthy had not been in the first rank of right-wing nationalist leadership. The death of Taft, the withdrawal of MacArthur to private life, and the cooptation of Nixon and, to a degree, Knowland gave McCarthy his opportunity to move forward. McCarthy was fated to lead an attack on the Eastern moderates of the Republican Party and to discover the limits of the reactionary surge. With unfortunate consequences for his political future, McCarthy would be hard pressed to find any substantive policy question on which to hang his offensive. There was no Alger Hiss known to be in the Administration, and Eisenhower did not lose Indochina. The basic political environment was also changing to the disadvantage of the right. The death of Stalin and the end of the Korean War inaugurated a period of steady relaxation in international tension which culminated in the summit conference of Eisenhower and Khrushchev at Geneva in 1955. There was also a Republican Administration, and the right could not count on opportunistic support from Republican moderates should it attempt to move against Eisenhower in the same spirit as against Truman. Although the Administration was dependent on the 25 per cent or so of the electorate that the right could deliver, Eisenhower also had great strength in the center. The 1952 election had already revealed a change in the public temper. The Republicans won the Presidency and the Congress, and three new right-wing Republicans, Goldwater of Arizona, Purtell of Connecticut, and Frank Barrett of Wyoming entered the Senate. But this time, three right-wing incumbents also lost— Kem of Missouri, Ecton of Montana, and Cain of Washington. Earlier, Brewster was defeated in the Republican primary in Maine. McCarthy himself won quite unimpressively in Wisconsin. He brought up the rear of the Republican ticket which was led by Fred R. Zimmerman, an anti-McCarthy Progressive, who won election as secretary of state.

Realizing McCarthy's potential to run amok, Taft had assigned Jenner, who was more amenable to party discipline, the chairmanship of the Senate Internal Security Subcommittee. However, McCarthy became chairman of the Government Operations Committee and quickly converted its Permanent Investigations Subcommittee into the grim reaper. As chief counsel and assistant counsel to the subcommittee, he hired promising young inquisitors—Roy Cohn, one of the prosecutors in the Rosenberg case, and Robert F. Kennedy, son of Joseph P. Kennedy, who was prone to share nationalist views on foreign policy. Through his committee chairmanship, Mc-Carthy had ready access to Internal Revenue records and other sensitive data. The Permanent Investigations Subcommittee got off to a fast start in 1953 with hearings on seventeen subjects of which the more important were trade with the Soviet bloc, subversion in the State Department information services and the Voice of America, infiltration of the Army, subversion in defense industries, and United Nations infiltration. The operations of the subcommittee were only a small part of a general post-war inquisition on the questions of Communism and subversion. During the 79th Congress, 1945–47, there were only four hearings in these fields. With the election of the Republican 80th Congress, 1947–49, the number increased to twenty-two investigations, conducted by six different committees. Even during the following Democratic Congresses, the 81st and 82nd, there were twenty-four and thirty-four investigations. The efforts of the Republican right from 1949 to 1953 were aided by the Southern Democrats who retaliated against the Truman Administration for its sponsorship of civil rights. With the election of the Republican 83rd Congress, investigations reached the unprecedented number of fifty-one. After 1955, the number of investigations declined to the levels of the 79th Congress.[7]

Given the role of the State Department in the right's theory of subversion, it was a natural object of investigation by Mc-Carthy. The focus on its information services and on the Voice of America was clear indication that McCarthy had taken it upon himself to prepare American propaganda agencies for their role in the strategy of liberation. With Raymond Swing, a left-of-center broadcast journalist as its chief commentator, the Voice of America was obviously in no shape to lead the contemplated offensive into Eastern Europe. In early 1953, McCarthy also bore in on the trading of U.S. Allies with Communist states. As long as the United States was engaged in a

shooting war with Communist countries on the Korean peninsula, this was a popular issue. McCarthy's staff "negotiated" an
agreement with Greek shipowners in London, who pledged not
to engage in trade with Communist nations. This episode provoked McCarthy's former political ally, Harold Stassen, who
was now Mutual Security Director, to criticize McCarthy for in-
terfering in the province of the Executive Branch. Dulles
promptly undercut Stassen by meeting with McCarthy and affirming that his actions were "in the national interest." Dulles
was made nervous by McCarthy since it was the Secretary of
State who had recommended Alger Hiss for the presidency of
the Carnegie Endowment. When Clement Attlee, now leader of
the opposition party in Great Britain, publicly wondered who
conducted American foreign policy, McCarthy was given the
opportunity to berate the British left.

A Republican Administration under a popular President
would be dangerous to McCarthy only if he confronted it directly or if it chose to attack him directly. Otherwise, it would
give McCarthy's activities an air of official sanction. Concerned
about the political consequences of a split in the party over the
issue of McCarthy, the Administration decided not to discipline
him, although he was distasteful to most of the White House
leadership including Eisenhower himself. By inaction, the Eisenhower Administration legitimated McCarthy. For the first
time, the polls in the early summer of 1953 showed that more
of the American people approved than disapproved the Senator. The Administration avoided a confrontation even when
McCarthy made a raid on the Central Intelligence Agency. Mc-
Carthy attempted to call William P. Bundy, a Washington lawyer and employee of the agency, to testify before his subcommittee. Bundy was the son-in-law of Dean Acheson and had
made a financial contribution to a defense fund for Alger Hiss.
The CIA informed McCarthy that under orders from Allen W.
Dulles, its director and the brother of the Secretary of State,
Bundy could not testify. Senator McCarthy took the CIA director to task for his uncooperative attitude. Vice President Nixon,
a friend of McCarthy and the Administration's principal con-

tact with him, then intervened, and McCarthy agreed not to press the issue.

In November, Herbert Brownell, U.S. Attorney-General, attempted to "take away some of the glamour of the McCarthy stage play." Brownell revealed that Harry Dexter White had been under close surveillance by the FBI as a suspected agent of Russian espionage, but that the Truman Administration had allowed his appointment to go through as executive director of the International Monetary Fund. In a televised reply, Truman admitted that his Administration had deleterious information concerning White but elected to allow him to continue in office as a means of advancing the investigation of espionage activities by intelligence agencies. When Truman accused the Eisenhower Administration of "McCarthyism," McCarthy took the opening to demand television time to reply to Truman. In his speech, McCarthy attacked not only Truman but directly criticized the Eisenhower Administration for not putting a stop to the "blood trade" between Communist China and the Allies of the United States, principally Great Britain through Hong Kong.

Far from taking the play away from McCarthy, Brownell had provided him with credibility. Just as Richard Nixon's success with the Hiss case tended to backstop McCarthy in his poorly documented forays against the State Department, so the White affair brought into some kind of focus McCarthy's frenetic investigating in 1953. McCarthy's rating in the Gallup Poll now rose to its highest point—50 per cent favorable, 29 per cent unfavorable—as the previously skeptical political center momentarily swung to his side. Brownell had also managed to set up a political challenge to his own Administration. White House sources characterized McCarthy's address as a "hat-in-the-ring" speech. McCarthy was now in the position of having to deny that he would contest the Republican Presidential nomination in 1956. The Gallup Poll took surveys which did not particularly encourage a McCarthy candidacy; only 9 per cent of those polled favored him over Eisenhower and only 5 per cent as a third party candidate.[8] But even to be considered in this light added to McCarthy's standing. Once again, the Administration dispatched Vice President Nixon to bring McCarthy into line. At a meeting with Nixon and Deputy Attorney-General William P. Rogers at Key Biscayne, Florida, on December 30, McCarthy agreed that he would direct his fire at the Democrats, not the Republican Administration, and that he would look into other matters besides Communist subversion.

Despite McCarthy's assurances to Nixon, the stage was set after the White incident for a hardening in the White House attitude since the strategy of accommodation had not deterred McCarthy. For reasons both of calculation and sympathy, the advocates of accommodation were Nixon, Rogers, and Major General Wilton B. Persons, a White House aide. The anti-McCarthy group in the White House was led by Sherman Adams, former governor of New Hampshire who functioned as White House "chief of staff" as Assistant to the President; Robert Cutler, president of Old Colony Trust Company in Boston who was Special Assistant for National Security; and C. D. Jackson, a vice president of Time, Inc., and publisher of *Fortune,* who was an advisor on "psychological warfare." The leader of Republican opposition in the Senate was Senator Flanders of Vermont.

Aligned against McCarthy in the Senate was the liberal/labor wing of the Democratic Party. This was the "Trojan horse" itself and the natural enemy of McCarthy and the Republican right. The National Committee for an Effective Congress established a "clearing house" to provide "technical assistance" to the anti-McCarthy forces. This venture was financed through the efforts of Paul Hoffman. From outside the Senate, William Benton also took an active part in organizing the anti-McCarthy forces. Flanders, Hoffman, and Benton had helped to found the Committee for Economic Development in 1942, a policy organization of internationalist business. In the Senate, the Republican right and the liberal Democrats were roughly evenly matched and a direct confrontation between the two could not be decisive. Except for Flanders, the Republican moderates were extremely reluctant to provoke a split in the party over the McCarthy issue. Senator Lyndon B. Johnson of Texas, the minority leader, attempted to encourage such a split by following the low-profile tactics which the Republicans had used against Roosevelt in the Supreme Court fight in 1937. Johnson attempted to rein in the Democratic liberals, lest they unite the Republicans by making a partisan issue of McCarthy. Johnson liked to refer to McCarthy as a "Republican problem."

The other political factor in the Senate was the Southern wing of the Democratic Party. The Southern Democrats had their own quarrel with the liberal Democrats over civil rights and domestic social policy. But they could not stand aside and allow the Republican right to demolish the Democratic Party, which was their national vehicle. As a Catholic and a Republican, McCarthy had no regional appeal. Nor were his politics popular with the Southern folk who revered the memory of Roosevelt and the New Deal. The region as a whole was internationalist and pro-British and not particularly sympathetic to the nationalist, pro-German perspective of the Republican right. For these reasons, the Southern Democrats began to move into active opposition to McCarthy.

In the summer of 1953, McCarthy hired J. B. Matthews as staff director of his subcommittee. A disillusioned former radical and a professional anti-Communist, Matthews had been research director for the Dies Committee and a consultant to the Hearst Corporation. As Matthews's appointment was announced, an article by him appeared in the right-wing *American Mercury,* "Reds and Our Churches," which attacked left-wing political activism among the Protestant ministry. Senator John McClellan, Democrat of Arkansas and a minority member of the subcommittee, was enraged by this affront to the patriotism of the Protestant clergy and with the other Democratic members of the subcommittee, Henry Jackson of Washington and Stuart Symington of Missouri, demanded that Matthews be fired. Officials of religious organizations, including the Southern Baptist Convention, denounced the appointment. This time, Nixon and Rogers joined with Emmet John Hughes, an anti-McCarthy White House speech writer, to arrange for a telegram to the White House from leaders of the National Conference of Christians and Jews protesting the Matthews appointment, which would receive a friendly Presidential response. The same day, McCarthy accepted Matthews's resignation. After this episode, the Gallup Poll showed that the American people were again more disapproving than approving of McCarthy.

In consultation with other Southern Democrats, McClellan now worked to undermine McCarthy's authority over his own subcommittee. When the Republicans on the subcommittee affirmed McCarthy's exclusive right as chairman to hire and fire staff, McClellan led Symington and Jackson off the subcommittee in a minority boycott, a political tactic unprecedented in the Senate. With the support of Senator Russell of Georgia, McClellan proposed in early 1954 that the Congress establish a single "Joint Committee on Subversive and Un-American Activities" which would unify all investigations in this area and exclude McCarthy completely. Senator Allen J. Ellender, Democrat of Louisiana, led a move to reduce the appropriations for McCarthy's committee. Finally, McCarthy capitulated, and the Republicans repealed the rule allowing him exclusive power to hire and fire staff. The Democrats rejoined the subcommittee under rules giving them more control of investigations, and the move to cut McCarthy's appropriations was dropped.

In the autumn of 1953, McCarthy pressed forward an effort to obtain the loyalty/security files of the U.S. Army. The Republican right had grown disillusioned with the military. The "Democratic Generals," together with Senator Russell who was chairman of the Armed Services Committee and perhaps the single most powerful Democratic Senator, had dealt with MacArthur on his return to the United States. As chairman of the Joint Chiefs of Staff, General Bradley had been an open advocate of the foreign policy of the Truman Administration. After the death of Roosevelt, General Marshall had been regarded by the right as the leader of the internationalist forces. The principal advocates of the "pro-Communist" China policy during and after World War II were not the junior- and middle-level State Department officials cast in the role by the right but the higher circles of the old War Department—Stimson, Marshall, and Stilwell. The right was also exercised by the presence of Communists in the Armed Forces. This issue might offer the means to strip the Democratic Generals of the cover of their uniforms and neutralize their political prestige. The Southerners could not be very happy about any such effort. More than 40 per cent of the officer corps was of Southern or Border state origin.[9] Marshall himself was a graduate of the Virginia Military Institute. The Eisenhower Administration also regarded this latest McCarthy venture with distaste. An investigation might not only undermine the U.S. military but affect the personal prestige of General Eisenhower. For long, the right had not dared to attack the Army directly. McCarthy dared.

In October, McCarthy began an investigation of subversion among civilian scientists employed by the Army Signal Corps Engineering Laboratories in Fort Monmouth, New Jersey. Typically, the case was second-hand and had already been exploited by HUAC. By January 1954, McCarthy was making an issue of it by threatening to subpoena the members of the Loyalty and Security Appeals Board, which had passed on the Fort Monmouth scientists. At the urging of the Republican members of the Permanent Investigations Subcommittee, McCarthy backed away from this demand. At this time, it came to light that McCarthy and his chief counsel, Roy Cohn, were attempting to secure favored treatment for David Schine, a consultant to the subcommittee and heir to an hotel fortune, who had been drafted into the Army. At a January 21 meeting attended by Herbert Brownell, Henry Cabot Lodge, and Army counsel John G. Adams, Sherman Adams asked the Army counsel to prepare a "chronology" of the efforts of McCarthy and Cohn to intervene on behalf of Schine.

In February, McCarthy continued his Army investigation by making much of the promotion of an Army dentist of left-wing affiliations, and insulting the man's commanding officer, Brigadier General Ralph Zwicker, before the committee. Robert T.

Stevens, the Secretary of the Army, who had used tactics of passive resistance with McCarthy, now openly denounced his conduct and ordered Zwicker, a highly decorated combat officer, not to reappear before McCarthy's committee. Nixon and Persons intervened to prevent a confrontation between McCarthy and the Army. They proposed a meeting between Stevens and the Republican members of the subcommittee—McCarthy, Dirksen, Karl Mundt of South Dakota, and Charles Potter of Michigan. At a "chicken lunch" at Dirksen's office, Stevens was induced to sign a "Memorandum of Understanding" which embodied McCarthy's viewpoint. In the ensuing melée, Stevens retracted his surrender, and the Administration released the damning chronology.

In a speech in Miami Beach, Adlai Stevenson ridiculed the Republican Party as a "political party divided against itself, half McCarthy and half Eisenhower." The Republican National Committee received free radio and television time to reply to Stevenson and chose Vice President Nixon to deliver the response. While answering Stevenson, Nixon disengaged from McCarthy by criticizing "reckless talk and questionable methods." Lines were now forming for an open confrontation between the Administration and McCarthy. The release of the chronology prepared the way for an investigation of the Army's charge against McCarthy and McCarthy's countercharge that the Army was using Schine as the means to forestall an investigation of itself. As the confrontation between the Army and McCarthy developed through the winter and spring of 1954, the popularity of McCarthy in the Gallup Poll steadily declined. The *Fortune* study, published in April, noted a decline in business support for McCarthy. Of corporate executives in Southern California, it remarked: "What underlies the congealing doubts of Los Angeles businessmen who only a year ago were unqualifiedly for McCarthy is a belief that he is a bungler who may, unless curbed, split the Republican Party."[10] Of the South: "Yet, even discounting political and religious bias, the Senator has made spectacularly little headway among the profoundly conservative businessmen of the South."[11]

With McCarthy and Cohn standing aside, the Permanent Investigations Subcommittee itself conducted hearings on the Army/McCarthy issues. Senator Mundt proposed that they be carried out on the confidential model of the MacArthur hearings. At the direction of Minority Leader Johnson, the Democrats demanded that they be not only open, but televised. Johnson was well aware of McCarthy's decline in public standing over the Army issue. There was also the precedent of the CBS broadcasts of Edward R. Murrow and Fred W. Friendly in March which allowed McCarthy to damn himself with his own words. The televised hearings dragged on inconclusively for two months and completed the abandonment of McCarthy by the political center. McCarthy was skillfully outpointed by Army counsel Joseph L. Welch. In opinion polls, 35 per cent of the people still approved him; he retained his basic support with the Republican right and some Catholic Democrats.

Still, there was no doubt who won the encounter. Roy Cohn resigned as chief counsel. McCarthy's attempt to replace him with former Senator Owen Brewster, defeated in the 1952 Republican primary in Maine, was rejected. Majority leader Knowland, who now regarded McCarthy as a liability, put a stop to McCarthy's effort to retreat to friendly territory by conducting an investigation of Communism in defense plants in Boston. In June, Senator Flanders introduced the resolution which, after modifications, became the vehicle for the eventual censure of McCarthy. This was too much for Knowland who would have preferred to encourage McCarthy to fade away. The Republican Policy Committee unanimously opposed the resolution. While Senator Dirksen organized the defense of McCarthy, Flanders of Vermont and John Sherman Cooper of Kentucky led the Republican anti-McCarthy forces. Fulbright of Arkansas and Monroney of Oklahoma led the Democratic opposition to McCarthy with the cooperation of other Democratic liberals.

In August, Knowland and Johnson agreed to refer the Flanders Resolution to a Select Committee appointed for that purpose. For the committee, they chose Senators who were acceptable to both men: Republicans Arthur Watkins of Utah, Frank Carlson of Kansas, and Francis Case of South Dakota and Democrats Edwin Johnson of Colorado, John Stennis of Mississippi, and Sam Ervin of North Carolina. One of the stipulations for membership was that the Senator not be on record as pro- or anti-McCarthy. With a Select Committee of this kind, Senator Johnson took a calculated risk. Its bipartisan character would not guarantee a result, but would give the recommendations of the committee more authority for that very reason. The members were all conservatives but not McCarthyites. It was an open question whether their conservatism would save McCarthy or their sense of propriety hang him. They were all from the South and West where McCarthy's popular appeal was not particularly great.

In the event, the Select Committee recommended censure of McCarthy on two counts of contempt of the Senate—refusal to appear before the Subcommittee on Privileges and Elections in 1952 and abuse of Brigadier General Zwicker before the Permanent Investigations Subcommittee. The focus on the procedures of the Senate itself was calculated to reduce the potential for political controversy and broaden the base for a censure vote. When the issue came to a head in late 1954, the Democrats voted unanimously for censure, 45 to 0, with only Senator John F. Kennedy of Massachusetts unrecorded. The Republicans split evenly, 22 for and against. Senator Saltonstall, majority whip and chairman of the Armed Services Committee, voted for censure, but the rest of the Republican leadership—Knowland, Bridges, Millikin, Dirksen—voted no. Outside Congress, the right organized an anti-censure movement, Ten Million Americans Mobilizing for Justice, the chairman of which was Lieutenant General George E. Stratemeyer, formerly Commanding General of the Far East Air Force.

The confrontation of the right with the Eisenhower Administration resulted in defeat. The reasons for failure were various. Fundamentally, the right did not command the political strength to overawe both the Democratic Party and the Republican moderates. Its Catholic/ethnic/blue-collar strategy added to the provincial base of the Republican right but not enough to insure victory. McCarthy's attacks on the Protestant clergy and the Army accelerated the development of a Southern opposition. His skirmishes with the Administration forced the Republican moderates into the open. The Eisenhower Administration also adjusted its policy in fundamental ways to the requirements of the right. There were no substantive issues of real promise. Although Eisenhower himself was exasperated enough with his chronic problems with the right by the summer of 1953 to speculate on the possibility of a third party *of the center* animated by the principle of "dynamic conservatism," this thought only indicated the basic differences in mentality between the center and the right, not the imminence of fission.

The right's confrontation with the Administration also suffered from the leadership of Senator McCarthy. For McCarthy, the issue of Communism in government had become an *idée fixe,* and he was unable to perceive that it had outlived its usefulness, much less to understand the consequences of the changes in the international climate. There was a touch of the absurd in McCarthy's effort to undermine the Democratic Party by embarrassing Republican administrators. The right followed McCarthy with considerable unease. When McCarthy openly denounced Eisenhower after his censure, many of the Republican Senators who had voted against his censure fell away from him. The right was forced to make its stand on the issue of McCarthy himself with disastrous results. McCarthy welcomed the personalization of the issue in his statement concerning the censure resolution:

> Let me say, incidentally, that it is not easy for a man to assert that he is the symbol of resistance to Communist subversion—that the Nation's fate is in some respects tied to his own fate. It is much easier, I assure you, to be coy—to play down one's personal role in this struggle for freedom. Self-effacement is always a comfortable posture.
>
> But I take it that you would rather I be frank than coy; that you would rather I acknowledge and accept the fact that McCarthyism is a household word for describing a way of dealing with treason and the threat of treason; and so I shall.[12]

In this statement, McCarthy freely predicted his own censure and asked who would benefit by it. The Communist Party would, of course, benefit, and therefore the Watkins Committee was the party's "involuntary agent." This notion of "objectively" serving the interests of the Communists without conscious understanding has been called the right's theory of "social Communism," equivalent to the Stalinist theory of "social Fascism." Senator Jenner shared this perception and believed that the Senate Internal Security Subcommittee should take its title to heart and investigate "conspiratorial influence on the Senate of the United States." The liberals or "anti-anti-Communists" would also benefit. This group dominated the "opinion-molding machinery of the United States" and in particular managed the "Luce empire."

In his valedictory, McCarthy briefly recapitulated the issues dear to the right—Yalta, Communist revolution in China, Dean Acheson's affection for Alger Hiss. He also recited the honor roll of those who had fallen in the fight against Communism—Martin Dies, Dr. William Wirt, and Joe McCarthy. During the 1954 off-year election campaign, the Republican National Committee was no longer interested in McCarthy. The speaking invitations no longer came. The Gallup Poll showed that a McCarthy endorsement would incline 43 per cent of the American people to vote against a candidate while only 19 per cent would be favorably influenced.[13] The Democrats regained control of Congress. McCarthyism had failed. The reaction was over.

11

THE GARGOYLES

There was a culture of Americanism just as there was a politics of Americanism. Both culture and politics emerged from the milieu of provincial Republicanism—from Main Street. If not ethnically homogenous in a strict sense, Americanist culture was certainly North European—Anglo-Saxon, German, and Scandinavian. It was built around the norms of free enterprise and small-town life. "Individualism" was valued as the expression of business initiative; it did not imply a mandate to explore the hidden places of the soul. Conformity and Individualism were not contradictory but the symmetrical expression of Puritan enterprise. Cultural reliance on the Protestant ethic was complicated in the 1950s by the new alliance with Catholic ethnic groups and the emergence of a Catholic right. This alliance required both the abandonment of one of the staples of old-style Americanism, anti-Catholicism, and a new crusade against "secular" irreligious trends which had often been associated in the right-wing mind with the old stereotypes regarding the swarthy-skinned peoples—laziness, degeneracy, and violence.

The enemy was the heterogeneous culture of the metropolis. The cultural influences emanating from the great cities were multi-ethnic. They conveyed no clear message unless it was a pragmatic tolerance which undercut the formation of a moral consensus. While the cities were the nerve centers of American capitalism, the political right regarded their populations as far from reliable standard-bearers of the Protestant ethic. The better elements were Anglo-Saxon and bourgeois, but they were not hard-working enough. The idle rich were soft and decadent. They also looked down upon their country cousins when they were not actively engaged in exploiting them. There were other elements of metropolitan culture which were insufficiently capitalist. The machine politics of the city often relied upon customary relationships and the *quid pro quo* rather than upon the infallible judgment of the marketplace. There were the trade unions which substituted group solidarity for individual worth. There were the government bureaucrats in the administrative centers who avoided the competitive struggle for the security of the civil service. All of these elements including the plutocrats drawing their monopolistic profits could be seen as part of a collectivist development. They were also parasites. They were repugnant not only for what they were, but for the burden they represented. Each passing year seemed to register an increase in the power of the public bureaucracies, the monopolistic corporations, the trade unions, and the political machines.

Since they were all "collectivist" from a *laissez-faire* perspective, these trends could be considered "left-wing." Actually, the influence of proletarian Socialist forces was not dominant among these various metropolitan tendencies which grew out of bureaucratic capitalism, the multi-national character of American culture, and other peculiarities of American history which, even in the absence of a strong Socialist movement, made the right feel under siege. Surveying the Democratic Party, the Republican right exaggerated the Socialist and Communist influences within it and doubted that the Democrats could be entrusted with the heritage of free enterprise. The South was the main Protestant element among the Democrats, but the region was tainted by anti-bourgeois traditions originating in the plantation system—paternalism and militarism. Its Anglican upper class did not embody the sensibility of the Reformation. The evangelical fundamentalism of its working class did not have the reassuring jingle of the countinghouse. Thus there was the paradox of a strong right-wing reaction, which based itself ideologically on the threat of Socialism, in a country where Socialist forces were relatively weak.

In this context, "Communist" and "left-wing" were symbolic epithets directed against the entire complex of bureaucratic capitalist, metropolitan, multi-ethnic, and Democratic forces feared and despised by the right. In the rogue's gallery, the *avant-garde* intellectuals occupied a prominent place. Most often, the cultural vanguardists espoused a vague *gauchisme* which arrayed them against the right. This anti-bourgeois posture was not actually rooted in Socialist working class politics but in the Romantic traditions of the middle-class intelligentsia. The haunts of the *avant garde* were not working class districts but the precincts of the nonworking, whether it be the wealthy or the *lumpen*. Of these areas, Marx remarked: "Alongside decayed *roués* with dubious means of subsistence and of dubious origin, alongside ruined and adventurous offshoots of the bourgeoisie, were vagabonds, discharged soldiers, discharged jailbirds, escaped galley slaves, swindlers, mountebanks, *lazzaroni*, pickpockets, tricksters, gamblers, *maquereaus*, brothel keepers, porters, *literati*, organ-grinders, ragpickers, knife grinders, tinkers, beggars—in short, the whole indefinite, disintegrated mass, thrown hither and thither, which the French term *la bohéme*. . . ."[1]

The politics of the Left Bank inclined to a rootless anarchism in which grand concepts of culture and utopia hovered above a social vacuum. Its social base was in *petit-bourgeois* artistic enterprise, the *demi-monde,* and the patronage of the rich. At the art gallery and the junk shop, the "establishment" and the "left" did seem allied in a conspiracy against the standards of the hard-working middle class. In the bohemian quarter of the city, there was concrete evidence of bourgeois complicity with social distintegration and moral decay which, according to the right, characterized the "modern age." In an essay in *Human Events,* E. Merrill Root argued the necessity to "clarify the mind and fortify the soul of America against the prevalent, disguised, largely triumphant, Culture of the Left. It is not (*as yet*) a fully Communist culture—but it is a culture of negation, despair, mockery, nihilism, a culture full of the virus of spiritual polio."[2] Root raised the cultural banner of Main Street: "Fortunately, many Americans already love and seek the life-sustaining Culture of the Right. They love *South Pacific* and *Oklahoma;* they know the greatness of Robert Nathan's *Portrait of Jennie;* they sustain their souls with the earth-tanged, resilient, life-rich poetry of Robert Frost; they acclaim the brave power of Taylor Caldwell."[3] Whatever may be said for the brave power of Taylor Caldwell, the rightist strictures against the *avant garde* had a certain point; by the middle of the twentieth century it was a cultural movement that was exhausted even in its own terms.

America's great cities were the catch-basins for the talented and the deviant from throughout the country, and there was a long-standing grudge between small-town America and its prodigals. But the right labored in its effort to connect all metropolitan forces with a relatively minor subculture. The cultural standards of the metropolitan upper class did not really derive from the underground. The convergence thesis of the upper and lower classes in an alliance against the middle class, particularly the provincial middle class, reflected an internal necessity of the right, which symmetrically linked its enemies. In the United States, the perspective was exacerbated by the regional tensions arising out of the pattern of American economic development. One of the stereotypes of the West testified to the effeteness of the East. In the early 1950s, homosexuality became a minor issue. The dismissals of personnel from the State Department on the grounds of "security" included a certain number of cases of homosexuality. This development provided an opening for the right to link up homosexuality, leftism, internationalism, and anything else that might catch its fancy. Senator McCarthy was not alone in this attitude. The notion of an "homosexual International" was formulated by Dr. R. G. Waldeck:

Welded together by the identity of their forbidden desires, of their strange, sad needs, habits, dangers, not to mention their outrageously fatuous vocabulary, members of this International constitute a world-wide conspiracy against society. This conspiracy has spread all over the globe; has penetrated all classes; operates in armies and in prisons, has infiltrated into the press, the movies and the cabinets; and it all but dominates the arts, literature, theatre, music and TV.

And here is why homosexual officials are a peril to us in the present struggle between West and East; members of one conspiracy are prone to join another conspiracy. This is one reason why so many homosexuals from being enemies of society in general, become enemies of capitalism in particular. Without being necessarily Marxist, they serve the ends of the Communist International in the name of their rebellion against the prejudices, standards, ideals of the "bourgeois" world. Another reason for the homosexual-Communist alliance is the instability and passion for intrigue for intrigue's sake, which is inherent in the homosexual personality. A third reason is the social promiscuity within the homosexual minority and the fusion it effects between upper class and proletarian corruption.[4]

During the McCarthyist reaction, a struggle took place within the institutions of culture—the schools, universities, the publishing industry, theatre, the press, radio, television, film and entertainment. In part, the objective of the right was to ensure that these institutions transmitted the culture of Americanism and to purge them not only of any leftist symptoms but of their general cosmopolitanism. The latter task was much the more difficult, since worldliness and skepticism were inevitable results of cultural activity which was self-conscious, institutionalized, and national, not to say international. For the rest, the objective of the right was to capture the cultural apparatus and use it against its political enemies. The press and electronic media were special targets.

The success of the rightist *Kulturkampf* was dependent upon the political balance of power. The grass roots movement in countless local communities took its cue from the Executive Branch of the federal government and, to a lesser degree, from the Congress, the courts, and state and local governments. The right-wing victory in the 1950 off-year election was the signal for a cultural reaction and the censure of McCarthy the beginning of its decline. Even during this period, the right never dominated either the American polity or its institutions of culture, but the cultural managers proved willing to appease the right by sacrificing those liberal and leftist elements which were most obnoxious to it. Market factors also influenced the purge. Firms and institutions which sold to provincial America were most sensitive to its political and cultural demands. Cultural activities of high visibility were especially attractive to political inquisitors anxious to make their way. The entertainment industry, particularly Hollywood, was an object of constant fascination for Congressional committees. For right-wing writers, the publishing industry was a special concern since they believed that their careers were obstructed by liberal bias. One of the claims of the China Lobby was that there was a network of left-wing intellectuals which monopolized the reviewing of books on Asia in the major newspapers and magazines. Of the impact of McCarthyism on the publishing industry, Harold Lord Varney noted with approval:

> One far-reaching consequence of the McCarthy Communist soften-up technique has been its impact upon the American world of ideas. The climate of American public discussions has been amazingly cleared since McCarthy began to fight. For the first time in two decades, the top magazines and publishing houses have become open to the writings of anti-Communists. The long grip upon the nation's communications media exercised by the literary Reds and Pinkoes has been broken.[5]

The foundations commanded the close attention of the right, as they appeared to embody the alliance of the establishment and the left. While the foundations often viewed themselves as agencies of social innovation, the right regarded them as instruments of cultural subversion. In 1952, Taft Republicans in the House, led by Representative Clarence Brown of Ohio, a political associate of Taft, supported a measure introduced by Eugene Cox, a rightist Democrat of Georgia, to investigate the foundations. The Taft group was interested in putting pressure on the Eastern internationalists behind Eisenhower. Dulles was associated with the Carnegie Endowment and Paul Hoffman with the Ford Foundation. The Democratic leadership in the House undercut the Cox Committee by loading it with members unsympathetic to the endeavor. In 1953, after the Republican victory, Representative Carroll Reece, Republican of Tennessee and Taft's Southern manager in 1952, revived the effort. Since the investigation could embarrass the new Administration, Speaker Martin also circumscribed it by reducing its appropriations and moderating its membership. Nonetheless, the Reece Committee delivered itself of a report attacking the cultural role of the foundations, particularly their influence on the social sciences.

The Reece Committee correctly described the foundations as devices to circumvent estate tax laws and to maintain family control of public-stock corporations. With no pretense to political innocence, the committee was most concerned with three foundations: the Reid Foundation whose donors controlled the New York *Herald Tribune,* the Eugene and Agnes E. Meyer Foundation whose namesakes owned the Washington *Post,* and the Ford Foundation which had recently established a subsidiary organization, the Fund for the Republic, charged with inquiring into the state of civil liberties in the United States. In its report, the Reece Committee maintained that the major foundations through interlocking relationships formed an "intellectual cartel" which dispensed "various forms of patronage which carry with them elements of thought control." In the social sciences, the cartel consisted of the Rockefeller foundations, Ford, Russell Sage, and several others. According to the committee report, the cartel or network controlled the development of the social sciences by funding clearing houses which claimed authority in certain fields—the American Council of Learned Societies, the American Council on Education, the National Academy of Sciences, the Institute of Pacific Relations, and like organizations. The clearing houses and foundations maintained an informal hegemony over the learned societies and scholarly journals through a network of personal associations and through their control of research funds. This network was, in effect, "restraining competition."

The Reece Committee discerned some undesirable patterns in the social science sponsored by the liberal cartel. It took exception to "moral relativity," "social engineering," "scientism," and for some reason, the "cultural lag theory." The right viewed these crypto-scientific trends as threats to the intellectual classicism and Christian roots of its world view. In the field of education, the committee was unhappy with foundation activities "tending to induce the educator to become an agent for social change and a propagandist for the development of our society in the direction of some form of collectivism." In the area of foreign policy, the committee argued that the

> net result of these combined efforts has been to promote "internationalism" in a particular sense—a form directed toward "world government" and a derogation of American "nationalism." Foundations have supported a conscious distortion of history, propagandized blindly for the United Nations as the hope of the world, supported that organization's agencies to an extent beyond general public acceptance, and leaned toward a generally "leftist" approach to international problems."[6]

The committee also named some names of the sort of people that foundation money was often going to—Gunnar Myrdal, Harold Laski, G.D.H. Cole, Lewis Corey, J.B.S. Hardman, George Soule, Freda Kirchwey, Bruce Bliven, Robert S. Lynd, and Paul H. Douglas. It was critical of the sponsorship by the Social Science Research Council and Carnegie of work by Stuart Chase who in an earlier study had coined the phrase, "New Deal."

A special anathema of the right was the Fund for the Republic. After leaving the presidency of the Ford Foundation because of tension with Henry Ford II over his political activities and managerial methods, Paul Hoffman became chairman of the board of the Fund for the Republic. After a brief reign by Representative Clifford P. Case, an anti-McCarthy Republican of New Jersey, Robert Hutchins, formerly chancellor of the University of Chicago and an associate director of the Ford Foundation, was designated president of the Fund. A leadership more repugnant to the right could hardly have been imagined. As a former director of the Marshall Plan and an Eisenhower organizer, Hoffman was a symbol of internationalism. Hutchins had led for more than twenty years the University of Chicago, a center of liberalism in the Midwest. The university and the Chicago *Tribune* had long been engaged in a vendetta. With money from Time, Inc., Hutchins had organized in the 1940s a Commission on the Freedom of the Press which inquired into the use and abuse of press freedom, economic concentration in the media, and other such matters. Colonel McCormick, who controlled a large share of the market, took this study as a personal affront and a threat to the First Amendment; a journalist for the *Tribune* wrote a book-length rebuttal of it. Hutchins was also suspect to the right for his association with liberal experimentation in education. Actually, his "Great Books" approach to higher learning was an effort to salvage traditional humanism rather than to manufacture Deweyite social engineers. He had also opposed intervention into World War II and had been associated with the America First Committee. But the right gave him little credit for these eccentricities.

When the Ford Foundation authorized $15 million for the Fund for the Republic in 1953, the right became alarmed. The Fund concerned itself with subjects relating to internal security and civil liberties—American Communism, the federal loyalty/security program, the radical right, segregation, blacklisting in private industry. In order to protect its tax-exempt status, the Fund confined itself to underwriting research on these issues. The Washington *Times-Herald* observed: "It is hard to discern what this expedition is intended to accomplish. All we have to say is that 15 million dollars would be a high price to pay to 'get' Senators McCarthy and Jenner and Rep. Velde."[7] The Fund soon received a letter of inquiry from Senator McCarthy asking for details. Subsequently, the Fund came under criticism from the Reece Committee, Hearst columnists, and the American Legion publication, *Firing Line.* The right was particularly incensed that the Fund would dare to consider the Americanism investigations of the Congress. The Fund helped to disseminate Telford Taylor's study in this area, *Grand Inquest.* Taylor was a retired general and a U.S. prosecutor at the Nuremberg War Crimes Tribunals. In 1951, the Republican right had attempted to block his nomination as Small Business Administrator.

The cultural struggle was even more overtly political as concerned the press. Unlike more esoteric cultural endeavors, the activity of the press had direct and immediate bearing on the course of political events. Practicing politicians were especially sensitive to the power which the press could exercise over their careers. Even when sincerely endeavoring to maintain a neutral posture, most newspapers and magazines could not escape some predisposition on the issues which the right regarded as crucial—internationalism, the New Deal, and secular cosmopolitanism. Given the capital requirements of modern publishing, most of the press occupied the political center, which meant that it tolerated the basic trends which were obnoxious to the right. By their very nature, the metropolitan dailies were arrayed against McCarthyism. National magazines were also in an inevitable opposition to provincialism. *Time* and *Life,* quintessentially modern publications, were anti-McCarthy.

Senator McCarthy was not without his allies within the press, particularly among those publications which catered to the provincial markets. The *Saturday Evening Post* and *Reader's Digest* were friendly to the right. The McCormick papers and the Hearst chain were right-wing dreadnoughts. Small-town papers in areas of Republican dominance often supported McCarthy. An occasional Democratic paper susceptible to McCarthy's Catholic influence endorsed him. John Fox, publisher of the Boston *Post,* remarked: "McCarthy's doing a good—a great—job. His business is dealing with rats, organized and articulate rats."[8] In 1953, twenty-eight cultural figures criticized the general press treatment of McCarthy as biased. In this group were the editors of *The Press* of Ashland, Wisconsin, and the *News-Herald* of Borger, Texas; the right-wing book publishers Devin Garrity and Henry Regnery; William Loeb, publisher of the *Union-Leader* of Manchester, New Hampshire; Frank Hanighen and Frank Chodorov, editors of *Human Events;* the columnist Frank Coniff; right-wing intellectuals such as Ralph de Toledano, Suzanne LaFollette, Eugene Lyons, William F. Buckley, John Chamberlain, John T. Flynn, and Victor Lasky; actors Ward Bond, Adolphe Menjou, and Charles Coburn; the playwright Morris Ryskind. Less predictably, Karl Hess, the press editor of *Newsweek,* and one rabbi endorsed the statement. The defense of McCarthy was also supported by the radio commentators Fulton Lewis, Jr., and Robert Hurleigh.[9] In general, the Mutual Broadcasting System was friendly to the right. Mutual donated radio time for "State of the Nation," a program developed by Facts Forum, an organization financed by H. L. Hunt, the right-wing Texas billionaire. Facts Forum was the prototype for sophisticated right-wing propaganda efforts. At this time it was tax-exempt and received $5 million in free radio and television time per year. It produced a radio and television show, "Answers for Americans," which was aired by the American Broadcasting Company. "Facts Forum," a radio show moderated by Dan Smoot, a former FBI agent, was carried by 222 radio stations. An interview program, filmed in Washington, was distributed to fifty-eight television stations. In addition, Facts Forum organized local chapters to carry on discussion groups, produced *Facts Forum News,* a monthly house organ of 60,000 circulation, maintained a free circulating library of 20,000 volumes, and distributed a public opinion poll to 1,800 newspapers, 500 radio stations, and members of Congress.[10]

In his career, Senator McCarthy was involved in an on-going feud with certain elements of the press. The political columnist Drew Pearson was an implacable opponent. During the course of his investigation of the overseas libraries of the State Department in 1953, McCarthy subpoenaed James Wechsler, editor of the New York *Post,* ostensibly on the grounds that he was an author whose works were included in the libraries. The *Post* was a liberal tabloid which had almost knocked Nixon off the ticket in 1952. As a young man, Wechsler had briefly been a member of the Young Communist League. Before his committee, McCarthy questioned Wechsler closely concerning anti-McCarthy editorials which the paper had run. Subsequently, Wechsler asked the American Society of Newspaper Editors to examine the record of the hearings to determine if press freedom had been endangered by McCarthy's interrogation. A special committee of the ASNE divided on the issue. Among the four editors of the eleven-man committee who concluded that Wechsler's charge was valid was J. R. Wiggins, managing editor of the Washington *Post.* In August, McCarthy addressed a letter to the other seven members of the committee requesting them to "investigate the extent to which . . . Wiggins, through his paper, The Washington Post, has prostituted freedom of the press by constant false, vicious, intemperate attacks upon anyone who dares expose any of the undercover Communists."[11] The editors declined McCarthy's request.

McCarthy then asked the Post Office Department to submit estimates of the cost of "subsidizing distribution" of the Washington *Post,* the *Wall Street Journal,* and the *Daily Worker,* the newspaper of the Communist Party. Though a member of the ASNE special committee, the editor of the *Wall Street Journal* was not one of the group critical of McCarthy. McCarthy said that he had "no complaint" against the Journal, but that it was the "organ of a group not exactly in financial straits." McCarthy's threat took on meaning from the issue of second-class postal rates. On August 15, Postmaster General Arthur Summerfield had asked from Congress an increase in the rates which would yield $19 million in additional revenue. In early 1954, McCarthy expanded his request for a study of postal rates to include "profitable" publications, particularly *Time* and *Life.*

In the early 1950s, the rise of television altered the balance of power within the media. Among newspapers, magazines, and radio, the right was well represented, though not dominant. In television, however, the two networks which dominated the industry, the National Broadcasting Company and the Columbia Broadcasting System, were not partial to the right. While somewhat friendlier, the American Broadcasting Company was by no means the counterpart of the Hearst Corporation. As a form, television was also a nationalizing influence and tended inherently to transmit cosmopolitan values, however vulgar. Since the America of the Republican right was a minority element, it did not pay the industry to gear programming to its tastes. Programming was also controlled by the networks and the advertising agencies in New York and reflected metropolitan cultural standards, though always within the parameters of commercial calculation. The local stations, which were independently owned, were more susceptible to right-wing influence. The stations of George A. Richards in Detroit, Cleveland, and Los Angeles were the outstanding cases. The Richards station, WJR in Detroit, broadcast the anti-Semitic and pro-Fascist Catholic priest, Father Charles Coughlin, in the 1930s. In the post-war period, Richards's licenses were challenged on the grounds of political advocacy and were ultimately renewed only after his death and promises of reform by his successors.

Economic concentration in the electronic media was gradually becoming a right-wing issue. In the 1930s and 1940s, attacks on the press generally came from the left. More than two-thirds of the national press by circulation opposed the Presidential candidacies of Roosevelt and Truman, although the Republicans argued that the working reporters transmitted a pro-Democratic bias in the news pages. Much of the Republican press was moderate in political tone. Although the largest chain, the Hearst papers, and the largest paper by circulation, the New York *Daily News,* supported the Republican right after the war, the Republican press tended for the most part to accommodate itself to the New Deal and internationalism as the crisis of the 1930s receded into the past. As was its custom, the right expressed its fear of decline and its general anxiety concerning the survival of its world through a purge of the left in the media, as it understood the left.

With financial assistance from Alfred Kohlberg, several former FBI agents in 1947 founded American Business Consultants, Inc., which published *Counterattack: The Newsletter of Facts on Communism.* In 1950, the firm put out *Red Channels: The Report of Communist Influence in Radio and Television,* which listed 151 people and the associations that the authors considered Communist or pro-Communist. Most of these people had endorsed Popular Front causes and organizations supported by the Communist Party but also by a broad range of other political forces. The Spanish Republic, anti-Fascism, racial justice, friendly relations with the Soviet Union, were typical issues. Among those listed were the composer Aaron Copland; the conductor Leonard Bernstein: singer Lena Horne; stripper Gypsy Rose Lee; actor Burl Ives, Zero Mostel, and Edward G. Robinson; broadcasters Alexander Kendrick, William L. Shirer, and Howard K. Smith; and the Federal Communications Commissioner Clifford J. Durr.

Red Channels was only the prototype for blacklists in the broadcasting industry. In 1950, Laurence A. Johnson, a supermarket owner in Syracuse, New York, who was active in the local American Legion post, entered the field. After election to office in the National Association of Supermarkets, Johnson became a national influence. Johnson's technique was to put pressure on the industry through the sponsors who were in turn intimidated by the prospect that local supermarkets would stigmatize their products as sources of funds for Communism. Since consumer products sold through supermarkets accounted for 60 per cent of the advertising revenue of the broadcast industry, the networks judged discretion to be the better part of valor. In 1953, Johnson joined forces with Vincent Hartnett, who had written the introduction to *Red Channels,* to form Aware, Inc. In an impressive display of individual initiative, Hartnett had turned blacklisting into a profitable business. Hartnett would charge firms in need of his services a per-name fee and would then make himself available to his victims whom he would help exonerate for a charge.

The networks dealt with the challenge from the right

through a strategy of preemptive purge. Feeling exposed by the liberalism of its programming in the 1930s and 1940s, CBS led the way. In 1950, it instituted a loyalty oath and in 1951 an executive with responsibility for security. Soon the "vice president in charge of treason" became a commonplace throughout the industry. In 1956, John Henry Faulk, a disc jocky for WCBS in New York, brought suit against Hartnett and Johnson after he was cited by Aware, Inc., for supposed Communist activities. Faulk had been elected vice president of the New York chapter of the American Federation of Television and Radio Artists on a non-Communist slate which repudiated Aware. In 1962 after the passing of McCarthyism and the election of a Democratic President, Faulk won his suit and helped to break the back of blacklisting in the industry.[12]

Edward R. Murrow, a member of the CBS board of directors, helped to finance Faulk's suit. Murrow enjoyed special influence at CBS. His "This Is London" broadcasts during World War II and efforts in building a European news staff had brought CBS to the fore in the field of radio news. He was a friend of William Paley, chairman of the board of CBS, who had served in London during the war as deputy chief of psychological warfare. In 1953, he was both a radio newscaster and coproducer with Fred W. Friendly of *See It Now,* a television series dealing with serious topics. Late in the year, he and Friendly began to investigate questions pertaining to civil liberties—"The Case Against Milo Radulovich, A0589839," which examined a security case in the Air Force, and "Argument at Indianapolis," which looked into a local dispute between the American Civil Liberties Union and the American Legion.

For these efforts, Murrow and Friendly came under attack from the right, particularly the Hearst paper, the New York *Journal-American,* and its television columnist Jack O'Brian. Some of the CBS local stations were unhappy. Undeterred, Murrow hired Raymond Swing, who had resigned from the Voice of America in protest against the McCarthyist purge, to write his radio commentaries. In March 1954, Murrow and Friendly took on McCarthy himself. They produced a program which relied upon film of McCarthy in action with a minimum of commentary, and followed up with a second program covering a hearing of the Permanent Investigations Subcommittee. Unable to secure corporate support, they advertised the programs with their own money. McCarthy accepted a CBS offer of time to reply, the effect of which was to give the impression of McCarthy engaging in a debate with McCarthy. With the assistance of Hearst commentator George Sokolsky and other advisors, the Senator produced a program in which he described Murrow as the "symbol, the leader and the cleverest of the jackal pack which is always found at the throat of anyone who dares to expose individual communists and traitors." The series of three programs demonstrated McCarthy's vulnerability to McCarthy and prepared the way for the televising of the Army/McCarthy hearings later in the spring.

The outcome of the right-wing offensive against televised liberalism, like that against cultural liberalism as a whole, was dependent upon the political balance of power within the country. As part of his program of accommodation of the right, President Eisenhower appointed in 1953 two pro-McCarthy commissioners to the seven-member Federal Communications Commission—Robert E. Lee and John C. Doerfer. The broadcast industry registered this shift to the right. Murrow's defeat of McCarthy in the spring of 1954 contributed to, and coincided with, McCarthy's general demise as a political force. The industry also registered this shift.

In the cultural reign of secular cosmopolitanism, there was much that was legitimate to criticize. Its liberalism could degenerate into libertinism; its tolerance could mask indifference. Its openness could be the excuse for opportunism and its humanism a front for exploitation. Cosmopolitan culture had a formal character. It could not provide cultural integrity or moral content because it was not a single culture but the terms of coexistence for an amalgam of many subcultures—ethnic, class, vocational—of the metropolis. Ironically, the function of the cities as the nuclei of capitalist development was responsible for much that gave offense to the cultural Puritanism of the right.

Commerce promoted an image of man as a monster with insatiable appetites for money, sex, and all good things, an image that was often enough a fair reflection of the human reality. As the points of entry for the immigrant masses, the cities also held large pools of poverty, the human results of which were not always pretty. Secular cosmopolitanism was vulnerable to criticism from any integrated viewpoint with ethical content. The right reacted to these phenomena from the particular standpoint of Puritan enterprise, which employed a master concept of "collectivism" to explain the cosmopolitan chaos.

III

THE NEW RIGHT

12

THE CATHOLIC TRADITION

The censure of McCarthy and the victory of the Democrats in the off-year election of 1954 marked the end of the reactionary wave of the early 1950s. These events also closed the political era which had begun with the Great Crash of 1929. The vapors of "McCarthyism" had failed to alter substantively the policies inaugurated in the Presidencies of Roosevelt and Truman. The New Deal and Fair Deal struck out in the direction of social democracy, under the power of trade unionism, and also served as the vehicle for an older tradition of middle-class Progressivism. While it did nothing to advance this cause, the Eisenhower Administration did not overturn it. As Walter Lippmann suggested, the Republican Administration may actually have legitimated the change by its attitude of toleration. The foreign policy of the United States was now firmly based on Europe-oriented internationalism, though Secretary of State Dulles did make some important concessions to the right in his strategic doctrine and style of execution. Were it not for the restraining influence of Eisenhower, he might well have altered it in substance as well, as in the abortive effort to intervene in Indochina.

Within the right, the attitude toward the New Deal and Fair Deal social policies did not change; they were Socialism at best, Communism at worst. In foreign policy, old nationalism was a dead letter. The new nationalism did not formally subscribe to the internationalist doctrines of free flow of trade and investment, much less support for the United Nations and aid to underdeveloped countries. Lacking a systematic view of the world, however, it tended to be dragged along behind internationalist policies. The salient feature of new nationalism was its militant anti-Communism, which severely circumscribed the flexibility of internationalist foreign policy. In the minds of the nationalists, there was a psychological link between their own domestic decline and the advances of international Communism. They did not share the expansive optimism of the internationalists who regarded the "Third World" as a new arena in which the United States and the Soviet Union competed for the allegiance of the uncommitted. The nationalists assessed Communist successes as a *net* loss to the "Free World." In this zero-sum game, Communist victory in one area could not be balanced by Western successes elsewhere.

The nationalist right was defeated in the early 1950s by the combined forces of the Eisenhower Administration, the Fair Dealers, and the Southern Democrats. But for the right, there were consolations. Politically, the New Deal/Fair Deal was a temporarily exhausted force. It had emerged out of economic crisis and world war. Times had changed. Economic prosperity and a cold peace did the liberal/labor forces no good. On the other hand, these same conditions were developing new allies for the nationalist right. Under the surface tranquility of the middle and later Eisenhower years, the right was regrouping for another bid for national power ten years after the fall of McCarthy.

The defection of a sizable minority of ethnic Catholics from the Democratic Party was a fact of political life in the 1950s. In part, it was based on discontent with foreign policy internationalism, particularly among the Irish and Italians whose national loyalties it had offended. More fundamentally, it represented the conservative animus of a new middle class which the wartime and post-war prosperity had elevated out of the urban tenements into the new suburban developments.

The successor to Joe McCarthy as leader of the Catholic right was not a politician but an intellectual—William F. Buckley, Jr. In 1951, at the beginning of the McCarthy period, young Buckley got off to a fast start in a highly successful career as a publicist with the publication of *God and Man at Yale: The Superstitions of "Academic Freedom."* Barely out of Yale University where he had been editor of the student newspaper, Buckley offered his conclusions concerning the failure of education at that institution. Noting that as a student he had struggled to no avail on behalf of "Christianity" and "individualism" against the forces of "secularism" and "collectivism," Buckley proposed that the Yale alumni intervene in the affairs of Yale and impose his program for him. This program consisted of the recognition of an "orthodoxy" of Christianity and individualism—as understood by the Republican right—which the Yale faculty would "inculcate" on pain of dismissal. Buckley explained:

> Let us examine the situation of Mr. John Smith, a socialist professor of economics at Yale, and survey his fate under my proposed plan. First of all, let us bar him from teaching because he is inculcating values that the governing board of Yale considers to be against the public welfare. No freedom I know of has yet been violated. We still cling to the belief in this country that, acting in good conscience, we can hire whom we like.[1]

In this case, the unfortunate Professor Smith was guilty of Socialist views. Like "Marx or Hitler, Laski or the Webbs, Huxley or Dewey," he was not an individualist. By his dismissal, no freedom that Buckley knew of was violated. Socialism would, however, have allowed many of the Yale faculty to escape the dragnet. It was "collectivism" that Buckley was really after and, it will be recalled, the main agent of collectivism was the New Deal Democrat. Buckley concluded his book:

> I shall not say, then, what specific professors should be discharged, but I will say some ought to be discharged. I shall not indicate what I consider to be the dividing line that separates the collectivist from the individualist, but I will say that such a divid-

ing line ought, thoughtfully and flexibly, to be drawn. I will not
suggest the manner in which the alumni ought to be consulted
and polled on the issue, but I will say that they ought to be, and
soon, and that the whole structure of Yale's relationship to her
alumni, as has been previously indicated, ought to be reexamined.[2]

There was still hope for the average Yale professor, since the
"dividing line that separates the collectivist from the individualist" was to be "thoughtfully and flexibly" drawn. Hope
began to fade for most of the Yale faculty when it emerged that
one of the "collectivist" economists denounced by Buckley was
Paul Samuelson, a neo-classical, Keynesian economist and author of a standard text, *Economics: An Introductory Analysis.*

For all its coyness, Buckley's program for a purge of the Yale
faculty based on the principles of "laissez-faire education" did
not differ in form from the practices of any dictatorship in the
Central American jungles or the Asiatic steppes. Only the
"orthodoxy" had been changed.

William F. Buckley, Jr., was particularly fitted to become the
leader of the new nationalist forces. His father, William F.
Buckley, Sr., was an Irish Catholic entrepreneur from Texas
who had built the family fortune on speculation in oil leases.
Buckley, Sr., was a family capitalist and thus a specimen of the
ideal type of the Republican Right. But the elder Buckley did
not build houses in Peoria or own everything in Sauk City. He
operated *abroad,* making his fortune in Mexico from which he
was expelled in 1921 in the era of the Mexican revolution by
the Obregon government. Buckley's main company, Pantepec
Oil, was supposedly named after a river which he had used to
make his getaway from Mexican revolutionaries. He subsequently moved on to Venezuela where he prospered under
the military dictatorship of General Juan Vicente Gomez, got
into difficulties under the democratic rule of Romulo Betan-
court. The founding father often tangled with the major oil
companies. Although they were his customers, he considered
them pusillanimous and opportunistic in their dealings with
foreign governments. The Buckley family's politics represented

the projection of the small business mentality into the international sphere. William Buckley, Sr.'s children—among them, William, Jr.—inherited, in equal shares, the family business, which was later controlled by a holding company, the Catawba Corporation.[3]

In the early 1950s, Buckley, Jr., operated within the McCarthy circle. In 1953, he wrote a speech for Senator McCarthy criticizing President Eisenhower's nomination of James B. Conant, president of Harvard, for High Commissioner of Germany. He was, at first, designated by McCarthy to answer the charges made by Edward R. Murrow in his television special in 1954, but the Wisconsin Senator finally decided to do the honors himself. Buckley's brother-in-law, L. Brent Bozell, a Catholic convert from Omaha, Nebraska, was an aide and speech writer to the Senator. With Bozell, Buckley coauthored an apologia for McCarthy in 1954, *McCarthy and His Enemies*.

In 1955, at the urging of William S. Schlamm, Buckley founded what became the official organ of the new right, *National Review*. Its outer circle of associates and contributors constituted a kind of rally of the American right, including heterodox figures such as Frank Chodorov, a right-wing anarchist, and Max Eastman, an atheist. But there was no doubt that *National Review* was dedicated to the propagandistic exposition of the principles of the new nationalism within the continuing traditions of Christianity, individualism, *laissez-faire* capitalism, and Americanism. After two years, its inner circle of editors consisted of Buckley, Bozell, Schlamm, James Burnham, John Chamberlain, Willmoore Kendall, and Suzanne LaFollette. As a young Anglophobe, Buckley, like the rest of his family, had opposed American intervention in World War II; Bozell had once been an innocent World Federalist from the provinces. Both were now new nationalists. James Burnham wrote a regular column on "The Third World War." Schlamm later explained the principles of the East European geo-politics in West Germany where his views found an appreciative, if chastened, audience. In 1957, Buckley hired William A. Rusher, formerly associate counsel to the Senate Internal Security Subcommittee under Robert Morris, as publisher of the magazine.

While *National Review* never achieved Buckley's ambition of imposing an orthodoxy on the United States, or even Yale University, it did become the arbiter on the right. In the 1950s, Buckley kept his magazine in basic opposition to the Eisenhower Administration, but he also steered clear of the right-wing fringe. Whittaker Chambers, his friend and Alger Hiss's adversary, attacked Ayn Rand's atheistic materialism in a book review in NR. Over the issue of religion, Max Eastman, a non-believer, severed his connection with the magazine. When *The American Mercury*, of which Buckley had once been associate editor, began to make noises about "Jewish international bankers," Buckley read it out of the ranks of the respectable right. Respectability did not exclude Joe McCarthy, whom the magazine regarded as an appropriate reviewer for a book by Dean Acheson.

Most notably, *National Review* repudiated the John Birch Society. In an editorial in the February 13, 1962, issue, "The Question of Robert Welch," the magazine maintained that Welch, the society's authoritarian leader, was "damaging the cause of anti-Communism" by his absurd theory that 60 to 80 per cent of the United States was pro-Communist. At this point, however, the magazine made a careful distinction between Welch and the society's membership which contained "some of the most morally energetic, self-sacrificing, and dedicated anti-Communists in America."

Welch founded the John Birch Society at a meeting in Indianapolis in 1958. Born on a farm in North Carolina, he attended the state university, the U.S. Naval Academy, and Harvard Law School, though failing to complete the programs of the last two. His business career in candy manufacturing was a mixed success. His own ventures failed, but he worked as an executive for E. J. Brock and Sons of Chicago and later for James O. Welch Company of Boston, a firm founded by his brother. For seven years, Robert Welch was a member of the Board of Directors of the National Association of Manufacturers. In the early 1950s, he was a passionate supporter of the

Presidential candidacy of Robert Taft and the investigations of Joseph McCarthy. The failure of both men and disenchantment with the centrism of the Eisenhower Administration led Welch into more extreme politics. In 1956, he made an address at a states rights conference in Memphis, which nominated T. Coleman Andrews, a former Commissioner of Internal Revenue in the Eisenhower Administration, for President.

The society was named for John Birch, a Baptist missionary to China. (Welch himself was born a Baptist.) During World War II, Captain John Birch did forward intelligence work for the 14th Air Force of Major General Claire Chennault. In an encounter with the Communists after the defeat of the Japanese, Birch was killed.

Clearly, John Birch was an appropriate political martyr for the Republican right, to which the JBS was oriented. Essentially, the principles of the John Birch Society were an intensified and paranoid version of those of Republican conservatives. The GOP right, which commanded the loyalties of some 20 per cent of the American electorate, suspected that the rest of the country was not only unenlightened but perhaps "collectivist" or "un-American." The Birch Society put the proposition even more baldly; anyone not in the right Republican camp was a pro-Communist pure and simple. Thus 60 to 80 per cent of America was pro-Communist.

JBS politics celebrated the familiar Republican idyll of 19th-century America—free enterprise with tariffs. The New Deal and all its works were damned. Woodrow Wilson's New Freedom, especially the income tax, did not escape criticism. In the John Birch Society, the small business mentality had free rein. The Communists alone were not the enemy, but big business as well. Both were actually a part of a larger world conspiracy masterminded by the "Insiders." These last had a genealogy going back to the "Illuminati" of the 18th century, who were supposed to have engineered the French Revolution. The Illuminati refer, of course, to the intellectual agents of the Enlightenment. This conspiracy theory was popular in the 19th century with the denizens of the provinces who were suspicious of secular cosmopolitan culture. It continued to titillate the rural folk mind in the 20th century.

The composition of the National Council of the John Birch Society in 1964 clearly revealed the ideological hegemony of small business. Two thirds of them were engaged in business activity, usually as heads of closely held family firms. They were "small" businessmen only by comparison to the major public-stock corporations run by management teams. These council members were substantial citizens and wealthy men. A surviving whiff of Old Guard Republicanism from big business was present. One of the council members was director of the First National Bank of Boston. The rest of the membership consisted of a professor and writer or two; a Catholic priest from Bridgeport, Connecticut, and Clarence Manion, former dean of the Law School of Notre Dame; retired Lieutenant General Charles B. Stone III, who had succeeded Claire Chennault as commander of the 14th Air Force; and Colonel Laurence E. Bunker, former aide to General Douglas MacArthur. In the early 1960s, Colonel Bunker was considered heir apparent to Robert Welch.

The Republican orientation of the JBS was also indicated by "One Dozen Candles," a collection of twelve books on the Communist conspiracy recommended for reading. These were right Republican classics by John T. Flynn, James Burnham, Senator McCarthy, J. B. Matthews, Arthur Bliss Lane, Garet Garrett, Major General Charles Willoughby (former chief of MacArthur's intelligence), and others. In 1961, two Republican Congressmen from Southern California confessed to JBS membership.

The Republican Party's national leadership regarded these recruits as a mixed blessing. The JBS exposed the party to the effective charge of right-wing extremism. While party moderates were openly hostile, the conservatives treated the society more gingerly. The JBS had a national membership of, perhaps, 75,000 after the Goldwater Presidential campaign of 1964 and considerable grass-roots popularity within the party. This popularity was worrisome, for the Birch Society was an authoritarian group run on a leader principle, which operated within Republican organizations. The society had a national network of reading rooms and book stores; a publishing house, Western Islands; and a magazine, *American Opinion*. Faithful to its premises, the JBS fought fire with fire, Communist cadre organization with right-wing cadre organization.

What also concerned the national conservative Republican leadership was that the John Birch Society parodied their views only in part; for the rest, it represented a rebirth of the *old nationalism*. The JBS viewed NATO as "useless and costly." Large defense expenditures were regarded by it with suspicion. So also were reciprocal trade agreements and foreign aid. The special fixation of the Birch Society was the United Nations, which embodied all that was anathema to it. The bitterness against internationalism was the source of Robert Welch's famous assertion, in *The Politician*, that Dwight Eisenhower, the protégé of George Marshall and conqueror of Taft, was a "dedicated, conscious agent of the Communist conspiracy." When the Vietnam War came along in the mid-1960s, the John Birch Society criticized it as just another pro-Communist feint, engineered by the Insiders. It took up the ambiguous refrain, familiar from the Korean War, that the U.S. should "either get in or get out." Though the society canonized Joe McCarthy and admired Barry Goldwater, it appreciated the repressive Americanism of these men rather than their new nationalist views.

What made the society particularly formidable was that it was not content to base itself in the Midwestern and Northeastern provincial Protestant citadels of the old nationalist right. It, too, reached out to other groups in American society with modern organization and slick propaganda. With its national headquarters in Belmont, Massachusetts, the society had a Catholic membership of 25 per cent. Cardinal Cushing of Boston gave the society his early blessing (later withdrawn). Although accused of anti-Semitism by the Anti-Defamation League, the society made efforts to keep such tendencies among its members under control. Conscious that religious and ethnic differences could limit the society's potential, Welch advocated a "religious synthesis" which all could accept as a basis for struggle against atheistic Communism. He practiced this precept as a Unitarian convert.

Founded by, named for, evangelical Protestants, the Birch Society reached out to this group which, like Catholics and Jews, had a Democratic heritage. The society established branch offices in the West and South, and had some organizing successes in cities like Los Angeles, Phoenix, Houston, and Nashville with large evangelical Protestant populations. Its immense success in Southern California probably owed more, however, to the Republican heritage of Midwestern migrants. Dressing up a provincial ideology in city clothes, the JBS flourished in the new white-collar suburbs.

National Review's broadside against Robert Welch in 1962 was in keeping with the views of Russell Kirk, Walter Judd, Fulton Lewis, Jr., Senator Goldwater, and others who had become concerned about JBS influence. In his gubernatorial campaign in California in 1962, Richard Nixon, whom the JBS despised for his Eisenhower apostasy in 1952, repudiated the society. In 1965, *National Review* again opened up on the Birch Society, this time the organization itself and not just its leader. Buckley and Burnham noted that the JBS took a squeamish view of the Vietnam War. *National Review*'s attack was part of a coordinated national Republican effort against the society. After a Birch candidate ran against Senator Karl Mundt, an ultra-conservative, in the Republican primary in South Dakota, Senator Thruston Morton of Kentucky, former national party chairman, Senator Everett Dirksen of Illinois, minority leader in the Senate, and Representative Gerald Ford of Michigan, leader in the House, attacked the society. Attacked by a Bircher who had become party chairman in his own county, Barry Goldwater advocated that its membership withdraw from the society. These Republicans were concerned about the advances of the society during the Goldwater Presidential campaign. This surge was particularly evident in California. Republican Party organizations, such as the Young Republicans, United Republicans of California, and the California Republican Assembly all acquired a strong Birch faction. Nineteen sixty-four proved to be the high watermark. Impeded by party attack, the national stigma of extremism, and the declining influence of the old nationalism, the society's advances were minimal for the rest of the decade.[4]

In 1956, the new nationalism faced a severe reality test and failed badly. Confronted by the Hungarian Revolution and the intervention of Russian troops, Secretary Dulles did not press Eisenhower to intervene. More striking, the new nationalists outside the Administration did not vigorously protest. The best *National Review* could do, after an initial editorial silence, was to circulate "The Hungary Pledge" on December 8 in which the signers promised not to deal with the Soviet Union or its puppet government in Hungary in any way and urged the U.S. government to do the same. This was an old nationalist response at best. In the January 19, 1957, issue of the magazine, an apparently sobered James Burnham asked "Liberation: What Next?" What was next was an "Austrian solution" to Soviet domination of Eastern Europe—reunification of Germany, the demilitarization of Eastern Europe, and a resulting drift of the area into the Western camp. How the Soviet Union was to be persuaded to surrender its dominions in return for nothing, Burnham did not say. Here was the pastoral version of liberation.

It is hard to avoid the impression that, when confronted with the reality of the Hungarian Revolution, the new nationalists suffered a failure of nerve. When the actual moment arrived, they were, to their credit, not ready to advocate military intervention in Eastern Europe and risk World War III. In their heart of hearts, they apparently counted on more circumspect men to save them from themselves. But after a respectable interval of a few years, *National Review* resumed its old air of bellicosity on the issue.

Though *National Review* was a nonsectarian publication, it inevitably came to be regarded under Buckley editorial control as an outlet for a right-wing Catholic tendency. The magazine's solicitude for the regime of Generalissimo Francisco Franco in

Spain was extraordinary and abiding. Bozell, the Omaha convert, later gave up on secular politics altogether and founded *Triumph,* a magazine advocating a version of militant Catholicism. In 1970, he was seen leading the "Sons of Thunder," arrayed in the red berets of Spanish Carlists, in an assault on an abortion clinic at George Washington University in Washington, D.C. Once again, Buckley found it necessary to separate himself from an extremist tendency.

National Review also had a sizable Jewish contingent, represented by men such as William Schlamm and Frank Meyer. After his departure from the editorial board, Willmoore Kendall complained that Catholics and Jews, newcomers to the Republican right, had pushed Midwestern Protestants out of influence on the publication. Quite often, the Jews were converts from left-wing radicalism, but not always. As an immigrant group which, like the Catholics, was emerging from lower working-class status, Jews were susceptible to the same new conservative tropisms. They, too, were not always happy about the new nonwhite immigrants pushing up against them from behind. They, too, were East Europeans who might have reason to oppose the Soviet Union.

Among them were small businessmen with the same bitterness against the labor unions and the wealthy establishment. Alfred Kohlberg, the textile importer, was chief organizer of the China Lobby. Roy Cohn was prosecutor of the Rosenbergs and counsel to Joe McCarthy's Senate committee. Marvin Liebman, a public relations man and ex-Communist, was the ubiquitous organizer of right-wing pressure groups—the Committee of One Million Against the Admission of Communist China to the United Nations, the American Committee for Aid to Katanga Freedom Fighters, Young Americans for Freedom, the Committee for the Monroe Doctrine. However, the Jews as a group remained far more loyal to the Democratic Party than recent Catholic immigrants. The war against Nazi Germany had wed them to the Democrats and alienated them from the right-wing Republicans. Historic oppression and an intellectual culture inclined them to liberal social views.

In the early 1960s, the right found itself on the defensive within the Catholic community. John F. Kennedy, a Catholic liberal, was in the White House, and a liberal Pope, John XXIII, was in the Vatican. American Catholics were, once again, voting heavily Democratic. Catholic liberals asserted that Buckley's "position on social matters is at grave variance with the social teachings of the Church, especially as expressed by Popes Leo XIII and Pius XI." In *The Catholic World,* Kevin Corrigan argued that Catholic doctrine was basically incompatible with the free market model of society. Leo XIII "held that society is not essentially the result of 'contract' but is a natural and organic community ordained by a higher authority, God Himself." The "new social philosophy" of the Church was, moreover, but a development of its age-old doctrine as expounded by Church fathers such as Saint Thomas Aquinas. "Fundamentally," Corrigan said, "it is a continuation of the great classical tradition of the Natural Law—the law that bids us as individuals and as societies to do good and to avoid evil." [5]

The Church was not formally aligned on the left. From the fundamentals of God, family, hierarchy, private property, and anti-Communism, it was possible to deduce a conservative, even extremist politics. The Fascist fellow-traveling of Father Charles Coughlin in the '30s and '40s had a Catholic orientation, even if perverse. The problem with "true liberalism" was that it was just not a part of Catholic culture. The free market philosophy had its historic origin in the Protestant Reformation and the rise of capitalism. With its precapitalist history, particularly its hegemony in the medieval period of the "Respublica Christiana," the Church found alien the values held dear by old American Protestants—the market, competition, the individual, the distinction between public and private, the social contract, the out-of-this-world God. Buckley demonstrated that he was infected with Protestant culture in his claim that the Catholic Church disapproved economic liberalism only to the extent that it pretended to be a philosophy of life rather than an economic practice. In fact, such a distinction was alien to the Church which stressed the "social and moral character of eco-

nomic life." The notion of a duality between the material world
and the religious life was typically Protestant.

This tension between the Catholic and Protestant cultures
was the source of the principal philosophical debate on the
right in the 1950s. The "libertarians" derived from the old
Protestant right. They defended Herbert Hoover's axiom that
political liberty was a function of economic liberty. The "traditionalists" were less interested in the free market philosophy.
Their conservatism was based upon an affection for home and
hearth. Economic liberalism was looked upon with some suspicion as a dynamic force tending to upset the not very immuta-
ble order of things, which, of course, it was. Theirs was a cultural conservatism in which the primary values were not
individualism, competition and freedom from regulation, but
God, family, and order.

The political basis for the emergence of a "traditional" conservatism in the 1950s was the tentative adherence of a minority of Catholics to the Republican right. Later, the crisis of the
Democratic Party in the South over the race issue gave traditionalism an additional impetus. Though small capitalism held
sway in the region, the South was the least urban section of the
country. Conservatism went over better if it was earthy.

The theorists of the "new conservatism" did not need to be
Catholics or Southerners. The point of view appealed to literary intellectuals for several reasons. First, it was redolent of the
land—not the land of the farmer, which was just another world
of grubby business calculation, but a more wonderful land of
lost virtue and uncorrupted Nature—the land, that is to say, of
the rolling hills of the college campus and the house in the
country. This "aristocratic" pose with its reverential attitude
toward the redundancies of Edmund Burke was nothing more
than literary romanticism warmed up. As such, it appealed to
the fantasy life of the educated middle class.

The potential for anti-capitalist heresy in romantic conservatism was great. It could not escape notice that capitalism was a
dynamic force tending to upset settled routines and to exploit
unused resources. Capitalism was also materialist; it was cold

and unspiritual. Polemical war between the "libertarians" and the "traditionalists" was not long in breaking out. For their champion, the libertarians had Frank Meyer, an ex-Communist. Russell Kirk, a free-lance intellectual, defended order, tradition, and being-in-itself. After many unkind things were said, Meyer put an end to the bloodletting with a new synthesis: "fusionism."

This newspeak formulation—given to the right by an old left-wing faction-fighter—reflected the underlying political realities. The academy did not provide the mass base for the right, and so in the larger scheme of things, romanticism was a diversion. Enough Catholics were emerging into the white collar middle class and into the petty capitalist world of insurance, real estate, retail commerce, and the like to make "libertarianism" respectable, if not formulated in too radical a fashion. Nor did the old Protestant right live by bread alone. It, too, believed in home and family, God and country, tradition and order.

The whole debate should be regarded for what it was: a surface phenomenon. The traditionalists were not the aristocrats they pretended to be. Neither were the libertarians believers in civil liberties. In the post-war period, their equation of government with tyranny gained credibility because of the existence of state tyrannies not only in the Communist countries but among the non-Communist backward countries of Asia, Latin America, and Africa. The thesis was not absurd. But these were other countries, other continents. In America, the "libertarians" had a consistent record since the 1930s of defending the free market while attacking the Bill of Rights. "True liberalism" was hostage to a reactionary historical development. Democratic freedoms were an obstacle to what the right regarded as its main task—revenge on the political enemies who had toppled it from power. Its "Americanism" was also xenophobic by tradition—hostile to cultures which were not Anglo-Saxon Protestant. Ironically, the drive for power was creating internal moderating forces. The old anti-Semitism and anti-Catholicism were no longer politic. New alliances with upwardly mobile immigrants softened the lines of the old Americanism. A new unity was forged around the general notion of "Christianity"—which placed Protestants and Catholics in the same camp against "secular" forces. Unfortunately, this liberalizing tendency was premised upon a hostile animus not only toward secular humanists but also nonwhites, the latest immigrants to the industrial cities. Americanism was dissolving as a specific form of Protestantism but regrouping as a united Christian front with a racist flavor.

Students and young people were most susceptible to the abstract claims of libertarianism. In 1953, two editors of *Human Events*, Frank Hanighen and Frank Chodorov, founded the Intercollegiate Society of Individualists with William Buckley as its first president. Modeled after the pre–World War I Intercollegiate Society of Socialists, ISI existed to counter Socialist ideas with "individualist" ones. Nothing more than a literary society, ISI did develop a membership of 2,500 on 300 campuses within its first year. In ISI, there was a genuinely liberal streak. In 1961, its magazine published an article attacking Buckley for alleged white supremacist views, super-nationalism, pro-colonialism, statism, and other sins. Still, the organization changed its name to the Intercollegiate Studies Institute in 1968 in response to the complaint that "individualists" made it sound radical.

In 1960, after the Republican convention and in the first glow of the Goldwater movement, the Buckley family founded a much more formidable student organization—Young Americans for Freedom. Convening at the Buckley estate in Sharon, Connecticut, the organization issued "The Sharon Statement," which affirmed free enterprise, states' rights, the Constitution, national sovereignty, and the like. Philosophically, the argument was still "That liberty is indivisible, and that political freedom cannot long exist without economic freedom." In the struggle with Communism, victory, not coexistence, should be the objective. By 1970, YAF had 70,000 members, having survived a small "libertarian" secession. Its national advisory board included seventy Congressmen.

In the same period, *National Review* prospered. By 1960, it had 30,000 readers. As the year of Goldwater approached, its circulation increased to 60,000 and, as a result of the Presidential campaign, climbed to 95,000 by 1965. Thereafter, its growth levelled off, and circulation did not surpass 100,000 until 1969. William Buckley's personal fortunes also improved. His newspaper column, "On the Right," was syndicated to more than 300 newspapers. Eventually, he acquired an interview program on public television, "Firing Line." He controlled Arlington House, a publisher of conservative books, and a more commercial venture, Starr Broadcasting, which owned a number of radio stations.

All in all, William F. Buckley, Jr., successfully imprinted his personality on the new nationalist right. Conservatives had long suffered from an intellectual inferiority complex because of dominance of the universities and organs of culture by their opponents. As an indefatigable polemicist and debater, Buckley took the fight into the camp of the enemy. He matched arrogance with arrogance, pomposity with pomposity, convolution with convolution. His was the style to emulate among young right-wing intellectuals.

13

SOUTHERN CALIFORNIA

There was nothing unusual about the Republican trend in the far West after World War II. Except for the anomalous South, the trend was national. Although the GOP actually won control only of the 80th and 83rd Congresses of 1947–49 and 1953–55, the apparent Democratic dominance would not stand examination. Taking the House of Representatives as a measure which quickly reflects a national trend, Democratic did not outnumber Republican Representatives *outside the South* until 1958. After the 1946 election, Republicans outside the South outnumbered Democrats by *three to one* in the House. The Democrats recovered in 1948, but were still in a minority in the North, West, and Midwest. The 1950–52 trend went against them, and they were soon down again by more than two to one outside the South.

As the New Deal flood receded after 1938 and even more after World War II, the Democratic Party gradually returned to its ancient, Southern channels. Until 1958, approximately half of the Democratic representatives in the House were from the South. In the Truman and Eisenhower years, ideological Democrats were restricted from moving very far on domestic reforms by their Southern conservative allies. But as the liberal/labor forces comprised barely a fourth of Congress, they were not going anywhere anyway. As long as it lasted, the assured Southern base gave the Democratic Party two advantages. For power political reasons, the Southern Democrats would be forced to act as a buffer between the Republican right and its enemy, the Democratic left. The Southerners would defend the party against partisan attacks in order to hold on to their committee chairmanships and political influence in Washington. Secondly, the Southerners still had a residual, though declining, commitment to internationalism. On foreign policy issues, they often stood on principle with the Northern liberals.

Premised on the fear of a renewed depression, the 1948 election was a great resurgence of the New Deal spirit in which the Democrats not only staved off Republican control of the White House but retook Capitol Hill. The election appeared to confirm the New Deal internationalist shift of power of the 1930s. From the perspective of the 1950s, Republicans might take a different view. They might regard the 1932–38 period as an episode. World War II, they might reason, had extended the Democratic lease in Washington artificially. Since the war, the Republicans had "really" been the majority party.

The Southern Democracy was an historical antique. On many issues—most significant domestic issues—Southern Democrats made common cause with the Republican right in a "conservative coalition." Eisenhower's victories showed that Southerners were susceptible to Republican conservatism in domestic policy when it was combined with an internationalist foreign policy. Outside the South, Eisenhower and Republican Congressional candidates swept the field.

The concept of a "Roosevelt revolution" must be qualified. The New Deal years were the beginning of a rising Democratic tide, but there were several cycles of advance and retreat before the Democrats could even lay claim to the "liberal Northeast" which continued, in fact, to be the Republican Northeast. The victories of the 1930s were followed by the fiasco of 1938; the 1948 triumph by McCarthyism. In 1958–60 arrived the third liberal Democratic surge which finally consolidated Democratic control of the industrial regions of the United States. The Democrats gained forty-eight seats in the House and fifteen in the Senate. They also won eight new governorships.

Rolling in with the third recession of the Eisenhower years, the 1958 election gave the Democrats—for the first time in the post-war period—a majority in the House of Representatives outside the South. Within the party, non-Southerners became a large majority of the party delegation. In the Midwest, the effects of the 1958 election were transient. As reflected in the House delegation, Midwestern politics quickly returned to their original, Republican shape. In the Northeast, however, the Democrats won a clear majority of the House delegation and held on to it with the additional impetus of a liberal Catholic in the White House. Even the Republican trend in 1966 barely affected this control. The "Liberal Northeast" had finally arrived.

In the West, the 1958–60 fulcrum was even more important. Half of the population of the West was in one state, California, and in California, the New Deal had failed to revolutionize state politics in the 1930s. Although party registration did gradually shift from three to one Republican to three to two Democratic after the Great Crash, it did not result in consistent Democratic victories at the polls. The turning point failed to turn. The preposterous EPIC ("End Poverty in California") campaign of Upton Sinclair for governor in 1934 ran straight into a massive radical-baiting campaign. Orchestrated by public relations experts, Clem Whitaker and Leone Baxter, the campaign against Sinclair became the model for dealing with threats from the left in California. The Democrats did win the governorship in 1938 for the first time in the 20th century, but it led to nothing. Earl Warren, the state's attorney-general, won the governorship in 1942 and was reelected twice.

The success of Earl Warren's political style—nonpartisan Progressivism—indicated that California continued to be Republican in spirit, even when its political mood was liberal. Party registration proved to be a surface phenomenon, since Republican Progressives during the governorship of Hiram Johnson before World War I had destroyed the machinery of party rule. Partisan offices and partisan primary were circumscribed. It hardly mattered if a citizen registered Democratic when Republicans could cross-file—and win, as Earl Warren did in 1946—in the Democratic primary or if offices up for election were nonpartisan, as was true for most local positions.

With its lack of party structure and its continuous migrations, California was peculiarly susceptible to public relations and mass media campaigns. Here originated the political management teams. Here, the press had unusual power. Although intensely conservative, the Hearst papers were not reliably partisan as to party. Republican politics were mainly influenced by a "press axis" of the Los Angeles *Times,* San Francisco *Chronicle,* and Oakland *Tribune.* The conservative Republican axis was put together by Kyle Palmer, political reporter for the *Times.*

If more than half of the population of the West was in California, more than half of the population of California was in a few counties in the southern half of the state. Forty per cent was in just one county, Los Angeles, the fastest growing metropolitan area in the nation in the 1950s. Southern California was an outpost of the Republican culture of the Midwest. It had begun as a barely habitable wasteland which had one attribute—climate—and thus became a center of winter tourism. When irrigation added water to the sun, the land was turned into an agricultural paradise, particularly for the cultivation of citrus fruit.

In the late 19th century, the first wave of migration to California consisted of the aged and the wealthy, who arrived in relative style by train. Early in this century, the economy of tourism was supplemented by oil strikes, motion pictures, and, of course, successive real estate booms. The prosperity attracted an internal migration to Southern California—the largest in American history—which consisted of people who were fairly prosperous already. With a little capital, they came in greatest number in the good economic years, not the bad ones. Principally, they migrated from the Midwest and Northeast— Illinois, New York, Ohio, Missouri, Kansas, Pennsylvania, and Iowa were the leading states. Southern California was the "New

Iowa." The famous migration of the "Okies" and "Arkies" in the 1930s was actually the smallest migration since the 1890s—another depression decade.

Naturally, the migrants brought with them the small-town culture of the Midwest. Los Angeles became famous as a city of villages with no urban heart. Home-owning, not renting, was the rule. Republican, small-town, Midwestern, pious—Southern California seemed to be founded on a rock. The reality was something else. For one thing, the region was in a perpetual boom and bust cycle. The old virtues did not hold up well when there was the promise of big money and the shadow of the apocalypse. For another, the constant migrations undermined any sense of place. Small-town stability could not flourish under conditions of anonymity. In 1960, 52 per cent of the people of California as a whole—and a higher percentage of the people of Southern California—were born in other states. Even this figure represented an improvement over 1930, say, when 66 per cent had been born in other states.

The physical conditions of the West were also not the physical conditions of the Midwest. Nature loomed all around, but for the most part, it was merely a spectacular backdrop. It was not inhabited. Southern California was a highly urban environment hemmed in by mountains, desert, and the ocean—an "island on the land." It was hardly an example of rural life tamed by little towns and the family farm. The family farm was largely absent in California where agriculture was dominated by corporate agribusiness utilizing rootless, migrant labor.

The same intensive urbanization was typical of other Western states. In the 1960s, the majority of the population of Arizona was in the Phoenix metropolitan area; most of the people of Colorado were in Denver; in Nevada, they were in Las Vegas and Reno; in Utah, they were concentrated in Salt Lake City. In the West, particularly the Southwest, nature was not domesticated as in the Midwest. Cities were set down like space colonies against a moonscape. The physical conditions of existence gave daily life a phantasmagoric quality.

There was a *strangeness* about the conservative Republicanism of Southern California. People brought the small-town culture with them, but somehow it did not apply. The evolution of conservatism in California was also affected by the state's economic development. In 1965, the state's largest industry was agriculture, with a value of $3.5 billion. Paradoxically, California agriculture was both advanced and capital intensive and backward and exploitative of labor. While the high-technology "factories in the field" were immensely productive, they made ruthless use of unskilled, migrant labor.

The labor was nonwhite, made up successively of Asians and Mexicans. Southern California had a race issue. The Republican North of the United States had largely escaped the race question which was the burden of the Democratic South, but Southern California linked the two worlds. Indeed, Southern California's agribusiness was often compared to the plantation system of the Old South. In some ways, it was worse. Since the migrant workers had no permanent residence, they were that much easier to disenfranchise. Under conditions of constant mobility from one harvest to another, their children could hardly be educated. They were in a poor position to utilize social services. They were paid practically nothing. In another context, a racist spirit manifested itself in what the American Civil Liberties Union characterized as the greatest single violation of civil rights in American history—the mass detention of Japanese in California after Pearl Harbor. One of the architects of the policy was state Attorney-General Earl Warren, the leading California liberal of modern times.

The second largest industry in California in 1965 was aircraft and other transportation equipment with an annual value of $3 billion. This industry was only one component of an immense military/aerospace industry in California, which was awarded 24 per cent of all federal defense contracts in 1965. However, aircraft was the nucleus. In the interwar period, the infant industry had gravitated to Southern California as a locale suitable in climate and topography to the testing and development of airplanes. World War II transformed this gentleman's sport into an industrial juggernaut. Douglas, Lockheed,

Northrup, North American, Consolidated Vultee, Ryan, Hughes—all had their bases of operation in Southern California.

The economic transformation that World War II wrought in California is difficult to imagine. The 1930s were, relatively, a slow decade for the state. Although the population expanded by 21 per cent, this was the lowest growth in the state's history. In 1940, the federal government expended $728 million in California, mainly for relief and pension programs. During the war years, the government spent *$35 billion*. Sixty per cent of federal prime contracts went for aircraft. The population grew by 30 per cent; per capital income doubled. Even so, California was not the leading defense contractor in the nation. In a war fought with vehicles, ordnance, and manpower, the traditional industrial states of New York and Michigan ranked first and second.

The Korean conflict was another conventional war. New York continued to be the leading contractor. But Korea was also a Pacific war. Air and sea power played important roles, and California was the embarkation point for the American military effort. While the state received under 9 per cent of defense contracts during World War II, its share rose toward 15 per cent in the early 1950s. What was decisive, however, for California's dominance of the military/aerospace industry was the advent of the nuclear and air age. In the early post-war years, the Air Force had the principal strategic nuclear role. With the technical revolution in missiles, California left all other states behind in the competition for military contracts. The aircraft industry assumed control of the missile market, while the development of space exploration also redounded to its benefit.

Building upon its aircraft industry, the state achieved preeminence in electronics and built a university system which generated the requisite reserves of technical manpower and the necessary research and development capability. By the middle 1960s, it received not only a quarter of all defense contracts but almost half of all contracts awarded by the National Aeronautics and Space Administration. To say that this role contributed to the state's economic development would be an understatement. Most military/aerospace expenditures were concentrated in Los Angeles, San Diego, and Orange counties in the south and Santa Clara County in the San Francisco Bay area. These counties generated 83 per cent of new manufacturing jobs in California between 1950 and 1962. They also attracted 62 per cent of the net in-migration of population.[1] The style of California's military/aerospace industry was determined by the character of the arms race. Technical innovation was continuous. The premium was thus on research and development and technical manpower rather than on existing plant and equipment. Like the migrations and the boom-and-bust cycle, the logic of the arms race kept Southern California in an amorphous cultural spin.

This military/aerospace complex dovetailed nicely with the political style of the new Republican right. Republican foreign policy was traditionally Pacific-oriented, while its strategic doctrine was slanted toward air power. The new nationalism was overcoming old guard inhibitions about military might. Of course, all this largesse flowed from the federal government which was supposed to represent a threat to free enterprise. A modification of doctrine was required. Defense expenditures were exempt from criticism; otherwise, the federal government was dangerous. Added to a Midwestern Republican heritage was a current economic interest in Republican new nationalism.

Truly, Southern California was the New Iowa. Since the Spanish-American War and the conquest of the Philippines, its destiny had been to give a relatively stagnant provincial Midwest a new lease on national influence. In *Southern California Country*, Carey McWilliams noted:

> After 1898 the Pacific became an American highway. There is no doubt that the year 1898 separates the old Los Angeles from the new. "As nearly as anything else," wrote Henry Carr, "this earlier period was punctuated by the Spanish-American War. When it began we were still a hick town. When it ended, we began to grow into a city."[2]

There were, then, several factors which made for a renascent and intense form of right-wing Republicanism in Southern California. There was its disoriented piety—a Midwestern Republican heritage under conditions of extreme transiency. There was the exuberance and militancy of new money—the outward sign of inward capitalist grace. There was its role as the embodiment of Pacific First and Air Power.

Finally, there were the Democrats. The first New Deal state administration in California—that of Cuthbert Olson in 1938–42—was ineffectual and failed to alter the patterns of California politics. Democratic registration or no, California politics continued in a Republican mode. The New Deal came late upon the scene in this state. The revolution did not strike until 1958. Senator William Knowland, Republican minority leader in the U.S. Senate and publisher of the Oakland *Tribune,* committed the colossal blunder of attempting to change jobs with Republican Governor Goodwin Knight and tying his campaign to a right-to-work proposition in a recession year. In the gubernatorial election, he was snowed under by Edmund G. Brown, Sr., a Catholic. Even more remarkably, the Democrats took control of the legislature. They proceeded, in 1959, to pass a legislative program which was compared to the New Deal's first hundred days. Among its more notable features were a $1.75 billion water bond issue, a master plan for higher education, and a fair employment practices commission. In the course of two terms, the Brown administration doubled state spending, from two to four billion dollars.

So the Republicans could be beaten even in California. But the very success of the Democrats ensured an intense right-wing Republican response. In California, the lateness of the New Deal revolution helped to account for the freshness of reaction. The critical election was not 1936, but 1958.

14

THE NEW SOUTH

The South stood apart from the political crisis of the 1930s and 1940s. It was not that the Great Depression, the Republican fall from power, the Second World War, the Cold War, and McCarthyism failed to affect the region. It was that for the South these events did not pose the same problem of structural identity.

The South suffered terribly from the depression; but deprivation was no stranger to a region in which the per capita income was barely half the national average. The undoing of the Republicans did not shake political arrangements; there were precious few Republicans to begin with. The "Roosevelt revolution" was far too leftist for the Bourbon establishment, but it did not object to the many benefits it received, such as agricultural subsidies and political patronage, and it had to adjust its style to Roosevelt's popularity with the Southern folk.

The South sent its sons to war, but it did not begrudge them, particularly on behalf of England. There were no doubts about the cause of European intervention—a vindication of the Wilsonian internationalism which Southerners had helped to create. The anti-Communism and European commitments of the Cold War certainly posed no crisis of conscience, while the "anti-Communism" of the McCarthyites, with its ravings against New Dealers and internationalists, was regarded as an alien circus.

The South stood apart because it had a distinctive history. It participated in these events without experiencing them as crises because its social and political structure varied from the national norm. This distinctiveness originated in the South's racial regime, the heritage of plantation economy and slave labor. In the Civil War of the 1860s, the South's social order came into cataclysmic conflict with a Northern capitalism based on free labor. The "Reconstruction" brought about by defeat in the war was incomplete. Remnants of the old system endured in the form of sharecropping, tenant farming, and white political control. By the 1930s, cotton agriculture in the Deep South was in a state of decay, but the old racial attitudes lingered.

Still, the South, particularly the Upper South, was not monolithically *ante-bellum* in its social arrangements. In his classic *Southern Politics,* V. O. Key sketched a tripartite political geography of the region. With their large, disenfranchised black populations, fearful white minorities, and plantation traditions, the black belts were Democratic and reactionary. The hill country's style of Democratic politics was populist because of comfortable white majorities and an impecunious economy. Alienated from the black belts and the Confederacy from the beginning for lack of a slave agriculture, the mountains went so far as to vote Republican on occasion. Yet, as Key explained, the "fundamental explanation of southern politics is that the black-belt whites succeeded in imposing their will on their states and thereby presented a solid regional front on the race issue." [1]

The historic irony is that the black belts were, if anything, stronger within the region after the Civil War than before it. Before the war, a reactionary regime based on slave labor and racial fear was contested by an independent, if not militant, democracy with roots in free-labor agriculture and commerce. After the war, an aborted Southern "nationalism" controlled the psychology of the region. Key noted,

> The War left a far higher degree of southern unity against the rest of the world than had prevailed before. Internal differences that had expressed themselves in sharp political competition were

weakened—if not blotted out—by the common experiences of The War and Reconstruction. And, however unreasonable it may seem, it follows—as even a sophomore can see from observing the European scene—that a people ruled by a military government will retain an antipathy toward the occupying power.[2]

The planters maintained their dominance of the South by forcing on the whole region the common experience of the lost war. Wartime suffering, military occupation, and Reconstruction succeeded where the principles of the Confederacy had failed in winning voluntary adherence to the Lost Cause. A common fate and a common stigma preserved the popular identification with the Bourbon ruling class in subsequent years. In the 1890s, rural populist democracy founded on an interracial alliance challenged the old order but was vanquished by race-baiting. In the reaction that followed, the black belt establishment successfully saddled the region with a system of racial segregation and a political system characterized by the disenfranchisement of most blacks and poor whites. For all intents and purposes, there was one-party rule. As it entered the 1930s, therefore, the South lacked the attributes essential to democratic government: a popular franchise and a two-party system.

The New Deal brought out the old populist spirit of the Southern masses without actually transforming the region's political system. Blacks were still disenfranchised and segregated. Though lying low, the Bourbons had not actually been driven from the seats of power. At the same time, there was no basis for a sharp reaction against the New Deal. Southern conservatives despised the social radicalism of the Roosevelt Administration, but they were too ambivalent to be effective against it. There was a general sympathy in the region for internationalist foreign policy. The fact that a Democratic Administration was in power meant that, to some degree, Southern Democrats were in power too.

The structural crisis in the South came after World War II, indeed, largely as a result of it. The crisis took the form of a transformation of Southern race relations, the "Second Reconstruction," and of the region's agricultural economy through an industrializing trend, sometimes inspiring the title the "New South." The federal government was the modernizing force. Washington demanded higher standards of racial justice and contributed to economic development by channeling funds, particularly for social welfare and the uniformed military establishment, into the region. This federal income expanded the market for local commerce and light industry. The role of federal contracts for military/aerospace *industry,* as distinct from the defense establishment proper, was important for some states, but for the South as a whole it was not above the national average.

These forces represented a threat to the existing order which was sufficiently great to call forth bitter reaction rather than business-as-usual conservatism. In response to the Second Reconstruction, the whites of the black belts rejected the national Democratic Party and defected to renegade Democratic or to right-wing Republican candidacies.

New South capitalism was more ambiguous than racial reconstruction in its effects. It was not a defensive reaction to a threat but a promise of wealth to be grasped with both hands. In one mood, the new capitalists and the suburban middle class gravitated to moderate Republicanism. In another, they were receptive to the doctrines of pure capitalism which were the stock-and-trade of the Republican right. Southern capitalism was in an early stage of development. The cultural level was low and the economic opportunities tangible. These were the materials for a regional Gilded Age.

In the Second Reconstruction, there were three watersheds: the Truman Administration's civil rights program in 1948, the U.S. Supreme Court's school desegregation decision in 1954, and the Civil Rights Acts of 1964–65.

The Democratic Party's civil rights commitment began to percolate during World War II. In the 1930s, President Roosevelt had preferred not to take a strong civil rights stand in order to hold white Southerners in line for the party. His economic programs were sufficient to begin to wean blacks away from their traditional Lincoln Republicanism. World War II greatly accelerated the pace of events by setting into motion vast population movements both into the armed forces and the war industries of Northern cities. These wartime movements raised the level of cultural sophistication and political consciousness of the black population. Even in the South, black voter registration increased from 5 to 20 per cent from 1940 to 1950. At the same time, the war brought the races into closer contact and created the potential for racial conflict between defensive whites and more demanding blacks. This potential was realized in 1943 in the Detroit race riots.

In 1941, black political leaders made themselves felt by demanding and getting a Fair Employment Practices Committee on pain of a "March on Washington." Two years later, Howard Odum, a University of North Carolina sociologist, and Jonathan Daniels, a White House assistant on leave from the Raleigh *News and Observer,* first proposed a race relations commission to President Roosevelt. It was not until late 1946 that Roosevelt's successor implemented the idea at the suggestion of an aide, David K. Niles.

In the interim, there were several key developments. The victorious conclusion to the war found a black population that was better off economically and had developed a stronger middle-class leadership. Abroad, the United States was in competition with the Soviet Union for the good will of the world's nonwhite populations. At home, President Harry Truman was under pressure from his left for the allegiance of black voters after the resignation of Secretary of Commerce Henry Wallace. All of these considerations were brought into high relief by Democratic defeat in the off-year election of 1946. Citing a wave of lynchings and other violence against blacks, President Truman created the President's Committee on Civil Rights.

In its 1947 report, *To Secure These Rights,* this committee took a bold line and, in effect, set the post-war civil rights agenda. Its "program of action" proposed not only anti-lynching legislation but recommended a civil rights division for the Justice Department, a Congressional civil rights committee, the desegregation of the armed forces and of the entire federal government. The committee suggested laws protecting the voting franchise and prohibiting discrimination in interstate transportation. It recommended a fair employment practices law, action against racially restrictive covenants, and federal funding sanctions against institutions which practiced discrimination. In early 1948, President Truman delivered a message to Congress that incorporated many of these proposals in an administration civil rights program.

The reaction from Southern Democrats was immediate. Within a week after the message, the Southern Governors Conference designated a committee under the leadership of Governor Strom Thurmond of South Carolina to meet with the U.S. Attorney-General Howard McGrath. The Administration's assurances were insufficient. The factions within the Democratic Party began to marshal their forces in preparation for a struggle over the civil rights plank of the party's 1948 platform. "White Jeffersonian Democrats" convened in Jackson, Mississippi, on May 10 to plan strategy. The leading figures were Governor Thurmond and Governor Fielding Wright of Mississippi, a political leader of the Delta planters. Mississippi and South Carolina, the states with the highest percentages of blacks, were proving to be the most adamant in their opposition to the civil rights program.

The Truman Administration attempted to mollify the Southerners by proposing a civil rights plank reminiscent of the generalities of 1944. Southern acceptance of this formula was not forthcoming; amendments were offered and voted down. In the ensuing polarization, liberal forces under the leadership of Hubert Humphrey, mayor of Minneapolis, rammed through a much stronger civil rights plank than the Administration version. A Southern insurgency in the fall election was ensured.

Southern "Dixiecrats" did not actually pursue a true third party strategy. Their intention was to take over the Democratic Party in the South and run electors pledged to vote for a "States Rights" ticket of Thurmond and Wright. The Dixiecrats succeeded in this purpose in the Deep South states—South

Carolina, Mississippi, Alabama, and Louisiana—but failed elsewhere, illustrating once again the differences in attitude between the Lower and the Upper South. The latter was quite often influenced by the independent spirit of the mountains and the base for Republican challenges which it offered. Most of these states were more highly industrialized, thus more urban, cosmopolitan in culture, and susceptible to influences and people from outside the region. Finally, the Upper South had significantly fewer Negroes in its population, thus less race consciousness.

The actual election followed this division. The Dixiecrats carried the Deep South states where they had appropriated the Democratic Party. Running as a third party, their best showing was 20 per cent of the vote in Georgia. The states that the Dixiecrats carried were the states with the highest percentages of blacks, and within these states, the Thurmond/Wright ticket ran best where the race issue was most salient—the black belts. Since the black populations in these areas were effectively disenfranchised, the States Rights ticket received overwhelming margins from race-conscious whites. The state of Mississippi voted 87 per cent for the States Rights Democrats; Alabama 79 per cent; South Carolina 72 per cent. The black populations in these states were 45, 32, and 38 per cent respectively. Nonetheless, only 19 per cent of all Southern voters supported the Dixiecrats, more evidence that there was more to the South than the black belts.[3]

All of this went on without reference to the Republicans, whose nominee was Governor Thomas Dewey of New York. Dewey had implemented a strong civil rights program in New York and received the virtually unanimous endorsement of the black press, although black voters preferred Truman by two to one. It was not until 1952 that the Republicans were able to exploit the discontent of the black belts. The Republican nominee, Dwight Eisenhower, had none of Dewey's militancy on civil rights, and the black belts in Deep South states, particularly Mississippi and South Carolina, gravitated toward him. But the Eisenhower phenomenon in the South was essentially moderate and urban. The Republican candidate carried the outer South states of Texas, Florida, Tennessee, and Virginia. His impressive gains in the Deep South did not translate into electoral votes.

This Republican tendency in the black belts was soon aborted by the Supreme Court's school desegregation decision in 1954. Eisenhower's steadfast indifference to the subject could not disguise the fact that the Supreme Court's Chief Justice was his appointee, Earl Warren, former governor of California. Eisenhower's popularity in the black belts thus proved to be an episode. The main channel of opposition to racial integration continued to be the Southern wing of the Democratic Party.

Senator Harry F. Byrd's "Organization" in Virginia took the lead in formulating opposition strategy to the Supreme Court decision. Virginia was not a Deep South state, and its black belt, Southside and rural Tidewater, did not dominate the state in population. By Southern standards, Virginia did not have a particularly high percentage of blacks—22 per cent. Nonetheless, the Byrd Organization did depend on the black belt for its core of support. It made up for its smaller black belt base by imposing on Virginia the most restrictive voting franchise in the nation.

It was Senator Byrd himself who brushed aside Governor Thomas B. Stanley's first statement of intent to comply with the Supreme Court decision and, in effect, forced Stanley's recantation. The Virginia General Assembly's response to the Court also proved to be too moderate for the senator. The assembly's Gray Commission proposed a pupil assignment plan based on ostensibly nonracial criteria, tuition grants for students who chose to attend private schools, even a local option to desegregate. The plan was evasive, but not openly extra-legal. In early 1956, Senator Byrd overtook the Gray Commission by laying down the line of "massive resistance." That summer, the General Assembly passed enabling legislation. The Governor was compelled to close any school under a court order to integrate. If a further court order required the school to reopen, the Governor would reply by cutting off state funds to the school.

The ideological spokesman for the Byrd Organization's massive resistance policy was James J. Kilpatrick, editor of the Richmond *News-Leader*. In a series of editorials in early 1956, Kilpatrick resurrected John C. Calhoun's discredited, *antebellum* doctrine of "interposition." The theory was that the states could "interpose" their own "sovereignty" between the federal government and the people when a question arose concerning an unconstitutional exercise of federal power. This superficially innocuous theory held that the Constitution was a "compact" among the states. Reserved to the states were all powers not specifically delegated. This was also the line of the "Southern Manifesto" ("Declaration of Constitutional Principles") which all but a few Southern members of Congress signed.

Though this theory did not logically require a theory of racial supremacy, it was historically associated with one. Race was also the current issue. Kilpatrick did not shrink, in a later book, from embracing a fully developed theory of racial superiority:

> The South earnestly submits that over a period of thousands of years, the Negro race, as a race, has failed to contribute significantly to the higher and nobler achievements of civilization as the West defines that term. This may be a consequence of innate psychic factors. Again, it may not be, but because contemporary evidence suggests little racial improvement, the South prefers to cling to the characteristics of the white race, as best it can, and to protect those characteristics, as best it can, from what is sincerely regarded as the potentially degrading influence of Negro characteristics.[4]

As long established by classical political theory, the "sovereign" must always be unitary; otherwise, the question arises of who the final authority is, and a conflict of sovereignties is inevitable. This was the problem with the Constitutional theory of the Southern resistance. "Interposition" was often seen as the genteel alternative to blatant race thinking. The truth was not that it was more respectable than racism, but that it was less; for it was an elaborate rationale for illegal action. It was no accident that interposition was originally formulated in circumstances leading toward civil war. The Southern Manifesto commended the "motives of those States which have declared the intention to resist forced integration by any lawful means." But what were "lawful means" when there was dispute about what was lawful? In the American political system, the Supreme Court is the final authority on what the Constitution means. It was precisely this authority of the Court that the Southern resisters challenged. The Southern Manifesto accused the Supreme Court of having substituted "naked power for established law." The resistance thus did not stop at saying the Supreme Court was wrong in its understanding, which was always possible. It maintained that the Court did not have the *authority* to decide what was "established law."

This point of view quickly translated into illegal acts not only by rioting mobs and nightriders, but by the state authorities. In February 1956, Autherine Lucy, a black woman, entered the University of Alabama under federal court order. When a riot developed, the state police intervened but also removed Lucy from the university. In the fall, Governor Allen Shivers of Texas sent in the Texas Rangers to deal with disturbances at public schools in Mansfield and Texarkana, which were under a court order to admit blacks. Again, the state authorities did not defend the right of blacks to attend integrated schools. Encouraged by these precedents, Governor Orval Faubus of Arkansas drifted into a similar policy in the Little Rock crisis in 1957. On the pretext of preventing violence, Faubus used the National Guard to obstruct the integration of the Little Rock schools. Finally alarmed by the open challenges to federal authority, the Eisenhower Administration put an end to this pattern by federalizing the National Guard and sending in the 101st Airborne Division to enforce integration. By his proclamation, President Eisenhower provided "Assistance for the Removal of an Obstruction of Justice Within the State of Arkansas."

"Massive resistance" in Virginia came to a similarly ignominious end. In the fall of 1958, after federal court orders to integrate, Governor Lindsay Almond ordered the schools of Warren County, Charlottesville, and Norfolk closed. Faced with the prospective end of public education, a moderate coalition speedily developed to oppose the massive resisters. On the same day, January 19, 1959, both the Virginia Supreme Court of Appeals and a federal district court found school closings unconstitutional under state and federal law.

The Republican Party had nothing to do with massive resistance and the illegality associated with it, but it risked falling heir to this tradition when it later competed successfully for the political allegiance of the black belts. Other affinities began to develop in the 1950s between Dixiecrats and right-wing Republicans. Since the order of things itself was threatened, Dixiecrat forces were attracted to extreme conspiracy theories of the McCarthyite type. In a notable speech in the spring of 1955, Senator James Eastland, Democrat of Mississippi, perorated on the "Communist associations" of the sociologists whom the Supreme Court had cited in footnote eleven of its desegregation decision. Eastland was chairman of the Senate Internal Security Subcommittee.

Southerners began to tire of foreign policy internationalism. The industrialization of the South was providing a growing base for protectionist sentiment. Most of the South's new industries, such as textiles, were labor-intensive and vulnerable to foreign competition. Ironically, black belt agriculture, where it still flourished, was a more reliable formation for a free trade policy because of its orientation toward export markets.

In the 1950s, the nonwhite countries of the "Third World" became more central to American foreign policy. In the midst of a racial crisis, Southern conservatives took a dim view of idealistic programs of aid to nonwhite underdeveloped countries and to the United Nations. In general, the defensive posture of the South, especially the Deep South, during the 1950s encouraged an attitude of retrenchment, even rancor, in foreign policy. Southern Congressmen still supported the Atlantic Alliance and large military budgets. But this orientation was consistent with new nationalism, as well as internationalism.[5]

In the Presidential campaigns from 1952 through 1960, the Republican Party made impressive progress. In 1952, Eisenhower carried Texas, Florida, Tennessee, and Virginia. In 1956, he added Louisiana to this number. In 1960, Richard Nixon was able to hold Florida, Tennessee, and Virginia, losing Catholic Louisiana to the Kennedy half and Texas to the Johnson half of the Democratic ticket. The premise of these advances was essentially moderate: a hard core of support in the mountains. But alone the Appalachian region could not be decisive.

The additional factor was supplied by the Southern cities. The strength of "Presidential Republicanism" in Southern metropolitan areas in the 1950s was a byword, but it was also a paradox illustrating the South's regional distinctiveness. Outside the South, the pattern was for the Democratic Party to base itself in the cities and the Republican Party to hold sway in the provincial areas. In the South, as long as the restiveness in the black belts was contained, the pattern was the reverse: Republican strength in the cities, Democratic dominance of the countryside. In a static comparison, differences between Northern and Southern cities stand out. The South did not have large Catholic and immigrant populations; organized labor was weak. But these factors could not entirely account for the weakness of Democratic liberalism in the cities. In the 1890s and 1930s, Southerners had shown themselves entirely capable of liberalism, even radicalism.

The salient difference between North and South was the stage of economic development. The South was the most rural region of the country. Its agriculture was the least advanced technologically. Although the South began to industrialize during World War II, the political culture of the new high-growth cities did not reproduce that of the North's mature metropolitan areas. For the rural Southern poor who migrated to them, the Southern metropolitan centers offered a new way of life and a much higher standard of living. For the middle class, both indigenous and newly arrived, the cities presented very real opportunities for enrichment.

This relatively early stage of economic development appeared to confirm conservative Republican more than liberal Democratic ideology. Under circumstances of rapid growth, the marketplace not only tested a person's mettle but rewarded him for it. The premises of conservative Republicanism were 19th century, but the South was in a 19th-century stage of development. Ironically, the "New South" cities were attracted by the political philosophy of the "Gilded Age" in the North—the *laissez-faire* doctrine which flourished over the dead body of the Old South after the Civil War.

In the Gilded Age, there was hard work and enterprise, but also vulgarity and cynicism. William C. Havard observed:

> The Whig mentality certainly survives among those who have most affected the growth of the new urban—or suburban— Republicanism in the South. In reading the pronouncements of many Southern financiers and businessmen and of the politicians from both parties who are attempting to translate business issue-orientations into public policy, one frequently feels that he has transmigrated into the McKinley era. In its most extreme extension and under circumstances in which the change is most rapid, e.g., in the case of Florida and former Governor Claude Kirk, both the environment and the pronouncements of its most prominent public spokesmen took on an air of unreality. Added to the unrelenting emphasis on the capacity of free enterprise and social Darwinism to provide a naturalistic solution to almost all the problems of a contemporary centralized society is an attitude which seems almost to deny the need of any regulative public institutions or even any concern for the *general* as opposed to the private welfare.[6]

It was the upper and middle classes of the cities that responded warmly to this new Republicanism. The blue-collar workers generally remained Democratic, though by unimpressive margins.

There were important qualifications to this image of a Southern boom in the 1950s. In employment and income, the South

Atlantic states—Virginia, Georgia, North and South Carolina—
were growing at a rate above the national average but not far
above it. Other states of the South, particularly the Deep South,
actually had growth rates below the national average. Mississippi and Arkansas were in a real economic depression. As one
tracks down the economic boom in the South and the impressive regional growth statistics, the prosperity tends to recede
from view until one reaches two states—Texas and Florida.
These states accounted for 60 per cent of Southern growth in
population and employment.[7]

There were similar variations in the strength and quality of
right-wing Republicanism in the cities of the region. Mountain
Republicanism provided a magnet for moderate Republicanism
in the cities of certain states. The possibility of an alliance with
a rural mountain Republicanism made of moderation a profitable political strategy for urban Republicans in the Upper
South. Eisenhower was able to carry Virginia and Tennessee by
combining mountain and city Republicans in a moderate coalition. North Carolina and several other states had mountain influences that helped to deflect right-wing Republicanism. But
in most of the Deep South, the tendency was the opposite. The
pull of the black belts was strong, and urban Republicanism
vibrated to Dixiecrat political ideology.

To find Gilded Age politics in its purest form, one has to
turn to Texas and Florida. These were the states with by far
the highest growth rates. Although East Texas and the Florida
panhandle influenced state politics in a rural Democratic direction, neither state was dominated by its Old South sections.
Neither state had a mountain base for traditional, anti-Dix-
iecrat Republicanism. In the 1950s, Eisenhower carried both
states for the cause of moderate Republicanism, but it was soon
to become evident that urban Republicanism without the brake
of the mountains had right-wing potential. In Texas, the go-go
city of Dallas was not just a bastion of "Presidential Republicanism" in the 1950s; it elected a conservative Republican Congressman in 1954 and reelected him thereafter. In 1961, John
G. Tower, a Republican of the right, won an upset victory in a

special election to fill the U.S. Senate seat vacated by Lyndon B. Johnson on his election as Vice President of the United States. The victory of Tower was built upon metropolitan majorities.

The boom in Texas was based on oil and gas and military/aerospace industry. Texas had the third largest urban migration in absolute numbers in the country in the 1950s, but its rural outmigration was also the nation's largest. Most of its urban work force was thus internally generated. Florida had an even higher growth rate than Texas, though it had only half the population. The migration to its cities was the second largest in numbers after California, but it had no net rural outmigration. Most of the people were coming from out-of-state, often from the Republican Midwest, and they brought their politics with them. Of the five million people in the state in 1960, more than 30 per cent had come to Florida in the 1950s alone.

Like Texas, Northern Florida had a Southern Democratic heritage. With a Jewish middle class, a strong labor movement, and nonwhite minorities, Miami had liberal Democratic politics similar to New York City's. But the rest of South Florida might have been Southern California. Climate was king, and the foundation for recreation, retirement, and tourist industries. There was also a budding aerospace industry. The migrants were often Republican white-collar workers or retired folk with some capital. Growth rates were high. Inapposite small-town values flourished amid the money-making, mobility, and anomie of the new suburbs. Still, except at the Presidential level, Florida remained safely Democratic throughout the 1950s. As in some of the boom states of the West—Arizona, New Mexico, and Nevada—urban Republicanism labored against a strong Democratic tradition in the countryside.

There were some premonitory indications. In 1952, William Cramer, a conservative Republican, was elected to Congress from a district that included Tampa and St. Petersburg. In 1962, Edward Gurney, the conservative Republican mayor of Winter Garden, won election to the Congressional district that included Orlando and Cape Canaveral, centers of the Florida aerospace industry. Like their cousins in Southern California, the white-collar wards of the federal government in the aerospace industry preferred their politics Republican, albeit with new nationalist spice.

15

BARRY GOLDWATER

In personality and style, Barry Goldwater was an unlikely successor to Joe McCarthy. That was his virtue. Where McCarthy was volatile, Goldwater was stable. Where McCarthy was steamy, Goldwater was healthy. Where McCarthy wielded a knife, Goldwater offered his hand. But the fact remains that the two were personal friends and shared a similar world view. McCarthy campaigned for Goldwater when the latter ran for the Senate in Arizona in 1952. On McCarthy's death, Goldwater declared: "Because Joe McCarthy lived, we are a safer, freer, more vigilant nation today. . . ." Goldwater inherited one of McCarthy's speechwriters, Brent Bozell, who ghosted *The Conscience of a Conservative.*

When McCarthy was on the verge of censure in 1954, Goldwater was one of his die-hard defenders. Goldwater attempted to save McCarthy by asking him to sign a written apology for his depredations as a way of heading off Senate action. McCarthy would have none of it. When, even after his censure, McCarthy persisted in his attacks on Eisenhower, Goldwater finally began to put some distance between himself and the Wisconsin Senator. But in the censure debate itself, Goldwater made it clear enough that he shared the substance of McCarthy's views. In a foray against the "unknown engineers of censure," Goldwater asked:

What kind of fight has it been? It is a fight which has been laden
with hypocrisy. The masterminds of this fight have said one thing
and meant another. Their propaganda has dripped with idealism,
high-mindedness, and lofty sentiments. Their deeds have come
from the darkness. As this fight has progressed, it has snowballed
to include wider and wider groups who hate McCarthy without
really knowing why that hate exists. All the discredited and embittered figures of the Hiss-Yalta period of American dishonor have
crawled out from under their logs to join the efforts to get even.
The news columns and the airwaves have been filled with their
pious talk about "civil liberties," "ethical codes," and "protection
of the innocent," while at the same time these people have dipped
in the smut pot to discredit Senator McCarthy and his work
against Communism.[1]

Barry Goldwater shared the old right's desperate view of the
New Deal internationalists. Still, there was something that set
him apart from the Midwestern leaders of the old right—Taft,
MacArthur, and McCarthy. These men were representatives of
a ruling group that had lost out decisively in the struggle for
national power. The regional base of this provincial business
elite was intact, and there was always the possibility that events
and new alliances might allow it to recoup. But defeat had left
its mark not only in the rancor but in the pessimism of its
outlook.

The optimism of Barry Goldwater was formed by a far different environment. In Arizona, a ruling Republican Party had
not been swamped by a Democratic tide; rather, it was the reverse. The Democrats were the traditional ruling party in Arizona. Their control of the countryside was similar to, and an
extension of, the rural Democracy that prevailed in the South.
After World War II, the Democrats found themselves hard
pressed by a new urban Republicanism of which Barry Goldwater became the leading representative. Goldwater was the
leader of a rising political force, not a declining one. He ex-
uded the optimism of a man who expected things to go well.

Barry Goldwater's uncle, Morris Goldwater, had actually
been one of the founders of the Democratic Party in Arizona, a
young state admitted into the union in 1912. Morris Goldwater

was a conservative Democrat of the old school, a "Jeffersonian Democrat." However, the nephew preferred the Republican Party in Phoenix, where he spent his early manhood managing the family department store. During World War II, he flew planes to the China-Burma-India theatre for the Air Transport Command.

When Goldwater was born, Phoenix had barely 30,000 people. Before the war, it had grown to more than 60,000—still no metropolis. It was wartime prosperity that transformed the city. By 1950, it had a population of more than 300,000; by 1960, more than 600,000; by 1963, more than 800,000. Phoenix developed on the basis of military installations, electronics, climate, water and power projects constructed by the federal government, and a fantastic in-migration. By 1960, two thirds of its citizens had come from elsewhere, mainly California, Illinois, New York, Ohio, and Texas. In its socio-economic profile of prosperity and migration, Arizona bore a close affinity to Southern California.

All of this was good for the department store and good for Barry Goldwater. It inclined him to a *laissez-faire* outlook of the most rigid sort, modified only by the "states rights" tradition of the old Democratic Party he had grown up in. In *The Conscience of a Conservative,* Goldwater-Bozell advocated the "prompt and final termination of the farm subsidy program" as a violation of free market principles. He proposed to "abolish the graduated features of our tax laws; and the sooner we get at the job, the better." He demanded that the federal government withdraw from "social welfare programs, education, public power, agriculture, public housing, urban renewal and all the other activities that can be better performed by lower levels of government or by private institutions or by individuals."

Goldwater's special province was labor. He opposed industry-wide bargaining and wanted all political activity by trade unions banned. Of course, he supported right-to-work. It was this issue which first involved him in politics after the war when he participated in a successful campaign to strengthen such a law in Arizona. In 1949, he made his formal entry into politics by running for and winning a seat on the Phoenix City Council on a good government ticket which aimed to clean out the corruption, prostitution, and gambling endemic to a frontier boom city.

In a Democratic state, this modest beginning was enough to make Goldwater a major figure in the Arizona Republican Party. In 1950, he managed the successful campaign of his friend, Howard Pyle, for governor. In 1952, Goldwater himself was elected to the U.S. Senate in a campaign, managed by Stephen Shadegg, a former Democrat, that stressed the danger of incipient Socialism in America. Goldwater became the second Republican Senator in Arizona's history as a state by defeating Ernest McFarland, no less than the Democratic majority leader. Goldwater's rapid ascent was assisted by the Eugene Pulliam newspapers, especially the Arizona *Republic* which later expressed for a time its editorial approval of the John Birch Society.

In the 1950s, Goldwater's career was that of a conservative back-bench Senator from a small state. Its most striking feature was a vendetta against Walter Reuther, president of the United Auto Workers, known as one of the more progressive unions in the country. Reuther had a political background as a democratic Socialist, though anti-Communist; he had expelled Communists from the UAW in the 1940s. But, because Reuther was in charge of the AFL-CIO's political arm, the Committee on Political Education (COPE), conservatives saw him as the embodiment of their theory of a Socialist takeover of America via a takeover of the Democratic Party by organized labor.

As a Republican member not only of the Senate Labor and Public Welfare Committee but of the Select Committee on Improper Activities in the Labor or Management Field, the "McClellan Rackets Committee," Goldwater pursued his interest in labor issues. Under its chief counsel, Robert F. Kennedy, the McClellan committee exposed corruption in the labor movement, particularly the Teamsters. The Republican minority on the committee, including Goldwater, perceived a partisan motive in the Teamsters investigation, since the union had endorsed Eisenhower for President in 1956. They demanded that equal attention be given to the UAW, which was a prominent contributor to the political campaigns of liberal Democrats. The Democrats responded that the presumed corruption was simply not there. In a minority report, the Republicans accused the committee of failing to investigate a "clear pattern of crime and violence" in UAW strikes and of conducting an inadequate investigation of the union's finances.

The McClellan committee investigations created a public demand for a labor reform bill. Goldwater's Democratic colleague on the committee, Senator John F. Kennedy of Massachusetts, took the lead. The first effort, the Kennedy-Ives bill, failed in 1958. The second, Kennedy-Ervin, passed the Senate by an overwhelming 95 to 1 vote in 1959. Goldwater cast the single vote, "the most important of my Senate career," against the bill. His view prevailed when the House rejected the bill and a stronger measure, Landrum-Griffin, was substituted.

Organized labor made the defeat of Goldwater a high priority in the off-year election of 1958. In a state in which local labor influence was not great, Goldwater turned this opposition to advantage by arguing that outside elements were trying to control the destiny of Arizona. Where tangible labor votes were involved, however, he did not hesitate to bid for their support. Thus, he competed for the endorsement of the Mine, Mill and Smelter Workers—a union expelled from the CIO as Communist-controlled—which had many members in Arizona's copper industry. Goldwater argued that Communists were not present in Arizona locals. Since the union did not in fact endorse him, a Democratic effort to tie Goldwater to the union misfired.

Goldwater's opponent was the still popular McFarland who had since been elected to two terms as governor. Goldwater defeated him by an improved margin. In the context of the devastating losses suffered by the Republicans in the 1958 election, Goldwater's victory moved him into the front ranks of the party. Nelson Rockefeller's election as governor of New York did the same for him. For the right, Goldwater's victory was inspiring because it was achieved on an ideological, anti-labor premise, a feat that William Knowland had tried and failed to accomplish in California. With Knowland defeated and Nixon co-opted into an Eastern internationalist Administration, the right needed a leader. Goldwater was next in line.

Senator Goldwater and Governor Rockefeller quickly developed into leaders of opposing political factions. Neither man was happy with the Eisenhower Administration, Goldwater criticizing it from the right, Rockefeller from the left. In 1960, Vice President Nixon, the prospective Republican Presidential nominee, attempted to promote harmony at the party's Chicago convention by vetoing Representative Melvin Laird, a conservative from Wisconsin, as chairman of the platform committee. Nonetheless, the committee received Senator Goldwater's remarks far more warmly than it did Governor Rockefeller's. Rockefeller threatened to repudiate the platform until Nixon visited him at his New York apartment and worked out the "Compact of Fifth Avenue," which chiefly provided for a stronger line on national defense, a more liberal one on civil rights. Goldwater was incensed by this "Munich."

Goldwater had his own moment of glory at the convention when his name was placed in nomination for President on the motion of the delegations of Arizona and South Carolina. Although Goldwater withdrew his name, he staked out a political claim for the Republican nomination in the future. It was significant that Goldwater's Presidential aspirations should have begun in South Carolina, where Gregory Shorey, Republican state chairman, and Roger Milliken, finance chairman and textile industrialist, had engineered the endorsement of the state convention. Goldwater recommended himself to the South Carolinians for several reasons. First, he had grown up as a "Jeffersonian Democrat," as many of them had. Second, he had a strong record of opposition to organized labor, a big issue in a state dominated by the militantly anti-labor textile industry.

Finally, Goldwater was right on race. "Despite the recent holding of the Supreme Court," Goldwater wrote, "I am firmly convinced—not only that integrated schools are not required—

but that the Constitution does not permit any interference whatsoever by the federal government in the field of education."[2] Goldwater had a relatively progressive personal record on race issues. He hired minorities at his department store and contributed financially to the Urban League and NAACP. He voted in favor of the Civil Rights Acts of 1957 and 1960. But he was prone to Constitutional inhibitions on major civil rights questions, such as the Supreme Court decisions ordering the integration of schools. "I believe," he said, "that it *is* both wise and just for negro children to attend the same schools as whites, and that to deny them this opportunity carries with it strong implications of inferiority. I am not prepared, however, to impose that judgment of mine on the people of Mississippi or South Carolina, or to tell them what methods should be adopted and what pace should be kept in striving toward that goal."[3] Goldwater was not a practicing racist; he believed in the Constitutional doctrine of states rights. This was good enough for the people of Mississippi and South Carolina. In 1964, Senator Strom Thurmond of South Carolina, States Rights Party candidate for President in 1948, announced that he was changing his Democratic registration to the "Goldwater Republican Party."

Goldwater made himself widely known and popular among party regulars throughout the country by his service as chairman of the Senate Republican Campaign Committee. In 1960, he published *The Conscience of a Conservative*. Published through the good offices of Clarence Manion, a member of the National Council of the John Birch Society, the book was an immense success and eventually sold over three million copies. Nonetheless, Goldwater was diffident about the possibility of a bid for the White House. The early work of organizing a Presidential campaign for 1964 fell to a "Draft Goldwater Committee," not all of whose leaders Goldwater knew well. Its founder was F. Clifton White, a renegade Dewey Republican from New York who had worked against Rockefeller's nomination in 1958. White's mentor in his ideological conversion was William Rusher, publisher of *National Review*, formerly of the staff of the Senate Internal Security Subcommittee. Utilizing national contacts acquired as Young Republican activists in the 1950s, White, Rusher, and Representative John Ashbrook of Ohio developed an embryonic draft organization in 1961. Prominent among its members were Roger Milliken, of Deering-Milliken; Charles Barr, a public affairs executive for Standard Oil of Indiana; and Robert Morris, formerly of the staff of the Senate Internal Security Subcommittee, now president of the University of Dallas. Eventually, Peter O'Donnell, Texas Republican state chairman, became the group's national chairman. Its finance committee was directed by three businessmen: Jeremiah Milbank III, William Middendorf, and J. D. Stetson Coleman.

More than organization would be required to win the nomination for Goldwater. According to the Gallup Poll, the clear favorite of Republicans was Governor Rockefeller, who was better known and more experienced in government than the Southwestern Senator. As of early 1963, Republicans preferred Rockefeller by a 49 to 17 per cent margin over Goldwater.[4] But in the spring, there were two critical developments. After a divorce, Rockefeller remarried Margaretta Fitler Murphy, a divorcee with four children. The American public was scandalized. And in April and May, there was a major and prolonged confrontation between black demonstrators, led by Martin Luther King, Jr., and local authorities in Birmingham, Alabama, over the desegregation of lunch counters. The Birmingham civil rights campaign inspired hundreds of demonstrations and led to thousands of arrests throughout the South. Governor Rockefeller was closely identified with civil rights, a favorite object of Rockefeller philanthropy. The atmosphere of racial unrest began to damage him with conservative voters.

The Gallup Poll of May 26 showed a reversal in the fortunes of Goldwater and Rockefeller. Goldwater was now the choice of Republicans by a 35 to 30 per cent margin. Goldwater also began to improve his standing in trial heats against President Kennedy, another champion of civil rights. In March, Goldwater was favored by only 27 per cent of the voters when matched against Kennedy. By the end of May, he commanded the support of 36 per cent, a substantial improvement.

For the Draft Goldwater Committee, the civil rights demonstrations of the spring and summer of 1963 and the conservative reaction against them represented a vindication of the "Southern strategy," which one of its members, William Rusher, had expounded in the pages of the *National Review* in February. Rusher argued that a conservative could win the Republican nomination and the Presidential election if he combined traditional areas of conservative strength in the Midwest and West with a renegade South.

Throughout 1961 and 1962, President Kennedy's popularity was proof against this hope. Whatever the outcome, foreign policy crises in Europe and the Caribbean tended only to rally the American people around the President. Despite a series of racial crises, Kennedy's poll ratings in the South were only marginally lower than in the nation as a whole. In the civil rights area, however, there was a potential problem. The civil rights crises of the 1950s placed the Southern racial regime against the "law of the land"—the decisions of the U.S. Supreme Court. The question of upholding law and order was crucial in swinging public opinion behind the school desegregation decision. The Kennedy Administration faced a more delicate problem. The civil rights movement had begun to oppose segregation with illegal tactics of civil disobedience in advance of federal statutes or court decisions finding segregated practices illegal. The law-and-order issue was now more problematic.

Such was the case with public accommodations and transportation. In 1961, the Congress of Racial Equality (CORE) tested segregation on buses by sponsoring "Freedom Rides" through the South. In Alabama, there was violence. U.S. Attorney-General Robert F. Kennedy intervened with federal marshals and was instrumental in obtaining an order of the Interstate Commerce Commission prohibiting segregation in interstate travel. The Administration survived this crisis politically intact.

Although the Freedom Riders were breaking the law, segregation was patently immoral; their pacifism also contrasted starkly to the violence of the reaction against them. Nonetheless, the Administration wanted to stay within the legal framework of the federal system and to hold on to its Southern political base. It channeled its own effort into the area of voting rights sanctioned by existing civil rights statutes and advised civil rights leaders to do the same.

In 1963, two years later, the Brimingham crisis inspired the Kennedy Administration to take a stronger stand on civil rights. On June 11, President Kennedy proposed a sweeping civil rights act covering public accommodations and employment. Reluctantly, the President gave his blessing to a "March on Washington" which brought 200,000 supporters of civil rights to the capital city. For these positions, the Administration had to pay a political price. An August 18 Gallup Poll had Goldwater beating Kennedy in the South by a percentage of 54 to 38, although another poll the next week had Kennedy comfortably ahead nationally by 59 to 35 per cent. Underlying this long lead were some disquieting strategic facts. In 1960, Kennedy had carried only three states, all small, in the far West. He might have real difficulty against a Western candidate, like Goldwater, who could carry the South.

Competing for the nomination of a conservative party, Rockefeller's situation had meanwhile become not merely troublesome but desperate. After a strident convention of the Young Republicans, dominated by the right, Rockefeller took the opportunity to deliver a manifesto declaring that the "Republican Party is in real danger of subversion by a radical, well-financed and highly disciplined minority." The New York governor took strong exception to the "Southern strategy":

> Completely incredible as it is to me, it is now being seriously proposed to the Republican Party that as a strategy for victory in 1964, that it write off the Negro and other minority groups, that it deliberately write off the great industrial states of the North (representing nearly 50 percent of the country's population), that it write off the big cities, and that it direct its appeal primarily to

the electoral votes of the South, plus the West and a scattering of other states.

The transparent purpose behind this plan is to erect political power on the outlawed and immoral base of segregation and to transform the Republican Party from a national party of all the people to a sectional party for some of the people.[5]

Rockefeller was sadly correct that the Goldwater forces were proposing to run on a "program based on racism or sectionalism." That this program was actually a product of "subversion" of the party by the "radical right" was a more dubious proposition. Rockefeller found this out when other party leaders failed to respond to his "Declaration of July 14" and when the conservative wing of the party took the document not as an attack on the "lunatic fringe" but as an attack on itself. In content, the views of the draft Goldwater group qualified as extreme but they were not generated from outside the party. The Draft Goldwater Committee was made up of party activists—state chairmen and finance chairmen, young Congressmen, political mechanics, and alumni of the Young Republicans. The same might even be said of the John Birch Society, which did not descend on the Republican Party from outside, but evolved from old nationalist elements within it.

As his political prospects improved, Senator Goldwater began to weary of the self-appointed managers of his destiny. He brought in his own "Arizona Mafia" to take control of the Presidential effort. The key men were Denison Kitchel, a friend and lawyer: Dean Burch, his former administrative assistant; and Richard Kleindienst, Arizona state Republican chairman. William J. Baroody, head of the American Enterprise Institute, provided a brain trust and a speechwriter, Karl Hess. Tony Smith, a former writer for *Human Events,* handled the press. Many of the draft Goldwater people stayed on, most notably, White and John Grenier, Alabama state chairman who was in charge of the Southern effort. A third leadership element consisted of conservative luminaries from Congress or the Eisenhower Administration, men such as former Senator William Knowland, who managed Goldwater's California campaign;

former Secretary of the Treasury George Humphrey, who managed Eisenhower; and Senator Carl Curtis of Nebraska, who hurled thunderbolts at Governor Rockefeller.

The summer of 1963 was the real high watermark of the Goldwater candidacy, the single moment when a Goldwater Presidency was conceivable, if not likely. It was also the historical moment when the South abandoned the Democratic Party at the Presidential level. By proposing major civil rights legislation, the Kennedy Administration had finally resolved the long-standing internal party conflict between blacks and Southern conservatives in favor of the former.

These facts were washed away by the blood of the Kennedy assassination. The Goldwater candidacy all but collapsed. By losing his political opponent, Goldwater also lost his foil—a symbol of the Eastern Establishment and Democratic liberalism which he could use to rally the South and West. President Lyndon B. Johnson, a Texan, would not do for these purposes. In early 1964, Johnson swamped Goldwater in the Gallup Poll by a 73 to 22 per cent margin in the South. Goldwater's strongest region was now the Midwest, the seat of traditional Republicanism.

As a corollary, the assassination revived Eastern candidacies as a counterstrategy to the Johnson Presidency. In the Gallup Poll, Rockefeller drew even with Goldwater. In fact, both candidacies were now crippled. The Republican ticket of 1960, Richard Nixon and Henry Cabot Lodge, came to the fore. Although well regarded by Republicans, Nixon was not considered a probable winner in a general election because of his unsuccessful campaigns for President in 1960 and for governor of California in 1962. Ensconced on Wall Street, he lacked a political base. Henry Cabot Lodge as the "Republican Kennedy" was the stronger possibility. Lodge stunned Goldwater with a write-in victory in the New Hampshire primary. However, the Lodge candidacy was too high-flying. He became the leader in the polls and a threat in the primaries but lacked organization, a critical weakness since most delegates were still to be had in state conventions and committees. His above-the-fray posture as ambassador to South Vietnam was too pat a repetition of the strategy he had helped to design for Eisenhower in 1952. When Rockefeller beat him in the Oregon primary, the Lodge campaign faded.

The Goldwater candidacy was a shadow of its former self. By May, Goldwater was the first choice of 14 per cent of Republican voters. His victories against second-rate opposition in Midwestern primaries were not impressive. But his organization continued to collect delegates by default in nonprimary states. As a result, the only chance of the moderates lay in a victory in the California primary, worth eighty-seven delegates to the winner and capable of reversing the trend elsewhere. After his victory in Oregon, Rockefeller forged ahead, but the weekend before the vote, a child was born to his new wife. Rockefeller lost in a close vote. Even so, he carried fifty of California's fifty-four counties. Goldwater's entire margin came from Southern California.

It mattered little that the new moderate hope, Governor William Scranton of Pennsylvania, outpolled Goldwater among Republican voters by two-to-one in the Gallup. Victory in California guaranteed Goldwater the nomination. This triumph was hardly the result of an invincible "movement." Had it not been for his marital problems, Rockefeller would certainly have been the nominee. As it was, the crippled Rockefeller candidacy was not strong enough to defeat Goldwater but was formidable enough to block the timely emergence of any other moderate candidacy.

In 1952, Eisenhower developed a Northeastern bloc to oppose Taft's Midwestern base and went on to compete successfully against him in the West and even in the South. In disarray, the moderates in 1964 were bottled up in the Northeast and never developed the potential that the polls and primaries consistently revealed. There were definite limits to Goldwater's popularity among the Republican rank and file. Where he marshalled genuinely new strength for the right was in the South. John Grenier delivered 271 out of 278 delegates to Goldwater by dint not simply of organization but of an historic crisis in

race relations. In the early 1960s, Alabama was a virtual battle-
ground. Goldwater brought his Southern and Western strategy
to fruition by winning California and Texas, the colossi of the
two regions. Together, the South and California (effectively
Southern California) accounted for almost half of all Goldwater's delegates.

The regional components of Goldwater's victory provided
the substance to the charge of extremism which Rockefeller
bravely repeated at the convention. Southern California's Republicanism was not the normal conservatism of the Midwest
which was losing some of its reactionary fire as memories of
past glory began to fade; the conservatism of Southern California was a super-heated version of the old-time religion. For
their part, the delegates from the Old Confederacy arrived at
the San Francisco convention covered with the dust of recent
battle with the federal government. The party was weak in
their region, and they had everything to gain and nothing to
lose from an ideological crusade. If these two groups were not,
strictly speaking, "outsiders" to the party, they must have
seemed like strangers to Republicans with the responsibilities of
government in stable regions.

Once outside the hothouse world of the Republican Party,
Goldwater discovered that his political opinions were no longer
assets in a campaign for national office against a popular incumbent president. His views on farm subsidies alienated the
farmers. His desire to make Social Security a voluntary system
alarmed the retired. His proposal to sell parts of the Tennessee
Valley Authority to private enterprise created a problem for
him in the Upper South. His labor views repelled the working-
man. His vote against the Civil Rights Act of 1964 made him
anathema to blacks. Outside the right wing of the Republican
Party, the American people were not receptive to conservative
fundamentalism.

Goldwater made some compensating gains in the South as
President Johnson pushed through the Civil Rights Act. In trial
heats against Johnson, his poll ratings in the region improved
by August to 40 to 51 per cent. In September, he moved past

Johnson, 47 to 46 per cent. However, any gains Goldwater realized as a result of reaction against civil rights legislation were neutralized by the popular response to his foreign policy views which were of paramount importance in a Presidential election.

As a new nationalist Republican, Goldwater naturally stressed air power and nuclear supremacy in his strategic attitude. He took a geneally dim view of arms control and in 1963 voted against the nuclear test ban treaty, an agreement which was popular with the American people. By remarking that nuclear weapons might be used to defoliate the jungles in the Vietnam War and by proposing that the decision to use nuclear weapons in Europe might be made below the Presidential level, Goldwater presented himself as a man who might make casual use of the nuclear arsenal. The Democrats exploited this negative public image.

In the aftermath of the Kennedy assassination, the American people were repelled by any hint of extremist violence. After the raucous Republican convention and his rationalization of "extremism in the defense of liberty," Senator Goldwater carried this stigma. Even the conservative press began to abandon him. For the first time since 1932, the Hearst newspapers endorsed a Democrat. Goldwater was left with a few diehards, such as the San Diego *Union,* the Richmond *News-Leader,* and the Chicago *Tribune.*

On election day, Goldwater won just under 39 per cent of the vote. He carried his home state of Arizona and five states of the Deep South—Mississippi, South Carolina, Alabama, Louisiana, and Georgia. The Goldwater strategy succeeded completely as a method of alienating the cities. Sixty-one metropolitan areas of more than 200,000 people contained 44 per cent of the American population. Goldwater could carry only four of them—Jacksonville, Florida; Tulsa, Oklahoma; Birmingham and Mobile, Alabama—and improve on Nixon's performance in one more, New Orleans, Louisiana. Goldwater was swamped not merely within the city limits of these metropolises but in the suburbs which Nixon had carried in 1960.[6]

Goldwater failed to develop compensating strength in the countryside. Outside the South, he lost the nonmetropolitan areas. He won only 80 per cent of the Republican vote as compared to Nixon's 95 per cent. He also was unable to win back much of the Catholic vote that Nixon had lost in 1960 to his Catholic opponent. Goldwater won 24 per cent of the Catholic vote, a small improvement over Nixon's 22 per cent. Neither compared to the 49 per cent which Eisenhower had won in 1956.

Of the 435 Congressional districts, Goldwater carried 60. Forty-four were in the South. For the rest, Goldwater carried six districts in Southern California, five in suburban Chicago, capital of the old right, and scattered districts elsewhere, including Arizona.

Goldwater's triumph was the Deep South. On his coattails, Republican Congressmen were elected in Mississippi and Georgia, five in Alabama. In South Carolina, one Democratic Congressman converted. But to win in the Deep South, Goldwater sacrificed the more racially moderate states of the outer South, which Eisenhower and Nixon had won. In Texas, two Republican Congressmen were defeated. In the Upper South, the traditional Republican vote in the mountains fell by ten percentage points. Goldwater's coalition was not the Eisenhower combination of the mountains and the new suburbs of the cities. Goldwater's vote was based in the rural black belts of the Deep South. Statistically, it correlated most closely not to the vote for Eisenhower or Nixon but to the States Rights Party of Strom Thurmond in 1948.[7] By sweeping the black belts, Goldwater improved on Nixon's showing in the eleven states of the Old Confederacy by 1.9 percentage points, though he still lost the region by a narrow margin. To achieve this result, Goldwater turned away the national black vote, which fell from 32 per cent Republican in 1960 to 6 per cent Republican in 1964.

16

THE COMEBACK
OF RICHARD NIXON

If the 1964 election was a fiasco for the Republicans, it was equally a breakthrough for the Democrats. Not since the 1930s had the majority party been able to enact extensive social legislation. Before the election, in 1964, the Democrats were able to pass anti-poverty legislation and the Civil Rights Act of 1964. After the election, in 1965, the Democratic Congress was even more active. The major landmarks were medical care for the aged, federal aid to education, a housing program, immigration reform, the Voting Rights Act, and aid to the depressed Appalachian region. In 1966, the momentum slowed, but the Congress did increase funding for existing programs and pass new legislation affecting the cities and highway safety.

Much of this success was owing to the legislative talents of President Lyndon B. Johnson. But the "Great Society" also benefited from the sectarian candidacy of Barry Goldwater in 1964. The Democrats gained thirty-eight seats in the House and two in the Senate, which gave them roughly two-to-one majorities in both chambers. The civil rights movement and the martyrdom of President John F. Kennedy provided moral impetus to the Democratic program. Still, the political advantage of the Democrats was delicate. What was lacking was a national crisis of the scale of the depression of the 1930s which would affect all Americans and mobilize them behind a reform program. Under the best of circumstances, President Johnson would have had trouble sustaining his plans.

What actually happened was near disaster. After campaigning as a peace candidate, Johnson chose in 1965 to commit American troops to the fighting in Vietnam. Troop commitments increased to 181,000 in 1965, to 389,000 in 1966, and to more than 500,000 in 1967. From the outset, these measures were not popular. The March 6, 1966, Gallup Poll showed the American people supporting Johnson's Vietnam policy by only a 50 to 33 per cent majority. By August 24 of the same year, the level of support had declined to 43 to 39 per cent. By October 25 of 1967, the American people judged it a mistake to have sent troops to Vietnam by a 46 to 44 per cent margin. The May 1, 1968, poll showed the American people divided evenly. Forty-one percent characterized themselves as "hawks" and 41 per cent as "doves" on Vietnam policy.[1] The war split the Democratic coalition that had supported the Great Society. The war also put pressure on the budget and made it difficult to fund programs. Finally, Johnson's desperate efforts to keep the war and the Great Society going at the same time let loose a serious inflation which altered the political and economic agenda in a manner favorable to Republicans.

On the face of it, the combination of anti-poverty legislation and civil rights had won over Afro-Americans for the ruling Democratic coalition. Already two-to-one Democratic, the black vote became nine and ten to one Democratic as a result of progressive legislation. But the efforts of the Democrats to absorb blacks soon ran into difficulties. Instead of pacifying black America, the new consciousness of equal rights seemed to fuel "black rage" over existing conditions. From 1964 to 1968, the urban, black ghettoes, North and South, were set aflame by riots. The worst of them were the Watts riot in Los Angeles in 1965 in which thirty-four blacks were killed by National Guard troops called in to restore order; the Detroit and Newark riots in 1967 in which forty-three and twenty-five persons were killed; and the nationwide—including Washington, D.C.—rioting that followed the assassination of Martin Luther King, Jr., in 1968. Emerging from the ghettoes and an atmosphere of violence were varieties of black nationalist and Marxist-Leninist ideology which challenged liberal Democracy for the allegiance of urban blacks.

These developments on the battlefields of Southeast Asia and urban America divided and demoralized the Democratic Party. The party distintegrated into three factions. Governor George Wallace of Alabama led Southern rural Democrats opposed to civil rights legislation and favoring a hard line on law and order. In the primaries of Wisconsin, Indiana, and Maryland in 1964, Wallace took his campaign with some success to the rural residents and blue-collar workers of the North. A second faction consisted of those strongly opposed to the war, strongly in favor of civil rights, and to some degree sympathetic with "black militants." This group, which consisted of both blacks and whites, found leaders in 1968 in Senator Eugene McCarthy of Minnesota and Senator Robert F. Kennedy of New York. Finally, there were the embattled New Dealers who favored civil rights, but supported the Vietnam War as an application of anti-Communist internationalism. The AFL-CIO unions were in this camp. Its leader was Vice President Hubert Humphrey.

War abroad and riot and assassination at home constituted a crisis that overshadowed the social reforms of the early Johnson years. Having lost both its right and its left wings, the New Deal coalition had trouble governing the country. Other political forces came forward to claim power. One such force was the "New Politics" which based itself in the anti-war movement. The theorists of this movement argued that the old Roosevelt coalition was moribund and that new trends in the labor force, primarily the decline of blue-collar and the rise of white-collar labor, were making for a liberalism different from the old, labor-oriented New Deal. The New Politics movement asserted that, in "post-industrial" society, "quality of life" issues, such as consumer safety and environmental quality, were taking precedence over economic, bread-and-butter questions. At its edges, the New Politics tended to merge with the counterculture which opposed industrialism for new values which stressed

community, spirituality, pacifism, experimentation with drugs
and a unisexual style. The counterculture was based in youth
ghettoes around universities and recruited from groups not
well integrated into the work force.

The other force seeking a new majority was the Republican
Party led by Richard Nixon. These two seemed an improbable
claimant. Nixon had been defeated for President in 1960 and
had lost an election for governor of California in 1962. The
Republican Party had been defeated by a close margin in 1960,
then routed in 1964. But in defeat, Goldwater had demonstrated that there were Republican possibilities in the Deep
South. In winning the Republican nomination, he had shown
the elan of Republicans from the new cities of the "Sun Belt"—
namely, Southern California, the Southwest, Texas, and
Florida.

For Nixon, the "comeback" began with the Goldwater election. Unlike moderate Republican governors who, for the most
part, put a maximum of distance between themselves and the
Goldwater candidacy, Nixon campaigned hard for Goldwater
across the country. In that manner he won the gratitude of the
Republican right in hard times. Nixon told William F. Buckley,
Jr., in 1967 that "Barry Goldwater found out you can't win an
important election with only the right wing behind you. . . .
But I found out in 1962 that you can't win an election without
the right wing."[2] In 1962 Nixon had repudiated the John
Birch Society and the extreme right in the Republican primary,
but had gone on to lose the governorship to Edmund G.
Brown, Sr. After serving as a faithful foot soldier in the Goldwater campaign, Nixon emerged, according to a January 17,
1965, Gallup Poll, as the first choice of the Republican county
chairmen for the next Presidential nomination. A March 24
poll showed Nixon even stronger among the party's rank and
file who preferred him by 36 per cent to Henry Cabot Lodge's
16 per cent, George Romney's 14 per cent, and Barry Goldwater's 11 per cent.

Nixon's problem—and his ambition—was to put together a
coalition that could win not only the nomination in 1968 but

also the election. Indeed, Nixon desired to use the occasion of the Democratic Party's disarray to construct a "new majority" that could win not only the 1968 Presidential election but succeeding Presidential and Congressional elections. His first efforts were crowned with success. In 1966, Nixon hired a young conservative editorial writer from the St. Louis *Globe-Democrat,* Patrick Buchanan, and committed himself to campaign nationally for Republican candidates in an enterprise known as "Congress '66." When voters repudiated the Democrats at the polls, Nixon was vindicated. In 1966, the Republicans gained forty-seven House seats, three Senate seats, and eight governorships. The GOP had not done so well since 1946.

By 1967, strong competition for the 1968 Presidential nomination had developed from Nixon's left. The Eastern moderates had united behind a Midwestern governor, George Romney of Michigan. For a time, Romney, who had the backing of Governor Nelson Rockefeller of New York, led both Nixon and President Johnson in the polls. But the well-meaning governor proved unable to sustain his campaign, which collapsed on the eve of the first Presidential primary in New Hampshire. Richard Nixon began his triumphal procession through the primaries virtually without opposition. Finally, in Oregon, Nixon had some real, though absentee, opposition from Governor Ronald Reagan of California. More than Nixon, Reagan was the heir of Goldwater as the leader of the right wing of the party. Reagan had inspired the conservative faithful with a nationally televised address during the 1964 campaign and in 1966 had won the governorship of California by almost a million votes.

Like Nixon, Reagan was a man of Southern California. Born in Tampico, Illinois, the son of an unsuccessful traveling shoe salesman, Reagan first worked as a sportscaster in Iowa. Then he came West to make his way as an actor in the motion picture industry. Politically, Reagan was originally an ADA liberal. He became disillusioned after World War II when, as president of the Screens Actors Guild, he encountered jurisdictional disputes with other unions and Communist influence within the guild. By 1952, he voted for Eisenhower. In 1954, he became host of the "General Electric Theatre" on television and pitched conservative ideology in tours of company plants. As Governor, Reagan led the reaction to the activist, New Deal-style government of the Brown years.

Even after Nixon's victory in the neighboring state of Oregon, Reagan was a threat by virtue of his control of the California delegation and his appeal in the South. Nixon moved to head off that challenge by meeting, like Rockefeller and Reagan, with Southern Republican state chairmen in Atlanta and impressing them with his views on race and national defense. "Southern Strategy," which amounted to protection of his right flank, was imperative both to Nixon's nomination and election. The support of Senator Strom Thurmond of South Carolina, former Dixiecrat candidate for President in 1948, stood him in good stead in both campaigns.

At the Republican convention in Miami, Nixon was nominated on the first ballot with 692 votes out of a possible 1333. Nixon had broad support in the South, Midwest, and West. Most of Rockefeller's 277 votes, beginning with his own New York delegation, came from the East. Almost half of Reagan's 182 votes were accounted for by his home state of California.

The bland campaign Nixon waged in the fall was based on the premise that the Democrats had defeated themselves by factional warfare at their Chicago convention. Nixon positioned himself to the right of Hubert Humphrey on law-and-order, refused to commit himself on Vietnam on the grounds that it would undercut negotiations, and waited for nature to take its course. This strategy almost put Hubert Humphrey into the White House, but Nixon managed to hold on and to win with 43.4 per cent of the vote in a three-way race with Humphrey, who won 42.7 per cent, and George Wallace, who gathered 13.5 per cent of the vote.

Some strategists in the Nixon camp were subsequently to argue that the 1968 results were really a conservative mandate. All that was necessary was to combine the Nixon and Wallace votes, and one had the impressive figure of 57 per cent voting for conservative candidates. The American Independent Party was to be viewed as a prelude, like other third parties in the past, to a realignment of the parties in America. The best known exponent of this view was Kevin Phillips, an aide to John N. Mitchell, Nixon's campaign manager, who made the argument in a book published in 1969 by Arlington House, *The Emerging Republican Majority*. Phillips argued that the main factor making for a Republican majority was race:

> The principal factor which broke up the Democratic (New Deal) coalition is the Negro socioeconomic revolution and liberal Democratic ideological inability to cope with it. Democratic "Great Society" programs aligned that party with many Negro demands, but the party was unable to defuse the racial tension sundering the nation. The South, the West and the Catholic sidewalks of New York were focal points of conservative opposition to the welfare liberalism of the federal government; however, the general opposition which deposed the Democratic Party came in large part from prospering Democrats who objected to Washington dissipating their tax dollars on programs which did them no good. The Democratic Party fell victim to the ideological impetus of a liberalism which had carried it beyond programs taxing the few for the benefit of the many (the New Deal) to programs taxing the many on behalf of the few (the Great Society).[3]

Phillips maintained that this revolt against the Great Society was essentially "populist": "The South, the West and the Catholic sidewalks of New York were the focal points. . . ." This new "populist conservatism" held the Great Society responsible for the urban riots. It also perceived the blacks and well-to-do allied in a "Negro-Establishment entente." According to Phillips, the Establishment no longer consisted of stuffy, conservative bankers:

> Today's Establishment is liberal: New Deal liberalism institutionalized. There is considerable confusion over this, especially among those who came of voting age before the Nineteen-Sixties. They will continue to be a majority of the electorate for many years, and they grew up thinking of the national Establishment as conservative. Until the Nineteen-Sixties, the Establishment *was*

basically conservative—the perpetuation of exhausted Coolidge-Mellon-Hoover politics—but in recent years, a new *liberal* Establishment has replaced it.

A full political cycle has passed since a conservative Establishment harassed the new administration of Franklin D. Roosevelt. Who can doubt that today's Establishment—the great metropolitan newspapers, the Episcopal and other churches, the Supreme Court, Beacon Hill and Manhattan's fashionable East Side—to some extent reflects the institutionalization of a successful New Deal, just as the Roosevelt-baiting press lords, industrialists and Supreme Court justices of the Nineteen-Thirties represented a weakening conservative Establishment rooted in the post–Civil War reign of industrial laissez faire and political Republicanism? A new Establishment—the media, universities, conglomerate corporations, research and development corporations—has achieved much of the power of the industrial and financial establishment dethroned politically by the New Deal. This new Establishment thrives on a government vastly more powerful than that deplored by the business titans of the Nineteen-Thirties.[4]

Thus, the "liberal Establishment" did not consist of banks and industrial corporations; rather, it was the "New Deal institutionalized." It controlled the cultural institutions and the communications industry—the "knowledge industry." It was dependent upon federal money and private endowments. Indeed, this Establishment ran the federal government itself.

Nixon and Mitchell denied that *The Emerging Republican Majority* was an authorized account of their political strategy, but the book did have a vogue in Nixon political circles. If Nixon had publicly endorsed the Phillips book, he would, in effect, have thrown in with the right wing of his party. The concept of a liberal establishment, the scorn for the Northeast, the hopes for an alliance of the West, South, and Catholics, the bluntness about race, the desire to compete for the Wallace vote, were all notions that were essential to a right-wing strategy for victory. But victory strategies, especially Southern strategies, came in different varieties. The first Republican to break through in the South was Eisenhower who won the Outer South states by combining mountain and urban votes. This was a quite different approach to the South than competing for black belt votes in the Deep South with thinly disguised race apppeals.

Nixon described himself as a "centrist." Faced with this choice, his instinct was to do both, to do neither, or to take a little bit from both sides of the question. This tendency was deeply rooted in his personal history and political career. Sociologically, Nixon had the profile of a conservative Republican. He grew up in the towns of Yorba Linda and Whittier in Orange County, a notoriously conservative area even for Southern California. His parents were Midwesterners who had migrated to California in search of a better life. Nixon's father had tried to make it as a lemon rancher and failed. He then made a modest success of a general store and gasoline station. In his memoirs, Nixon described his father as a "hard line Ohio Republican."

Yet Nixon's father was capable of liberal moods, and Nixon's mother was a Quaker. The father voted for Robert LaFollette, Sr., a liberal Republican who was running on a third party Progressive ticket in 1924. Young Nixon's favorite professors at Whittier College were also liberal: "The populist elements of my father's politics, the Progressive influence of Paul Smith, the iconoclasm of Albert Upton, and the Christian humanism of Dr. Coffin gave my early thinking a very liberal, almost populist, tinge."[5] As a result of experience as a college debater, "I became a convinced free trader and remain so to this day."[6]

From Whittier, Nixon went to Duke to study law and then returned home to join a law practice. After an unhappy experience at the Office of Price Administration, he served during World War II with the South Pacific Combat Air Transport Command. By the time Nixon was elected to Congress, his politics had evolved in a more conservative direction. His voting record showed him to be slightly to the left of the regulars, but not liberal enough to qualify him as a liberal Republican. In other words, his record made him a "centrist"—understood as the center of the Republican Party—which placed him well to the right on the American political spectrum.

Nixon became famous for the Red-baiting campaigns he ran against Jerry Voorhis for Congress and Helen Gahagan Douglas for the Senate. These campaigns were not original. His effort to tie Voorhis to the Political Action Committee of the Congress of Industrial Organizations was a standard Republican tactic in 1946. His "Pink Lady" campaign against Douglas in 1950 was modeled on the "Red Pepper" tactics that George Smathers used to defeat Claude Pepper in the Democratic Senatorial primary in Florida. The choice before the electorate, Nixon said, was nothing less than one between "freedom and state socialism." These tactics identified Nixon with the right wing of his party.

This identification was strengthened by the Hiss case. As a member of the House Un-American Activities Committee, Nixon took the lead in the investigation of Alger Hiss's relationship with a former Communist functionary, Whittaker Chambers. The accused was president of the Carnegie Endowment for International Peace. Conservative Republicans were anxious to establish a relationship between Communism and internationalist foreign policy. The Hiss case, which led to Hiss's conviction on a charge of perjury, seemed to do this and made a hero of Nixon on the right.

Curiously, Nixon considered himself an internationalist. One of his most important experiences as a Congressman was to serve on the Herter Committee which investigated Europe's need for aid. "Most of my advisers in California were pleased with my appointment," Nixon reported, "but they wanted the committee's report to disown the bipartisan Truman-Vandenberg foreign policy that was being promulgated in Washington to support the Marshall Plan."[7] In fact, the Herter Committee visited Europe and made a report strongly endorsing aid on the scale of the Marshall Plan. In a poll, Nixon discovered that 75 per cent of his constituents were opposed to foreign aid, but he went ahead and voted for the Marshall Plan anyway after making an effort to educate his district.

Because of his views on foreign policy, Nixon immediately responded to the internationalist candidacy of General Dwight

Eisenhower. Thomas Dewey, governor of New York and former Republican nominee for President, saw Nixon as the ideal running-mate for Eisenhower. Nixon was young and associated with a major issue for the Republicans—Communism in government. As a Californian identified with the right, he would provide both geographic and political balance to the ticket, while at the same time having the right views on foreign policy. Finally, Nixon had proved to be a gut fighter in political campaigns and could perform this distasteful chore for Eisenhower. "In a sense," Nixon later wrote, "the hero needed a point man."[8]

As Vice President, Nixon served as the Administration's emissary to the right wing of the party. Only very reluctantly did he repudiate the performance of Joe McCarthy. Nixon also led the party in its "rocking, socking" off-year election campaigns in 1954 and 1958, but was not able to show much in the way of results. Because of this conservative, partisan identity, there was an effort, led by Harold Stassen, to remove him from the ticket in 1956, but nothing came of it. Instead, Nixon developed into the heir apparent to Eisenhower.

In the 1960 campaign for President against Senator John F. Kennedy of Massachusetts, Nixon was convinced that he faced the "most ruthless group of political operators ever mobilized for a presidential campaign." Comparing himself to his opponent, Nixon found:

> Our differences were distinct. He preached the orthodox gospel of government activism, making sweeping promises and issuing rhetorical challenges to leap ahead into an era of new leadership and social welfare. I carried the banner of constructive post-war Republicanism, bred of conservative beliefs that a healthy private sector and individual initiative set the best pace for prosperity and progress. But beyond these differences, the way the Kennedys played politics and the way the media let them get away with it left me angry and frustrated.[9]

The 1960 defeat evidently left Nixon embittered. It was one more episode in which the media and the establishment had done him dirty. In 1952, the New York *Herald Tribune* and

Eisenhower's advisors had wanted to drop him from the ticket as a result of the affair concerning a private contributors' fund to defray his expenses as a Congressman. In 1956, "White House intrigues" had kept him on edge regarding his place on the ticket. Now the media and the Kennedys had kept him out of the White House. "From this point on," Nixon wrote, "I had the wisdom and wariness of someone who had been burned by the power of the Kennedys and their money and the license they were given by the media. I vowed that I would never again enter an election at a disadvantage by being vulnerable to them—or anyone—on the level of political tactics."[10]

Nonetheless, Nixon did not enter the White House in 1969, bent on a vendetta against the "liberal Establishment." Both his staff and his policies were a mixed assortment. His staff consisted mainly of friends, experts, and associates from Southern California, New York (where he practiced law while out of office), and the Eisenhower Administration. His policies were a mixture of retrenchment and modest progress. The tendency was not to crusade against the New Deal or the New Politics but to coopt them, particularly the New Dealers who were upset with the "new isolationism" in foreign policy and the sectarian flamboyance in domestic policy of the New Politics. Senator Henry Jackson, Democrat of Washington, was asked to become Secretary of Defense. Hubert Humphrey was offered the U.S. ambassadorship to the United Nations. Both men declined. On the other hand, Daniel Patrick Moynihan, a Harvard professor and a former Assistant Secretary of Labor, accepted a high staff position in the White House.

For a year and a half, Moynihan was influential with President Nixon and made a lasting impression with his notion that Nixon could preside, like Prime Minister Benjamin Disraeli in 19th-century England, over a spell of "Tory reform." Moynihan himself was whipsawed between his preference for progressive social measures and his distaste for the cultural style of the new liberals. Moynihan made a not very convincing case that his design for welfare reform, the Family Assistance Plan, was conservative in principle because it delivered hard cash to

the recipients rather than social services provided by bureaucrats. One could easily reverse the argument. The plan put
more people on the dole. It redistributed income. Yet the FAP
did have work incentives. Welfare reform became the centerpiece of the Nixon Administration's domestic efforts in 1969.

In *The New Majority*, Patrick Buchanan evoked the flavor of
the early months of the Nixon administration:

> His victory pledge to "bring us together," his Inaugural call for
> Americans to "go forward together," were models of reconcili-
> ation and restraint. His White House staff was structured to re-
> flect the nation's political diversity with Goldwater conservatives in
> uneasy harness with Ripon liberals, and Rockefeller Republicans
> like Henry Kissinger entering the Presidential service alongside
> Kennedy Democrats like Daniel Moynihan.
>
> To achieve a truce, an armistice with his adversaries, the Presi-
> dent in effect offered more: to forego the victor's prerogative of
> purging the Democratic bureaucracy and to renew the lease on
> most of the Great Society programs dear to their hearts. In
> exchange, he sought a decent interval to initiate and carry out his
> plan to end with honor American involvement in the Vietnam
> War.
>
> Eight months into his presidency, the unwritten understanding
> collapsed.[11]

Buchanan maintained that the "political truce with the nation's Liberal Establishment had been broken by them, not by
him" over the Vietnam War. In October 1969, hundreds of
thousands of people protested the war in a nationwide "Moratorium." Compared to previous war protests, the Moratorium
was more widely tolerated and encouraged. This is the event
that Buchanan believed was the violation of the "unwritten understanding" Nixon had with the governing class of the country. The "Liberal Establishment" was to leave the President
alone in foreign policy and the President would leave the Liberal Establishment alone in domestic policy.

Whether the "Liberal Establishment" was ever aware of the
terms of this "truce" is doubtful. In any event, President Nixon
confronted the anti-war movement and prevailed with his "Silent Majority" speech of November 3, 1969. After it, Nixon's

Gallup Poll rating climbed from 56 per cent approval to 68 per cent approval in a month's time. In the speech, the President defined the "Nixon Doctrine" which he had first suggested to reporters on the island of Guam the previous summer:

—First, the United States will keep all of its treaty commitments.
—Second, we shall provide a shield if a nuclear power threatens the freedom of a nation allied with us or of a nation whose survival we consider vital to our security.
—Third, in cases involving other types of aggression, we shall furnish military and economic assistance when requested in accordance with our treaty commitments. But we shall look to the nation directly threatened to assume the primary responsibility of providing the manpower for its defense.[12]

The Nixon Doctrine was a renewal of Eisenhower-Dulles foreign policy. The United States would continue to assert itself as a great power, particularly in the Pacific, but it would avoid committing its ground troops against the bottomless well of Asian manpower. The United States would defend its interests through the use of air and sea power and through its substantial wealth. Ground troops would be held back as a worldwide strategic reserve. America's allies in Asia and elsewhere would be expected to supply the manpower in their own defense.

President Nixon told reporters on his stopover in Guam that "if we are going to have peace in the world, that potentially the greatest threat to that peace will be in the Pacific." He cited precedents: "Also, as we look over the historical perspective, while World War II began in Europe, for the United States it began in the Pacific. It came from Asia. The Korean War came from Asia. The Vietnamese war came from Asia."[13] However, in an article for *Foreign Affairs* before his election as President, Nixon made clear that he did not regard Asia as only a source of danger. While China must be contained, it was still possible to make overtures to the Chinese, for "we simply cannot afford to leave China forever outside the family of nations." In his attitude toward Asia, there was a touch of the messianic spirit traditional with Republicans:

Poverty that was accepted for centuries as the norm is accepted no longer. In a sense it could be said that a new chapter is being written in the winning of the West: in this case, a winning of the promise of Western technology and Western organization by the nations of the East. The cultural clash has had its costs and produced its strains, but out of it is coming a modernization of ancient civilizations that promises to leap the centuries.[14]

Symbolically, the President ruled the country, in part, from his "Casa Pacifica" in San Clemente, California.

The main obstacle to this lovely vision was Vietnam where Nixon had inherited a ground war from the Democrats. The President clearly hoped to apply the Nixon Doctrine to Vietnam as well. In this case, the United States could not move forward guided by the doctrine. In addition, the strategic balance no longer permitted a nuclear ultimatum modeled on Eisenhower's action toward China in 1953. The United States would have to back into the principles of the doctrine by undoing American involvement in a ground war. It would have to "Vietnamize" the war. As Secretary of Defense Melvin Laird, the apostle of Vietnamization, always pointed out, Vietnamizing the war did not necessarily mean ending it. As Vietnamese were substituted for Americans in the ground fighting, the United States would make itself felt by immense applications of air power. Nixon had made known his preference for air and sea power in fighting the war as far back as 1965.[15] Unlike Korea, the United States would not permit privileged sanctuaries to the enemy, particularly if they were minor powers. It would bomb Cambodia and any part of North Vietnam, if necessary. It would invade Cambodia and permit the invasion of Laos. The U.S. would also try to put pressure on Hanoi by striking a bargain with the Soviet Union.

There were profound weaknesses in this policy. The regimes in North Vietnam and South Vietnam were not well matched. That was why American ground troops had been necessary in the first place. It was unlikely that bombing could make up the difference of 500,000 American soldiers. Then there was the anti-war movement at home. The Nixon policy would require time, time that domestic politics at home might not make available.

Like Johnson before him, Nixon came to see the anti-war movement as a prime threat to his war policy and to the viability of his presidency. In an October 7, 1969, column for the Washington *Post*, David Broder suggested that the anti-war movement was trying to do to Nixon what it had done to Johnson—drive him out of office. Entitled "The Breaking of the President," this column was closely read within the White House. Broder aside, Nixon became incensed at what he considered a pattern of media sympathy with the anti-war movement. If the President's Silent Majority speech was a low-key confrontation with the movement, Vice President Spiro Agnew expressed things in more direct terms. A few days after the Moratorium, in New Orleans, Agnew deplored the protest demonstrations which he saw as an expression of a "spirit of national masochism," which was encouraged by an "effete corps of impudent snobs who characterize themselves as intellectuals." At the end of October, in Harrisburg, Pennsylvania, Agnew put things in grand, new majority terms:

> Think about it. Small bands of students are allowed to shut down great universities. Small groups of dissidents are allowed to shout down political candidates. Small cadres of professional protesters are allowed to jeopardize the peace efforts of the President of the United States.
>
> It is time to question the credentials of their leaders. And, if in questioning we disturb a few people, I say it is time for them to be disturbed. If, in challenging, we polarize the American people, I say it is time for a positive polarization.
>
> It is time for a healthy in-depth examination of policies and a constructive realignment in this country. It is time to rip away the rhetoric and to divide on authentic lines. It is time to discard the fiction that in a country of 200 million people, everyone is qualified to quarterback the government.[16]

In November, in Des Moines, Iowa, Agnew took the fight to the media. Invoking the Silent Majority speech, Agnew complained that the President's "words and policies were subjected to instant analysis and querulous criticism" by the television networks. He took the American Broadcasting Company to task in particular for letting W. Averell Harriman, a Paris negotiator under the Democrats, comment on Nixon's address. "Like Coleridge's Ancient Mariner," Agnew said, "Mr. Harriman seems to be under some heavy compulsion to justify his failures to anyone who will listen."[17] Six months later in Cleveland, Agnew expanded the indictment of Harriman and conjured up the spirit of the early 1950s: "As one looks back over the diplomatic disasters that have befallen the West and the friends of the West over three decades at Teheran, Yalta, Cairo—in every great diplomatic conference that turned out to be a loss for the West and freedom, one can find the unmistakable footprints of W. Averell Harriman."[18] Finally, in Montgomery, Alabama, a week after the Des Moines speech, Agnew completed the cycle of denunciation by attacking the Washington *Post* and New York *Times*.

The Silent Majority speech of Nixon and the diatribes of Agnew marked the end of the balanced, moderate government of Nixon's first nine months. Vice President Agnew conjured up a new vision: the politics of "positive polarization." President Nixon, whose speechwriters put words in Agnew's mouth, now calculated that, if he could force an electoral division along the lines of the anti-war movement and counterculture, the results would be highly favorable to the Republican Party. So, why not "rip away the rhetoric and divide on authentic lines"?

17

THE SILENT MAJORITY

Even before the enunciation of positive polarization by Agnew, there were some prefigurative episodes in the Nixon Administration. In pursuit of a de-Americanized war, President Nixon ordered early in his Administration the bombing of the enemy's sanctuaries in Cambodia. The military logic of this move was unassailable. The problem was that Cambodia was a neutral country and Nixon lacked the authority to order acts of war on her. Consequently, the bombing of Cambodia was a closely held secret, and the United States Air Force kept secret records on the course of these operations. It was not surprising that the Administration was obsessed by the possibility of "leaks" on this subject. When the inevitable report of the bombing appeared in the New York *Times* in the spring of 1969, the White House panicked and asked the FBI for seventeen wiretaps of newsmen and strategically placed aides, especially members of Henry Kissinger's National Security Council staff. When White House relations with FBI Director J. Edgar Hoover deteriorated, the White House became fearful that these wiretap reports would be used against it. Assistant Attorney-General for Internal Security Robert Mardian obtained them in 1971 from William C. Sullivan, an Administration ally who was head of the FBI's Domestic Intelligence Division. Subsequently, Hoover fired Sullivan. The Administration found a job for Sullivan as director of the Office of National Narcotics Intelligence within the Justice Department.

The Nixon Administration's struggle with the FBI was typical of its relations with the permanent bureaucracy in Washington as a whole. The White House saw itself not as the accepted head of government but as an outpost in enemy territory. Each foot of ground outside the gates had to be won by fire and sword. To some degree this attitude was common to any new administration in Washington. In *A Thousand Days* Arthur Schlesinger, Jr., noted:

> In the thirties conservatives had bemoaned the expansion of the federal government as a threat to freedom. Instead they should have hailed the bureaucracy as a bulwark against change. The permanent government soon developed its own stubborn vested interests in policy and procedure, its own cozy alliances with committees of Congress, its own ties to the press, its own national constituencies. It began to exude the feeling that Presidents could come and go but it went on forever. The permanent government was, as such, politically neutral; its essential commitment was to doing things as they had been done before. This frustrated the enthusiasts who came to Washington with Eisenhower in 1953 zealous to dismantle the New Deal, and it frustrated the enthusiasts who came to Washington with Kennedy in 1961 zealous to get the country moving again.[1]

This same zeal existed within the Nixon Administration. The Republican *philosophy* of government preached that limited government was good and big government was bad. Conservative Republicans, men like Robert Mardian, who was Goldwater's Western regional coordinator in 1964, thus found themelves in a paradoxical position in 1969. They were the symbolic heads of everything they despised.

If anything, this attitude grew stronger as time went by. Nixon entered office determined to strengthen Cabinet government, but he soon realized that Cabinet government meant playing the game by the bureaucracy's rules. The primary goal of the second term came to be a reorganization that would humble the bureaucracy. Control would mean centralizing decision-making power in the White House, and it would mean determining the personnel several layers deep within the departments and agencies. Thus Nixon demanded the resignation of *all* noncareer officials the day after his reelection victory in 1972.

The model for reorganization was the National Security Council. From the outset, President Nixon and his Assistant for National Security Affairs, Henry Kissinger, made the NSC the main forum for decision-making in the foreign affairs area. The Department of State, the Department of Defense, the Central Intelligence Agency all had to go through the NSC mechanism in order to set policy. The NSC staff prepared the anlayses and proposals, and Henry Kissinger chaired the key interdepartmental committees in the national security area. In 1970, a Domestic Council with John Ehrlichman as director was established on the NSC model. However, the Domestic Council never achieved in the domestic sphere the authority of the National Security Council over foreign affairs. This form of organization posed Constitutional problems because the real authority was in the White House. White House personnel did not have to be confirmed by the Senate and could claim executive privilege if summoned to testify before Congress.

Another shift to the right that predated the proclamation of "positive polarization" by Agnew was the application of "Southern strategy" to civil rights. In this area, Nixon made an attempt in the campaign to pursue what he thought was a moderate position by advocating "freedom of choice" plans as a form of gradual integration. This advocacy was feckless since the Supreme Court had already found on May 27, 1968, in the *Green* case that freedom of choice was not adequate.

Once in office, Nixon and his associates quickly discovered that the legal realities were quite different than they had imagined. Under pressure from party chairmen in the South and Harry Dent, a former aide to Senator Thurmond, in the White House, the Administration searched for a way to slow down the pace of integration. On July 3, after much pulling and hauling, Attorney-General John N. Mitchell and Secretary of Health, Education and Welfare Robert Finch announced that the Administration would now rely less on fund cut-offs by HEW and more on court suits in order to achieve the integration of the schools. Such an approach would shift the burden of enforcement onto the courts.

Later in the summer, Finch intervened in the case of thirty-three school districts in Mississippi which had already developed plans acceptable to HEW and asked the federal courts to slow down the process and thus reverse his own department and previous court findings. This action provoked protests by lawyers in the Civil Rights Division of the Department of Justice, several of whom resigned. The U.S. Commission on Civil Rights was also critical of the Administration's performance in the civil rights field. The Mississippi case made its way to the Supreme Court which reversed lower court rulings and ordered that integration must take place "at once."

Finch was unable to withstand the struggles over civil rights in his department. The leaders of the conservative faction were his executive assistant, L. Patrick Gray, a veteran of the 1960 Nixon Presidential campaign, and HEW's general counsel, Robert Mardian. The leaders of the liberal group were Jack Veneman, a California liberal and Under Secretary, and Leon Panetta, a former aide to Republican Senator Thomas Kuchel of California, and director of the Office of Civil Rights. In early 1970, under pressure from the White House, Panetta was fired. In a letter, HEW employees demanded clarification of U.S. civil rights policy from President Nixon, who issued a long statement on March 24. Not long after, Finch himself was kicked upstairs to the position of Presidential Counsellor. Since Finch, as a longtime friend and aide to Richard Nixon, was regarded as titular leader of the moderate forces within the Administration, his removal from HEW in 1970 was a serious setback for the moderate cause.

In the Justice Department, John Mitchell, a former law partner of Nixon in the New York firm of Nixon, Mudge, Rose, Guthrie, Alexander & Mitchell, struck a blow for Southern strategy when he recommended that the Voting Rights Act of 1965 not be renewed for another five years. Since its enactment black voter registration in the South had increased from

29 to 52 per cent. The Administration argued that the act was regional legislation, since its formulae effectively ruled out all states but six Southern ones. The Justice Department prepared a substitute measure which would apply to all states but which would also critically weaken enforcement procedures. States would no longer have to obtain the prior approval of the U.S. Attorney-General for any change in their voting laws. The House of Representatives passed the substitute measure, but it failed in the Senate. Mitchell had better luck with "preventive detention" and "no knock" provisions of a crime bill for the District of Columbia. Preventive detention would allow certain dangerous criminals to be detained without bail before trial, and no knock would allow police with a search warrant to enter a home without prior announcement under some circumstances. The law, the District of Columbia Reorganization and Criminal Procedure Act of 1970, was intended to make of the nation's capital a model of criminal procedure. It affected a black majority city.

Mitchell, along with Harry Dent, also produced nominees for the U.S. Supreme Court to fulfill Nixon's theory that the Court needed more "balance" and that the South needed a conservative, not just Hugo Black, to represent it. The nomination was to replace Abe Fortas who had resigned under a cloud of financial impropriety. Thus, when the Administration proposed Clement F. Haynsworth, a South Carolinian on the Fourth Circuit Court of Appeals, liberal Democrats quickly turned the tables on the Republicans and questioned the propriety of Haynsworth purchasing the Brunswick Corporation's stock after having ruled on a case involving it. The Haynsworth nomination failed. President Nixon then instructed Dent to "go out and this time find a good federal judge farther down South and further to the right."[2] Dent came up with G. Harrold Carswell of Florida, recently confirmed by the U.S. Senate for the Fifth Circuit Court of Appeals. The Carswell nomination also failed. President Nixon denounced these results:

> I have reluctantly concluded—with the Senate as presently constituted—I cannot successfully nominate to the Supreme Court any Federal appellate judge from the South who believes as I do in

the strict construction of the Constitution. Judges Carswell and Haynsworth have endured with admirable dignity vicious assaults on their intelligence, their honesty, and their character. They have been falsely charged with being racist. But when all the hypocrisy is stripped away, the real issue was their philosophy of strict construction of the Constitution, a philosophy that I share, and the fact that they had the misfortune of being born in the South.[3]

In the calculus of Southern strategy, defeats could be as important as victories if they dramatized the Administration's positions to the Southern voter. The Haynsworth and Carswell nominations failed, but they failed spectacularly. Mitchell failed to derail the Voting Rights Act and had to accept a compromise measure, but no one missed the point of the exercise. The Administration was overruled by the Supreme Court in its effort to slow down the pace of integration. Undaunted, the Administration tried to take the credit when the more rapid pace of integration was accepted by the South.

In 1968, Richard Nixon won the states of the Outer South, not the Deep South which was carried by George Wallace. Nixon's one Deep South state was South Carolina. His strength was thus the reverse of Barry Goldwater's. In the first eighteen months of the Administration, a Southern strategy evolved which indicated that Nixon was not content with five Outer South states but was ready to contend with George Wallace on his own terrain. The Nixon forces also involved themselves directly in Alabama politics. Wallace had been succeeded as governor of Alabama by his wife Lurleen. When she died in office, she was succeeded by Lieutenant Governor Albert Brewer who became independent of Wallace. In a closely contested Democratic primary for the gubernatorial nomination, H. R. Haldeman, White House chief of staff, and Herbert Kalmbach, Nixon's personal lawyer, funneled $400,000 into the Brewer campaign against Wallace. Haldeman also obtained and then leaked to political columnist Jack Anderson information concerning an Internal Revenue Service investigation of George Wallace and his brother Gerald Wallace. Nonetheless, Brewer lost the primary.

In the spring of 1970, President Nixon ordered American intervention against Vietnamese Communist units in Cambodia. Nixon tried to repeat the success of the Silent Majority speech by announcing the "incursion" in a televised address on April 30. However, the public did not respond to the Spenglerian rhetoric of the speech: "My fellow Americans, we live in an age of anarchy, both at home and abroad."[4] Mr. Nixon's speechifying was also in the service of an extension of the war rather than the "Vietnamization" of November 3 of the previous year.

Initially, Nixon seemed unaware of the difference in public response. The next day, he referred to student protesters as "bums." He had cause to regret this remark when on May 4th four students were shot and killed by the Ohio National Guard at Kent State University. Nixon actually tried to reach out to young protesters in an early morning visit to the Lincoln Memorial on May 9th, the dawn of a peaceful protest of 100,000 people. Elsewhere hundreds of schools were closed down or given over to teach-ins on the "Second Indo-China War." At Jackson State, a black school in Mississippi, two black students were killed by the authorities during a demonstration. The country was in the grip of a crisis, and the Nixon Administration was plainly shaken by the massive protests. Some members of the Administration publicly called for a change of course. Commissioner of Education James Allen declared: "We just must withdraw from there as rapidly as we can. The war is having a disastrous effect on the young people of this country."[5] In a letter made public, Secretary of the Interior Walter J. Hickel called on Nixon to silence Agnew and realize that "youth in its protest must be heard." Nixon himself appointed a commission on campus unrest, chaired by former Governor William W. Scranton of Pennsylvania. Regarding its conclusions as too soft, Nixon later put some distance between himself and his commission.

Once recovered from the initial shock of the student response to the Cambodian intervention, Nixon reacted in terms calculated to promote his "new majority." In New York, Mayor John V. Lindsay ordered City Hall's flag flown at half-staff after the Kent State killings. When anti-war students marched on City Hall on May 8 they were intercepted by construction workers who beat them up and raised the flag to full staff. On May 11, two thousand construction workers marched in support of Nixon and the war in the Wall Street district of the city. More "hardhat" demonstrations in other parts of the country followed.

On May 26, President Nixon received twenty-two union leaders including Peter J. Brennan, president of the Building and Construction Trades Council of New York, and Thomas Gleason, general president of the International Longshoremen's Association. From them, Nixon accepted a white hardhat with the words "Commander-in-Chief" printed on the front.

Such gestures were part of Nixon's "Northern strategy," "blue-collar strategy," or "Catholic strategy." The three overlapped. Nixon was determined to recover the support among Catholic blue-collar workers in the North that Republicans enjoyed before the advent of the Kennedy Presidency. His chief aide for such matters was Charles W. Colson, who played an important role in the executive clemency for James R. Hoffa, imprisoned former president of the Teamsters Union. Later, at the end of his first term, Nixon designated Peter Brennan as his Secretary of Labor. The critics within his Administration did not fare so well. Allen was fired in early June; Hickel was let go a few months later.

On June 5, the President and members of his staff met with the leaders of the major intelligence agencies: the Federal Bureau of Investigation, the Central Intelligence Agency, the Defense Intelligence Agency, and the National Security Agency. Nixon directed this group to investigate methods of dealing with the new threats represented by the anti-war movement, New Left terrorists, and the black movement. The White House representative on this committee was Tom Charles Huston, a former president of the Young Americans for Freedom and a veteran of Army counterintelligence.

On June 25, the Interagency Committee on Intelligence (Ad Hoc) submitted its "Special Report," along with a covering

memorandum by Huston recommending the relaxation of restrictions on techniques which were "clearly illegal," such as
mail openings and surreptitious entries. Huston also proposed
a permanent interagency committee to coordinate domestic intelligence and carry out the recommendations of his "plan."[6]
The intelligence agencies including FBI officials in this field,
William C. Sullivan and Charles D. Brennan, were strongly in
favor of Huston's recommendations. In part, they desired Presidential approval for new initiatives; in part, they wanted the
Presidential imprimatur for activities already under way. Sullivan, who was in close touch with Huston, wanted to resume the
"black bag jobs" or surreptitious entries which had been ter-
minated in 1966. The CIA already had a program of mail
openings and was deeply involved in domestic intelligence
through "Operation CHAOS." The National Security Agency
was covering the international communications of thousands of
Americans.

A week after the submission of the report, President Nixon
issued a decision memorandum approving all of Huston's recommendations. The only member of the committee to object
was J. Edgar Hoover, the FBI Director. In 1966, Hoover had
ordered cutbacks in the FBI's use of intrusive techniques including black bag jobs, mail covers, and electronic surveillance.
The FBI was also the principal domestic intelligence agency.
Hoover was therefore not enamored either of the restoration
of intrusive techniques or the plan to "coordinate" the domestic
intelligence activities of the various agencies. Hoover went to
Attorney-General Mitchell, who supported him in his views.
Five days after approving the "Huston plan," President Nixon
rescinded this approval and recalled the memoranda.

The defeat of the Huston plan, which would have removed
all restraints on intrusive intelligence techniques, was undoubtedly a victory for civil liberties. But the episode took place in a
context of massive intelligence programs for domestic surveillance. Since 1956, the FBI had operated COINTELPRO
(Counterintelligence Program), a program of disruptive actions
directed against the Communist Party, USA and against Com-

munist fronts. After three civil rights workers were murdered in Mississippi in 1964, the program was extended to the Ku Klux Klan. After the Newark and Detroit riots in 1967, the program was put in operation against black nationalists. After the Columbia University rebellion in 1968, it was extended to the New Left. In addition, the FBI had hundreds of thousands of names on file under various surveillance programs.

By law the CIA was prohibited from exercising "internal security functions." Nonetheless, during the Vietnam War period, President Johnson and later President Nixon were anxious about the "international connections" of the American left. In addition to two studies of this question in 1967 and 1969, the agency launched Operation CHAOS in 1967. CHAOS ultimately developed files on 7,200 Americans, as well as a general name index of 300,000. The CIA also opened a quarter of a million letters from 1953 to 1973.

After the Army was called in to cope with the Detroit riot and the Pentagon demonstrations of 1967, the Army Chief of Staff approved a plan to collect information on civilians. At one time, the Army had 1,500 operatives in this area. Under public pressure, the program was closed down in June 1970. According to Joseph Califano, a White House aide, the Newark and Detroit riots in 1967 were a "shattering experience" for the Johnson White House and were the occasion for a major effort to improve intelligence gathering. At the direction of Attorney-General Ramsey Clark, Assistant Attorney-General John Doar organized the Interdivision Information Unit to prepare a "master index on individuals, or organizations, and by cities" from all pertinent government agencies from the Community Relations Service to the CIA. By 1970, the IDIU was processing 42,000 reports a year from various government agencies.

While the Nixon Administration approved of these programs, it can be blamed for originating only one of them. In 1969, Tom Charles Huston and Arthur Burns, acting on Nixon's behalf, complained to Internal Revenue Service Commissioner Randolph Thrower that "tax-exempt funds may be supporting activist groups engaged in stimulating riots both on the campus and within our inner cities."[7] In response, the IRS formed the Special Services Staff to do tax investigations of people under suspicion. The names usually came from the FBI or the IDIU. The investigations were undertaken for political, not tax reasons. Before its abolition by Commissioner Donald Alexander in 1973, the SSS maintained files on 11,000 individuals and organizations.

After the episode of the recalled decision memorandum, H. R. Haldeman in August transferred responsibility for domestic intelligence issues to John Dean, the new White House counsel and a protégé of John Mitchell. Dean proposed the creation of an Intelligence Evaluation Committee using the IDIU as a "cover." The IEC attempted to improve coordination of the federal government's intelligence efforts. Substantively, what the intelligence agencies had been doing they continued to do.

When Nixon denounced the U.S Senate for rejecting his nominees for the U.S. Supreme Court, he was careful to add "as presently constituted," for he did not plan to accept a liberal Senate as his fate. Going into the 1970 off-year election, the Democrats controlled fifty-seven seats in the Senate, the Republicans forty-three. Nixon desired that the Republicans win seven additional seats; then they could organize the Senate with the Vice President supplying the tie-breaking vote. The Vice President would also be the engine by which the Republicans would prevail in the election. Nixon had plans for more "positive polarization." No less than four of Nixon's own aides—Bryce Harlow, Martin Anderson, Patrick Buchanan, and William Safire—were assigned to the Agnew campaign. On September 9, Nixon called these men into his office and gave them and other political aides a long briefing: "There's a realignment taking place. Agnew can be a realigner. If he can appeal to one third of the Democrats, we'll win two-thirds of the races. In all your preparing you are talking to the swing vote, the independent voter. That's 5 percent of the people. What we do in this campaign will have an enormous effect on 1972."[8]

The next day, Vice President Agnew took the word to

Springfield, Illinois. The "new majority" was rising up in wrath against the "radical liberals" in the U.S. Senate. "Radical liberal" was a new and important coinage. The Communist Party in the United States was moribund, and there was no advantage in attempting to tie Democrats to Communists. But there was a very active New Left. Vice President Agnew's task was to put the onus of radicalism on the Democrats. "We have to force them to repudiate the left, which loses them votes," President Nixon had explained, "or else to take the left—which gives us the center."[9] This campaign against radical liberalism also translated into a campaign against the Liberal Establishment. Agnew declared:

> Here in Illinois, and across America this fall, there is occurring a second critical phase in the historic contest begun in the fall of 1968—a contest between remnants of the discredited elite that dominated national policy for forty years and a new national majority, forged and led by the President of the United States—a contest to shape the destiny of America.[10]

In his fusillades, Agnew risked splitting his own party. In New York, Senator Charles Goodell, a Republican, was running against a liberal Democrat, Richard Ottinger, and a third party candidate, James L. Buckley, a Conservative and the brother of publicist William F. Buckley, Jr. As a member of the House of Representatives, Goodell had been a staunch conservative Republican, but once appointed to the Senate by Governor Nelson Rockefeller to succeed the martyred Robert F. Kennedy, Goodell became a strong anti-war liberal. For this reason, the White House had no use for him and allowed Agnew to attack him openly and to indicate a preference for Buckley. Goodell lost and Buckley won, but the price the White House paid was to alienate liberal Republicans who felt threatened by the Goodell purge.

During the early stages of the campaign, President Nixon was on a foreign tour. When he returned to Washington, he could not resist the temptation to involve himself directly in the campaign. He had, after all, been the Republicans' chief national campaigner in the off-year elections of 1954, 1958, and 1966. He proceeded to campaign in twenty-three states in three weeks. In San Jose, California, there was an incident in which demonstrators threw rocks at him. Nixon decided to make the most of this occurrence, and in an October 31 speech in Phoenix, Arizona he denounced the "appeasement" of demonstrators and the "creeping permissiveness in our legislatures, in our courts, in our family life, and in our colleges and universities." Yet once more he announced, "The time has come to draw the line. The time has come for the great silent majority of Americans of all ages, of every political persuasion, to stand up and be counted against appeasement of the rock throwers and the obscenity shouters in America."[11]

This speech was televised nationally on the eve of the election. The tape was of poor quality, and Richard Nixon made a bad impression as he delivered a strident stump speech. The Democrats had their Vice-Presidential candidate of 1968, Senator Edmund Muskie of Maine, make a quiet appeal from his home in Maine. It was Muskie who appeared the more "Presidential." The results of the election were mixed. The Republicans lost nine seats in the House but gained two in the Senate. They defeated some "radical liberals" in the Senate, such as Goodell and Albert Gore of Tennessee, but they were routed in the gubernatorial elections, with a net loss of eleven. Except for the governorships, it was a respectable performance for the party in power in an off-year election, but it was by no means a grand "realignment." In the Gallup Poll, Senator Muskie, who had previously run well behind Nixon in trial heats, now ran even.

Nixon sensed that he should take a more constructive approach. Agnew, the realigner, fell into disfavor. John Connally, former Secretary of the Navy and former governor of Texas, joined the Administration as Secretary of the Treasury. There was immediate speculation that Agnew might be dumped in 1972 in favor of Connally. As a conservative Democrat from Texas, Connally was consistent with the new majority and with Southern strategy.

In his State of the Union for 1971, Nixon maintained an edifying tone. He announced that his Administration had "six great goals" in domestic policy. The most surprising of these was the "full employment budget," which in Keynesian economic theory meant a budget which would be in balance at full employment. In practice, this meant a budget in deficit at less than full employment—a heresy according to Republican economics. But Herbert Stein, one of the members, later the chairman, of Nixon's Council of Economic Advisors had pointed out in *The Fiscal Revolution* that Keynesianism did not necessarily imply big government. It only required stimulative deficits at less than full employment. This goal could be reached by tax reductions as easily as by increases in federal spending. In a rare televised interview with four correspondents on January 4, Nixon said, "I am now a Keynesian in economics."[12]

Nixon had not abandoned traditional Republican doctrine. The centerpiece of the speech was revenue sharing by which the federal government would return funds to the states. Five billion dollars would be in the form of "general revenue sharing" which could be used for any purpose by the states and localities. Eleven billion dollars would be in the form of "special revenue sharing" which would be earmarked for certain purposes, such as urban development or manpower training. Most of the money for special revenue sharing would come from the abolition or consolidation of existing federal categorical grants. This proposal had large implications for federal social spending, which would be reduced in favor of more state and local spending. The states and localities would have broad discretion in how to use the revenue sharing funds. Congress took a dim view of revenue sharing, especially special revenue sharing, precisely because it involved a shift in authority.

Nixon also wanted to reorganize eight of the federal government's domestic Cabinet-level departments into four super-departments: Human Resources, Community Development, Natural Resources, and Economic Development. He wanted to pass a 37-point program concerning the environment. The creation of the Environmental Protection Agency symbolized Administration concern in this area. He proposed nothing concerning national health insurance, but he did have a health program that involved greater stress on preventive care and more funds for cancer research. Finally, Nixon still wanted to reform the country's welfare system. These were the six great goals: the full employment budget, revenue sharing, executive reorganization, an environmental program, health proposals, and welfare reform. Together, Nixon claimed, they constituted a "New American Revolution."

Nixon maintained this moderately progressive tack until June 13 when the New York *Times* began to print the "Pentagon Papers," an official record of America's involvement in the Vietnam War up to 1968. Nixon's initial reaction was to pass off the papers as a political embarrassment to the Democrats whose exploits they documented. However, Nixon's Assistant for National Security Affairs, Henry Kissinger, insisted that this wordy security breach endangered current negotiations with China and North Vietnam. When the FBI determined that the papers had been leaked by Daniel Ellsberg, Kissinger was even more upset. Before Nixon had assumed office, Kissinger had asked the Rand Corporation for a study of the "options" in Vietnam. Rand had, in turn, put Ellsberg in charge of the pre-Inaugural project. Kissinger's alarmist view of the Pentagon Papers prevailed in the White House. The government went to court to get an injunction to stop the publication of the papers. Two weeks later, the Supreme Court ruled in favor of the press, and the publication of the papers resumed.

The other step which the White House took was to set up a Special Investigations Unit to plug leaks. Because of the nature of its work, this unit became known as the "plumbers." It was directed by David Young, an assistant to Kissinger, and by Egil Krogh, an assistant to John Ehrlichman. Krogh was involved in drug control matters and hired from this field two men: Walter Minnick of the Cabinet Committee on International Narcotics Control, which Krogh directed, and G. Gordon Liddy, an assistant to the Secretary of the Treasury. Another man, E. Howard

Hunt, was a White House consultant who came to the unit on the recommendation of Charles Colson.

The White House had high hopes for Daniel Ellsberg. Krogh was told by President Nixon to read his book, *Six Crises,* especially the chapter on Alger Hiss, and to absorb its lessons. The White House hoped to discredit Ellsberg, but through Ellsberg, it hoped to reach others: Leslie Gelb, director of the Vietnam History Task Force which produced the Pentagon Papers; Paul Warnke, who had served as an Assistant Secretary of Defense for International Security Affairs; and Morton Halperin, who had been Warnke's deputy. Finally, the White House operatives wanted to discredit Clark Clifford, a former Secretary of Defense and a very big fish indeed.[13] These men formed a dovish group in the Department of Defense in the last years of the Johnson Administration. On June 28, Ellsberg was indicted for theft of government property and for unauthorized possession of documents related to the national defense. The mission of the Special Investigations Unit was vague. In a note on Ellsberg, John Ehrlichman wrote: "Goal—Do to . . . JFK elite the same destructive job that was done on Herbert Hoover years ago."[14] The Ellsberg case had other ramifications. Assistant Attorney-General for Internal Security Robert Mardian and J. Fred Buzhardt, general counsel to the Pentagon and a former aide to Senator Thurmond, met with members of the House Armed Services Committee to promote the idea of hearings to reveal a radical conspiracy.

Hunt and Colson were already at work doing a "destructive job" on the Kennedys. Colson was a Republican from Massachusetts and a professional Kennedy hater. Hunt was a retired CIA agent who had been involved in the Bay of Pigs operation and was chagrined at the failure of President Kennedy to provide air cover. At first, the White House was interested in pursuing the Bay of Pigs but later backed off, perhaps because Richard Nixon had been involved in invasion planning in the last months of the Eisenhower Administration. The White House turned to Vietnam as a more fruitful area. Hunt was instructed to study the Pentagon Papers for negative material. The coup which overthrew and led to the death of Ngo Dinh Diem became the focus of the search. At a press conference on September 16, Nixon declared that "I would remind all concerned that the way we got into Vietnam was through overthrowing Diem, and the complicity in the murder of Diem. . . ."[15] On Ehrlichman's authority, Hunt was given access to State Department cables during the relevant period. Finding that the originals did not live up to expectations, Hunt faked two cables at the suggestion of Colson. The White House was also anxious to obtain CIA files on the Bay of Pigs and the Diem coup, and finally did when President Nixon personally remonstrated with CIA Director Richard Helms. The White House hoped to find "complicity in the murder of Diem," a Catholic, on the farfetched calculation that such complicity would damage the Kennedys with the Catholic vote in the United States. Eventually, the White House gave up on this pseudo-historical excavation.

The immediate problem was Ellsberg. The plumbers decided that Ellsberg's psychiatric records would be helpful in his undoing. Ellsberg's psychiatrist, Dr. Lewis J. Fielding, had already refused to give these to the FBI on the grounds of doctor/patient confidentiality. The plumbers refused to accept this result and determined on a "black bag job," a break-in at Fielding's office. On the night of September 3–4, Hunt and Liddy, together with some Cuban-American operatives recruited by Hunt in Miami, broke into Fielding's office. Three White House aides were ultimately convicted of crimes as a result of the break-in. John Ehrlichman was convicted of violating Fielding's civil rights and of lying to a grand jury. Liddy and Krogh were also convicted on a civil rights charge. Colson pleaded guilty to obstruction of justice for his efforts to discredit Ellsberg.

Whatever its other merits might have been, the "New American Revolution" did not provide the impetus that Richard Nixon needed to win reelection. It was in the field of foreign policy that Nixon made major breakthroughs. Nixon remained faithful to his internationalist heritage. Upon assuming office in 1969, Nixon and Kissinger began a carefully orchestrated program of relaxation of restrictions on trade and travel with the People's Republic of China. This program culminated in 1971 with the elimination of all restrictions on travel to China and the termination of the twenty-one-year-old trade embargo with China. The lifting of the trade embargo in April coincided with the acceptance by a U.S. table tennis team of a Chinese invitation to visit. These events inaugurated a brief era of "ping pong diplomacy." Then in July, Nixon announced that he would personally visit China some time before May 1972. Several weeks later, Secretary of State William P. Rogers declared that the United States would not oppose the admission of Communist China to the United Nations, though it would oppose the expulsion of Nationalist China.

Nixon's visit to China in late February 1972 was a great political success. He was the first American President to visit the People's Republic of China. In May, Nixon made a visit to the Soviet Union. He signed no less than seven agreements with the Soviets in the fields of space exploration, medical research, trade, the environment, incidents at sea, technology, and strategic weapons. The Strategic Arms Limitation Treaty or SALT was undoubtedly the most important. In 1968, Nixon had campaigned as a strong critic of the deterioration of the strategic balance between the United States and the Soviet Union. However, SALT I conceded Soviet quantitative superiority in several strategic fields and relied upon American qualitative superiority to make up the difference.

"Peace" was the byword of the Nixon reelection effort in 1972, and the "opening" to China and *détente* with the Soviet Union were broadly popular policies, although they did lead to the "suspension of support" by some conservative intellectuals grouped around the *National Review*. This peace, however, did not necessarily extend to the home front. When H. R. Haldeman, President Nixon's principal aide, was interviewed in January by Barbara Walters on NBC's "Today" show, he was asked how Mr. Nixon regarded criticism, particularly criticism from the U.S. Senate. He answered that, if criticism included

Nixon's and Kissinger's Vietnam peace efforts, it should be considered "consciously aiding and abetting the enemy." In other words, it would have to be considered treason.

Southern strategy still determined how the Administration handled sensitive racial issues. On April 20 of the previous year, the Supreme Court had found that bussing was a permissible means of achieving racial integration. Nonetheless, Nixon felt no compunction about publicly breaking with the Court whose decisions he was constitutionally bound to enforce. On March 16, 1972, in a nationally televised address, Nixon proposed legislation which would put a "moratorium" on bussing. Once again, Nixon had responded to political pressure from his right. Two days earlier, Governor Wallace had won the Florida primary in which an anti-bussing referendum had passed.

Muskie had finished fourth in Florida, and his campaign was in some trouble. The Maine Senator had defeated Senator George McGovern of South Dakota by an unimpressive margin in the neighboring state of New Hampshire. When Muskie went on to lose two Eastern primaries, Massachusetts and Pennsylvania, his campaign collapsed. This development left Senator McGovern and Governor Wallace as the strongest candidates in the race. Wallace was shot while campaigning in Maryland, and McGovern was left as the front runner. In the spring, the polls showed McGovern, the anti-war candidate, to be competitive with Nixon, whose approval ratings never went much above 60 per cent, even at their best.

However, the elimination of the Wallace candidacy, while helpful to McGovern in the primaries, also stood to benefit Nixon in the general election. The ideal projected by Kevin Phillips and John Mitchell of combining the 1968 Wallace and Nixon votes now seemed to have been realized. Nixon was also much strengthened by his foreign policy successes in 1972. A program of wage and price controls, inaugurated in 1971, shored up Nixon's weak economic flank.

McGovern was damaged by some heavy political punching by Senator Hubert Humphrey of Minnesota in the California primary. Humphrey raised the question of McGovern's views on defense, and although McGovern won the primary, many voters were plainly troubled by McGovern's plans for cutting billions from the defense budget. McGovern was probably not helped by the television exposure of the Democratic convention as a festival of the New Politics. His choice of a running-mate proved to be a disaster. Senator Thomas Eagleton of Missouri had a history of mental illness, including shock treatments. McGovern awkwardly dumped him in favor of Sargent Shriver, a former OEO and Peace Corps director who was a Kennedy in-law. After the convention, McGovern came under heavy fire from the press for his guaranteed income plan. The net result of these events was that the McGovern candidacy, viable in the spring, was a hopeless case in the autumn.

In McGovern, the Nixon Administration got a New Politics candidate who could serve as the perfect foil for New Majority tactics and rhetoric, although Nixon would be careful to maintain a more Presidential posture than in 1970. Nixon took the view that the "Eagleton matter and the way McGovern conducted his campaign may have affected this election by five points, no more. This election was decided the day he was nominated. The issue in this election was his views."[16] In any event Nixon won in a landslide. He won 61 per cent of the popular vote and every state except Massachusetts and the District of Columbia. But this landslide hardly affected the Democratic Congress. The Republicans gained twelve seats in the House, but lost one in the Senate and one among the governorships. The realignment was still elusive.

In a preelection interview with Garnett (Jack) Horner of the Washington *Star-News,* Nixon explained his plans for his second term by comparing them to Franklin D. Roosevelt's accomplishments:

In domestic policy, if you look at the Nixon proposals in the first four years—and I can assure you, Jack, that when you look at them over the next four years, this will be known as an Administration which advocated—and if we get the proper support in the Congress after the election, was able to accomplish—more significant reform than any Administration since Franklin Roosevelt's in 1932; but reform in a different direction. Roosevelt's reforms led to bigger and bigger power in Washington. It was perhaps needed then. The country's problems were so massive they couldn't be handled otherwise.

The reforms that we are instituting are ones which will diffuse the power throughout the country and which will make government leaner, but in a sense will make it stronger. After all, fat government is weak, weak in handling the problems.[17]

The New Deal and the 1930s were still the yardstick by which Nixon wanted to measure the historic significance of his Presidency. In his memoirs, Nixon repeated this theme of "reform in a different direction":

At the beginning of my second term, Congress, the bureaucracy, and the media were still working in concert to maintain the ideas and ideology of the traditional Eastern liberal establishment that had come down to 1973 through the New Deal, the New Frontier, and the Great Society. Now I planned to give expression to the more conservative values and beliefs of the New Majority throughout the country and use my power to put some teeth into my New American Revolution.[18]

Not only were Presidents Kennedy and Johnson thought of as the heirs of Roosevelt but the Congress and the federal bureaucracy were considered to be ideological instruments of the Democrats. This New Deal tradition was identical with the "liberal establishment," now referred to as "Eastern" by the conservative populists. Using conservative rhetoric as an indicator, the establishment would also have had to include the institutions of culture and communication: the universities, the foundations, and the media, particularly those institutions which were elite, metropolitan, and Eastern and served national and international clienteles. The conflict between conservatives and the establishment was partially characterized by Patrick Buchanan: "So, the problem simply stated is that the Lords Spiritual and the Lords Temporal in the society are at sword's point."[19]

Nixon never had the opportunity to "put some teeth into my New American Revolution." He was faced, instead, by Watergate. The break-in at the Democratic National Committee headquarters had its origin in the desire of Nixon and his campaign director, John Mitchell, for a political intelligence capability as a part of the Committee To Re-elect the President. Gordon Strachan, an assistant to H. R. Haldeman, and Jeb Magruder, second-in-command to Mitchell, asked John Dean to find a general counsel for CRP who could also serve as director of a political intelligence operation. After considering David Young of the Special Investigations Unit and Fred Fielding, his own assistant, Dean finally settled on Gordon Liddy on the recommendation of Egil Krogh. Later, Howard Hunt joined his old comrade from the Special Investigations Unit in this new intelligence enterprise.

In the late spring and early summer of 1972, the CRP intelligence operatives made no less than four attempts—only one of them successful—to break into and wiretap the offices of the Democratic National Committee. On the fourth attempt, June 17, five men were caught and arrested by Washington police. The men included James McCord, a CIA veteran who was CRP's director of security, and Bernard Barker, an alumnus of the Fielding burglary. Liddy and Hunt, who had planned the operation, were implicated later.

Since the Democratic National Committee was not the command center for the McGovern Presidential campaign, the priority it had for the Watergate burglars raised questions. Hunt and Liddy told their men that they should search for evidence of ties to Communist Cuba or left-wing organizations within the United States. This advice was consistent with conservative thinking about "radical liberalism" and probably seriously meant. Lawrence O'Brien, chairman of the DNC, had a particular fascination for the CRP apparat. His phone was unsuccessfully tapped during the third break-in episode. O'Brien had been on the Howard Hughes payroll to the sum of $15,000 a month. Most likely, O'Brien was retained as a lobbyist in Hughes's crusade to overturn a court decision that had stripped him of control of Trans-World Airways. Richard Nixon was obsessed with Howard Hughes because the revelation of a $200,000 loan to his brother, Donald Nixon, had hurt him both in the 1960 campaign for President and the 1962 campaign for governor of California. Both of these campaigns were unsuccessful. The Nixon people may well have wanted to turn the tables on the Democrats and uncover a Hughes scandal. Finally, O'Brien was an old Kennedy operative and an effective critic of the Nixon Administration. The Kennedy connection automatically qualified O'Brien for the close attention of the Nixon men.

Within a week of the apprehension of the five men, an effort was under way to conceal the relationship of CRP officials to the Liddy intelligence operation and to stop the criminal investigation at the level of Liddy and Hunt. On June 23, President Nixon himself approved a plan to have the CIA intervene with the FBI. This plan suggested itself because of the association of some of the men apprehended at the Watergate complex with the 1961 Bay of Pigs operation of the CIA. Nixon was also concerned that the source of the money used to finance the burglary not be traced back to the CRP via Mexico. On the afternoon of June 23, Vernon Walters, Deputy Director of the CIA, told the new FBI Director, L. Patrick Gray, that an FBI investigation into Mexico would jeopardize CIA operations. The taped record of Nixon's involvement in this ploy, which lasted only two weeks before the FBI resumed its investigation of the money chain into Mexico, became the "smoking gun" which indicated his vulnerability to a charge of obstruction of justice. At an August press conference, Nixon prophetically remarked: "What really hurts is if you cover it up." [20]

In the short run, Watergate failed to develop into a major scandal. Only Hunt, Liddy, and the five burglars were indicted. The incident was not an issue in the election. The Administration found the votes to derail a threatening investigation by Wright Patman's House Banking and Currency Committee. But the Senate persisted. At the end of the year, Senator Edward Kennedy's Judiciary subcommittee on Administrative Practices and Procedure conducted a low-profile investigation which laid the groundwork for a Senate Select Committee the next year, the Ervin Committee, after its chairman, Senator Sam Ervin of North Carolina.

In February and March of 1973, the cover-up began to unravel. At his confirmation hearings before the Senate, FBI Director Patrick Gray revealed that he had given FBI reports on the FBI investigation of Watergate to John Dean, White House counsel. At this point, Dean was functioning as the orchestrator of the White House cover-up. Gray later admitted that he destroyed documents from Howard Hunt's White House safe, which had been passed to him. His nomination was withdrawn.

At this juncture, Nixon was convinced that he was the target of an Establishment cabal. He told Dean:

> They are, they're, they're going to Watergate around in this town, not so much our opponents, but basically it's the media, uh, I mean, it's the Establishment. The Establishment is dying, and so they've got to show that after some rather significant successes we've had in foreign policy and in the election, they've got to show, "Well, it just is wrong because this is—because of this." In other words, they're trying to use this to smear the whole thing.[21]

Keeping in mind the equivalence for Nixon of the Establishment and the New Deal coalition, there was something to his claim that the "Establishment is dying." In 1972, neither candidate was heir to the New Deal tradition. Yet, neither the New Politics Democrats nor the New Majority Republicans were able to fill the vacuum. The result was political stalemate or *ad hoc* coalitions which shifted from issue to issue. The grand Watergate coalition which forced President Nixon to resign resembled the New Deal coalition in its breadth. Southern Democrats and moderate Republicans joined liberal Democrats on liberal terms in order to deal with a national crisis. Ultimately, the Watergate coalition realized the worst premonitions of the Nixon men. Many of them were convinced that they were brought down by a CIA conspiracy.[22] They reached this conclusion by speculating that the men with CIA backgrounds whom they willingly employed were double agents and that other men who played a key inside role in Nixon's fall were CIA plants. In conservative thinking, the Central Intelligence Agency is liberal internationalism made flesh and thus a premier Establishment institution.

The burglars were indicted. Through the summer and fall they remained silent. In early 1973, they were convicted. On March 19, James McCord transmitted a letter to Judge John J. Sirica in which he made these assertions, among others:

1. There was political pressure applied to the defendants to plead guilty and remain silent.
2. Perjury occurred during the trial in matters highly material to the very structure, orientation and impact of the government's case, and to the motivation and intent of the defendants.
3. Others involved in the Watergate operation were not identified during the trial, when they could have been by those testifying.
4. The Watergate operation was not a CIA operation. The Cubans may have been misled by others into believing that it was a CIA operation. I know for a fact that it was not.[23]

Judge Sirica proceeded to hand down harsh "provisional sentences" to the other defendants which would be reexamined three months later. By this procedure, he hoped to elicit further information from the defendants.

John Dean, knowing his own culpability, was made highly nervous by these developments. He also feared that he would be set up as a scapegoat by his White House colleagues. Eventually, he retained a lawyer and began to negotiate with prosecutors for immunity. On April 30, he was formally fired by President Nixon. But the cover-up was hemorrhaging. Nixon had to accept the resignations of John Ehrlichman and H. R. Haldeman. John Mitchell had left CRP the year before, within two weeks of the Watergate break-in. In the Gallup Poll, Nixon's approval rating had fallen 20 points since a January reading of 68 per cent.

In the hearings of the Ervin Committee, which were open and televised, John Dean was the star witness because he was the point of contact with the President himself. But the Watergate tide began to ebb in early summer because the commit-

tee was unable to develop any additional evidence to corrobo-
rate Dean's charges. Then on July 16, Alexander Butterfield, a
Presidential aide, revealed the existence since 1971 of a tape
recording system within the Oval Office. The tapes could verify
the allegations of the Watergate principals. Indeed, Nixon valued them for this purpose; he hoped to catch Dean in perjury.
After Butterfield's testimony, Nixon had only one week to destroy the tapes legally. When the Ervin Committee and Archi-
bald Cox, who held the newly created Office of the Special
Prosecutor, subpoenaed several of the tapes, they became evidence and their destruction became a crime.

But Nixon refused to obey the subpoenas, and Cox went to
court. Nixon appealed a lower court order to surrender the
tapes and proceeded to order his Attorney-General, Elliot Richardson, to fire Cox. Since Richardson had testified before the
Senate that he would not fire Cox except for misconduct in office, Richardson refused. Richardson was therefore fired himself. His deputy, William Ruckelshaus, also refused and was
fired in turn. Solicitor General Robert H. Bork finally dispatched Cox. At this, public opinion intervened. The White
House was buffeted by a "firestorm" of negative comment. It
was in a poor position to defend. Nixon's Gallup rating was
down to a below-sea-level rating of 27 per cent. Vice President
Agnew had already departed office after pleading *nolo contendere* to one count of tax evasion in a case in which he was accused of taking kickbacks from Baltimore contractors.

Having fired two officials in the Justice Department in order
to be rid of a special prosecutor and the tapes issue, Nixon was
forced by the firestorm to hand over the tapes and accept a
new special prosecutor, Leon Jaworski, a Houston attorney.
The whole process of impasse over additional tapes began
again, except that now the House Judiciary Committee had
begun to consider impeachment. In the spring of 1974, Nixon
did offer some edited transcripts which were inadequate legally
but which damaged Nixon politically by revealing him as pro-
fane in private. Nixon stated that he would abide by a "definitive" decision by the Supreme Court on the sixty-four addi-

tional tapes requested by Jaworski. The suggestion was that there were some circumstances under which he would not consider a Supreme Court decision definitive. This ploy probably helped to ensure a unanimous verdict by the Court in favor of the special prosecutor's argument. The Supreme Court decision finished Nixon because one of the June 23 tapes was the "smoking gun"—hard evidence that Nixon had involved himself in an obstruction of justice. At that point, even conservative Republican opinion began to turn against Nixon. In the House Judiciary Committee, moderate Republicans and Southern Democrats were already leaning toward liberal Democrats in their consideration of impeachment. On July 27, the committee voted 27 to 11 in favor of its first article of impeachment concerning the obstruction of justice in the Watergate break-in. In subsequent days, the committee voted 28 to 10 for a second article concerning the abuse of power and 21 to 17 for a third article having to do with the defiance of subpoenas.

After the Supreme Court decision and the vote of the House Judiciary Committee, President Nixon was advised that he would most probably be impeached by the House and that he had only fifteen votes in the Senate, less than the one third he needed to survive a trial. On August 9, Richard Nixon resigned his office. He was pardoned by his successor, Gerald R. Ford, for any criminal offenses committed while in office. H. R. Haldeman, John Ehrlichman, John Mitchell, and Robert Mardian had been indicted the previous March and were variously convicted of conspiracy, obstruction of justice, and lying under oath. John Dean pleaded guilty to obstruction of justice and defrauding the government.

Richard Nixon never admitted any criminal wrongdoing. In answer to an interrogatory from the Senate Select Committee on Intelligence in 1976, Nixon expounded this legal theory:

> It is quite obvious that there are certain inherently governmental actions which if undertaken by the sovereign in protection of the interest of the nation's security are lawful but which if undertaken by private persons are not. . .
>
> . . . (It) is naive to attempt to categorize activities a President

might authorize as "legal" or "illegal" without reference to the circumstances under which he concludes that the activity is necessary. . . .

In short, there have been—and will be in the future—circumstances in which Presidents may lawfully authorize actions in the interests of the security of this country, which if undertaken by other persons, or even by the President under different circumstances, would be illegal.[24]

In short, the "sovereign" is above the law. But in the United States, the sovereign is not constitutionally above the law and the sovereign is not the President, but the people.

It is undeniable that the Watergate break-in had less adverse impact on American democracy than the major domestic security programs inaugurated in the Johnson years. The peculiar vulnerability of the Nixon Administration to Watergate arose not from the greater heinousness of the break-in but from the fact of direct CRP involvement in the crimes of break-in and wiretapping and of direct White House involvement in the further crime of obstruction of justice. Had the White House left to the security bureaucracies the sordid details of illegal operations it would have been free to deny explicit authorization of them, and Richard Nixon would never have had to resign. But the Republicans were suspicious of the security bureaucracies which they believed had a liberal internationalist or Democratic bias. They were determined to create their own intelligence capabilities in CRP and the White House. The conservative Republicans were thus brought low by their own political anxieties.

What was also distinctive about the Watergate break-in was the target. Liberal Democrats were not accustomed to the government defining them as subversive. Nonetheless conservative Republicans had regarded New Deal Democrats since the 1930s as little better than fellow travelers. In a different context, Vice President Agnew stereotyped the new liberals of the 1960s as "radical liberals"—an updating of the same argument. CRP operatives went into action against the McGovern campaign on this premise.

Richard Nixon, who regarded himself as an Eisenhower internationalist, tried to fit these partisan considerations into the traditional framework of national security. But the liberal international definitions of subversion—whatever intrinsic value they may have had—were much narrower than the conservative Republican, and Nixon's efforts bent this framework out of shape. In addition, the serviceability of "national security" itself was being called into question by the unpopularity of the Vietnam War which had never been democratically legitimated by a Congressional declaration of war. Richard Nixon shared the burden of the Vietnam War with Lyndon Johnson and ultimately the crisis of the "imperial presidency" which the war brought on engulfed them both. The loss of popularity within his own party forced Johnson to renounce a reelection campaign. The sanctioning, even if after the fact, of illegal tactics against the anti-war candidacy of George McGovern inexorably led to the resignation of Richard Nixon. The unorthodox combination of conservative Republicanism and internationalism, which had served Nixon so well throughout his career, proved finally to be his undoing in the peculiar political conjuncture known as Watergate.

NOTES

PART I

Chapter 1

1. Frank S. Meyer, "The Recrudescence of American Conservatism" in William F. Buckley, Jr., ed., *American Conservative Thought in the Twentieth Century* (New York, 1970), p. 78.
2. The distinction between "urban" and "rural" areas is misleading, since the Census defines an urban area as a place with a population of only 2,500 or more. I use the Census definition of a Standard Metropolitan Statistical Area as a population concentration of 50,000 or more as equivalent to "metropolitan area." "Provincial" designates areas of less than 50,000. See V. O. Key's discussion of "Sectionalism, Urbanism, and Party" in *Politics, Parties and Pressure Groups* (New York, 1952) for an analysis of the relationships among urbanization, class politics, and the vote for the Democratic Party.
3. The idea of a "system of 1896" derives from the theory of "critical elections" first expounded by V. O. Key in 1955 in the *Journal of Politics.* In "The Functional Approach to Party Government" in Sigmund Neumann, ed., *Modern Political Parties* (Chicago, 1956), E. E. Schattschneider explains the party realignment of 1896 and the "revolution of 1932." Walter Dean Burnham has continued this tradition in "The Changing Shape of the American Political Universe" in the *American Political Science Review* (March 1965) and *Critical Elections and the Mainsprings of American Politics* (New York, 1970).

4. Joe Martin (as told to Robert J. Donovan), *My First Fifty Years in Politics* (New York, 1960), p. 66.
5. Samuel I. Rosenman, ed., *The Public Papers and Addresses of Franklin D. Roosevelt*, 13 vols. (New York, 1938), Vol. 5, p. 233.
6. *Ibid.*, p. 232.
7. Angus Campbell, Philip E. Converse, Warren E. Miller, Donald E. Stokes, *The American Voter* (New York, 1960), pp. 357–58.
8. John T. Flynn, *The Decline of the American Republic* (New York, 1955), p. 93.

Chapter 2

1. Herbert Hoover, *Addresses Upon the American Road 1933–38* (New York, 1938), p. 138.
2. *The Freeman*, October 2, 1950, p. 5.
3. Quoted in Robert Green McCloskey, *American Conservatism in the Age of Enterprise, 1865–1910* (New York, 1951), p. 49.
4. John T. Flynn, *The Road Ahead* (New York, 1949), pp. 8–9.
5. *Ibid.*, p. 10.
6. *Ibid.*, p. 9.
7. Harold Lord Varney, "Is Roosevelt a Socialist?" *The American Mercury*, October 1936, pp. 209–10.

Chapter 3

1. See George H. Mayer, *The Republican Party 1854–1966* (New York, 1967), pp. 469–70.
2. Edwin Emery, *The Press and America* (Englewood Cliffs, N.J., 1972), p. 461.
3. See George Wolfskill, *The Revolt of the Conservatives* (Cambridge, Mass., 1962), pp. 198–223.
4. George H. Mayer, "The Republican Party, 1932–1952," in Arthur M. Schlesinger, Jr., ed., *History of U.S. Political Parties*, 4 vols. (New York, 1973), Vol. 3, p. 2268.
5. George H. Gallup, *The Gallup Poll: Public Opinion 1935–1971*, 3 vols. (New York, 1972), Vol. 1, pp. 52, 55.
6. *Ibid.*, p. 57.
7. *Ibid.*, pp. 51, 62, 94, 105.
8. See Walter Goodman, *The Committee* (Baltimore, 1969).
9. James T. Patterson, *Congressional Conservatism and the New Deal* (Lexington, Ky., 1967), pp. 325–52, for the pattern of conservative voting.
10. House Select Committee on Lobbying Activities, *American Enterprise Association* (Washington, D.C., 1950).

11. U.S. Department of Commerce, Bureau of the Census, *Statistical Abstract of the United States, 1974* (Washington, D.C., 1974), p. 436.
12. Seymour Martin Lipset, *Political Man* (Garden City, N.Y., 1960), p. 242.

Chapter 4

1. Jerome E. Edwards, *The Foreign Policy of Col. McCormick's Tribune 1929–41* (Reno, Nevada, 1971), p. 49.
2. For the relationship among section, party, metropolitan area, control of the White House, and foreign policy attitudes, see George L. Grassmuck, *Sectional Biases in Congress on Foreign Policy* (Baltimore, 1951); Ralph H. Smuckler, "The Region of Isolationism," *American Political Science Review* (June 1953), pp. 386–401; and Leroy N. Rieselbach, *The Roots of Isolationism* (Indianapolis, Ind., 1966).
3. U.S. Department of Commerce, Bureau of the Census, *Historical Statistics of the United States from Colonial Times to 1957* (Washington, D.C., 1960), pp. 48–67.

Chapter 5

1. Herbert Hoover, *Addresses upon the American Road, 1940–41* (New York, 1941), p. 35.
2. William Henry Chamberlin, *America's Second Crusade* (Chicago, 1950), p. 51.
3. *Ibid.*, p. 197.
4. On the interventionist committees, see Walter Johnson, *The Battle Against Isolation* (Chicago, 1944).
5. Henry R. Luce, "The American Century," *Life* Magazine, February 17, 1941, p. 62.
6. *Ibid.*, p. 65.
7. *Ibid.*
8. *Ibid.*
9. Robert A. Taft, symposium on "The Future of the Republican Party," *The Nation*, December 13, 1941, p. 612.
10. *Ibid.*, pp. 611–12.
11. On the America First Committee, see Wayne S. Cole, *America First: The Battle Against Intervention 1940–41* (Madison, Wisc., 1953).
12. *Ibid.*, pp. 15–16.
13. Hoover, p. 93.
14. Cole, p. 85.
15. New York *Times*, August 6, 1941.
16. See Cole, pp. 104–31.

17. Louis L. Gerson, *The Hyphenate in Recent American Politics and Diplomacy* (Lawrence, Kan., 1964), pp. 128–29.
18. George Morgenstern, *Pearl Harbor: The Story of the Secret War* (New York, 1947), p. 329.
19. Joint Committee on the Investigation of the Pearl Harbor Attack, *Minority Report* (Washington, D.C., 1946).
20. D. Clayton James, *The Years of MacArthur*, 2 vols. (Boston, 1970), Vol. 1, p. 574.
21. Douglas MacArthur, *Reminiscences* (New York, 1964), p. 97.
22. Forrest C. Pogue, *George C. Marshall: Education of a General* (New York, 1963), p. 280.
23. *Ibid.*, p. 278.
24. On the Draft MacArthur movement, see Arthur H. Vandenberg, Jr., ed., *The Private Papers of Senator Vandenberg* (Boston, 1952), pp. 75–90; and D. Clayton James, *The Years of MacArthur*, 2 vols. (Boston, 1975), Vol. II, pp. 422–40.
25. James, Vol. II, p. 435.

Chapter 6

1. See H. Bradford Westerfield, *Foreign Policy and Party Politics* (New Haven, 1955), pp. 150–53.
2. *Congressional Record*, 79th Congress, 1st Session, p. 7441.
3. *Ibid.*, p. 7442.
4. A rough index of the balance of the factions within the Republican Party in Congress is provided by the percentage of times Congressmen voted with their party on key roll calls. Moderate Republicans would tend to vote more often against their party. Of the forty-six Republican Senators in office in 1952, only three— Wayne Morse of Oregon, James Duff of Pennsylvania, and George Aiken of Vermont—actually voted more often with the Democrats in the post-war period, 1945–52. A larger group of eight, including Lodge and Saltonstall of Massachusetts, Flanders of Vermont, and Tobey of New Hampshire, voted with their party from 50 to 70 per cent of the time. Twenty-seven Senators, including Millikin of Colorado, Jenner of Indiana, Taft of Ohio, Bridges of New Hampshire, and McCarthy of Wisconsin, voted with their party more than 80 per cent of the time. Between these groups, a group of eight, including Knowland and Nixon of California, supported their party on from 70 to 80 per cent of the key votes. In the House, only two Republicans, Jacob Javits of New York and Usher Burdick of North Dakota, voted more often with

the Democrats. A group of twenty-two supported the party on 50 to 70 per cent of the key votes, while a much larger bloc of 140 voted with their party more than 80 per cent of the time. The rest voted with the party on 70 to 80 per cent of the key roll calls. See *Congressional Quarterly Almanac* (Washington, D.C., 1952), pp. 67–68.

5. William S. White, *The Taft Story* (New York, 1954), p. 85.
6. George H. E. Smith, "Bipartisan Foreign Policy in Partisan Politics," *American Perspective* (Spring 1950), p. 162.

Chapter 7

1. Barbara W. Tuchman, *Stilwell and the American Experience in China* (New York, 1972), p. 432.
2. Tang Tsou, *America's Failure in China* 2 vols. (Chicago, 1967), Vol. I, p. 203.
3. Alfred Kohlberg, "China Via Stilwell Road," *The China Monthly* (October 1948), p. 286.
4. For the text of the Yalta Agreement on the Far East, see U.S. Department of State, *United States Relations with China* (Washington, D.C., 1949), p. 113.
5. *Ibid.,* p. 582.
6. *Ibid.,* p. 382.
7. *Ibid.,* p. 383.
8. *Congressional Record,* 79th Congress, 2nd Session, p. A4494.
9. *Ibid.,* p. 2764.
10. On the Institute of Pacific Relations, see John N. Thomas, *The Institute of Pacific Relations* (Seattle, 1974); Internal Security Subcommittee of Committee on Judiciary, U.S. Senate, *Institute of Pacific Relations* (Washington, D.C., 1952); and, American Institute of Pacific Relations, *Commentary on the McCarran Report on the I.P.R.* (New York, 1953).
11. Mark Tsai, "Now It Can Be Told," *The China Monthly* (September 1948), p. 255.
12. Charles Wertenbaker, "The China Lobby," *The Reporter,* April 15–29, 1952; see also Ross Y. Koen, *The China Lobby in American Politics* (New York, 1974), p. 63.
13. *Congressional Record,* 81st Congress, 1st Session, p. 12290.
14. *Ibid.,* pp. 1950–51.
15. *Ibid.,* p. 8406.
16. *United States Relations with China,* p. xvi.
17. *Ibid.*
18. Tang Tsou, Vol. II, p. 510.

PART II

Chapter 8

1. *Congressional Record,* 81st Congress, 2nd Session, p. 1541.
2. See Jules Weinberg, "Priests, Workers, and Communists," *Harper's,* November 1948, pp. 49–56; and Richard J. Ward, "The Role of the Association of Catholic Trade Unionists in the Labor Movement," *Review of Social Economy* (September 1956), pp. 79–101.
3. *Official Report of the Proceedings of the Twenty-fourth Republican National Convention* (Washington, D.C., 1948), p. 24.
4. See Robert Griffith, *The Politics of Fear: Joseph R. McCarthy and the Senate* (New York, 1970), p. 96. For the facts of McCarthy's political career, I rely on Griffith's excellent account.
5. George H. Gallup, *The Gallup Poll: Public Opinion 1935–1971,* 3 vols. (New York, 1972), Vol. 2, for the dates indicated.
6. *Ibid.,* September 25, October 4, 1950.
7. See Nelson W. Polsby, "Towards an Explanation of McCarthyism," *Political Studies* (October 1960), pp. 250–71; and Louis H. Bean, *Influences in the 1954 Mid-term Elections* (Washington, D.C., 1954).
8. See the summary of McCarthy's voting record in "What Kind of Senator Is McCarthy?" *Congressional Quarterly,* April 30, 1954, pp. 525–36.
9. See Michael Paul Rogin, *The Intellectuals and McCarthy: The Radical Spectre* (Cambridge, Mass., 1967), pp. 86–94.
10. Gallup for dates indicated.
11. *Ibid.* for dates indicated.
12. *Ibid.,* January 15, March 15, May 24, June 9, 1954.
13. Seymour Martin Lipset and Earl Raab, *The Politics of Unreason: Right-wing Extremism in America, 1790–1970* (New York, 1970), pp. 224–35; and Angus Campbell and Homer C. Cooper, *Group Differences in Attitudes and Votes: A Study of the 1954 Congressional Election* (Westport, Conn., 1974).
14. Martin Trow, "Small Businessmen, Political Tolerance, and Support for McCarthy," *American Journal of Sociology* (November 1958), p. 274.
15. Charles J. V. Murphy, "McCarthy and the Businessman," *Fortune,* April 1954.
16. Gallup, June 23, 1954.
17. *Congressional Record,* 81st Congress, 2nd Session, p. 1954.
18. "Taft and McCarthy," *Life,* October 1, 1951, p. 32.
19. *Time,* October 22, 1951, p. 24.

Chapter 9

1. *Department of State Bulletin,* January 23, 1950, p. 115.
2. *Congressional Record,* 81st Congress, 2nd Session, p. 14916.
3. *Ibid.,* p. 14929.
4. Quoted in Eric F. Goldman, *The Crucial Decade—And After* (New York, 1961), p. 125.
5. *Congressional Record,* 81st Congress, 2nd Session, p. 4120.
6. *Ibid.,* p. 4121.
7. George H. Gallup, *The Gallup Poll: Public Opinion 1935–1971,* 3 vols. (New York, 1972), Vol. 2, February 23, 1949; December 22, 1950.
8. Dean Acheson, *Present at the Creation* (New York, 1970), p. 623.
9. Herbert Hoover, *Addresses upon the American Road 1948–1950* (Stanford, Calif., 1951), pp. 208–9.
10. *Ibid.,* p. 205.
11. *Congressional Record,* 82nd Congress, 1st Session, p. 58.
12. *Ibid.,* pp. 1258–59.
13. Harry S Truman, *Memoirs: Years of Trial and Hope,* 2 vols. (Garden City, N.Y., 1956), Vol. 2, p. 440.
14. Courtney Whitney, *MacArthur: His Rendezvous with History* (New York, 1956), p. 467.
15. *Ibid.,* p. 466.
16. Hearings before the Committee on Armed Services and the Committee on Foreign Relations, U.S. Senate, *Military Situation in the Far East* (Washington, D.C., 1951), Appendix J, pp. 3191–92.
17. Whitney, pp. 496–97.
18. *Congressional Record,* 82nd Congress, 1st Session, p. 4123.
19. *Military Situation in the Far East,* p. 267.
20. *Ibid.,* p. 82.
21. *Ibid.,* p. 3598.
22. *Congressional Record,* 82nd Congress, 1st Session, p. 6599.
23. *Ibid.,* p. 6592.
24. Whitney, pp. 514–15.

Chapter 10

1. Robert A. Taft, *A Foreign Policy for Americans* (Garden City, N.Y., 1951), pp. 17–18.
2. John Foster Dulles, "A Policy of Boldness," *Life,* May 19, 1952, p. 148.
3. *Official Report of the Proceedings of the Twenty-fifth Republican National Convention* (Washington, D.C., 1952), p. 313.

4. Robert A. Taft, "Letter on the Republican Convention, 1952: To Douglas MacArthur," Arthur M. Schlesinger, Jr., gen. ed., *History of U.S. Political Parties*, 4 vols. (New York, 1973) Vol. III, p. 2391.
5. Quoted in William Costello, *The Facts About Nixon* (New York, 1960), p. 90.
6. New York *Times*, September 13, 1952.
7. Robert Griffith, *The Politics of Fear: Joseph R. McCarthy and the Senate* (New York, 1970), p. 328.
8. George H. Gallup, *The Gallup Poll: Public Opinion 1935–1971*, 3 vols. (New York, 1972), Vol. 2, January 17, 1954.
9. Morris Janowitz, *The Professional Soldier* (New York, 1964), p. 89.
10. Charles J. V. Murphy, "McCarthy and the Businessman," *Fortune*, April 1954, p. 192.
11. *Ibid.*, p. 187.
12. *Congressional Record*, 83rd Congress, 2nd Session, p. 15952.
13. Gallup, May 2, 1954.

Chapter 11

1. Karl Marx, *The Eighteenth Brumaire of Louis Bonaparte* (New York, 1963), p. 75.
2. E. Merrill Root, "The Culture of the Left," *Human Events*, February 4, 1953.
3. *Ibid.*
4. R. G. Waldeck, "Homosexual International," *Human Events*, April 16, 1952.
5. Harold Lord Varney, "The Truth About Joe McCarthy," *The American Mercury*, September 1953, p. 10.
6. Report of House Special Committee To Investigate Tax-Exempt Foundations and Comparable Organizations, *Tax-Exempt Foundations* (Washington, D.C., 1954), p. 19.
7. Quoted in Thomas C. Reeves, *Freedom and the Foundation: The Fund for the Republic in the Era of McCarthyism* (New York, 1969), p. 49.
8. Charles J. V. Murphy, "McCarthy and the Businessman," *Fortune*, April 1954, p. 190.
9. New York *Times*, April 6, 1953.
10. "McCarthy, Hunt, and Facts Forum," *The Reporter*, February 16, 1954, based on "The Facts About Facts Forum" series in the Providence *Journal*.
11. *Congressional Quarterly Almanac, 1953* (Washington, D.C., 1954), p. 342.
12. On the purge in the broadcasting industry, see Erik Barnouw, *A

History of Broadcasting in the United States, 3 vols. (New York, 1968, 1970), Vols. II–III.

PART III

Chapter 12

1. William F. Buckley, Jr., *God and Man at Yale* (Chicago, 1951), p. 86.
2. *Ibid.,* p. 197.
3. See Charles Lam Markmann, *The Buckleys: A Family Examined* (New York, 1973).
4. See Benjamin R. Epstein and Arnold Forster, *The Radical Right* (New York, 1967); J. Allen Broyles, *The John Birch Society* (Boston, 1964); Alan F. Westin, "The John Birch Society" in Daniel Bell, ed., *The Radical Right* (New York, 1964); Seymour Martin Lipset and Earl Rabb, *The Politics of Unreason* (New York, 1970).
5. Kevin Corrigan, "God and Man at *National Review,*" The Catholic *World,* January 1961, pp. 206–12.

Chapter 13

1. See James L. Clayton, *The Economic Impact of the Cold War* (New York, 1970), and Roger E. Bolton, *Defense Purchases and Regional Growth* (Washington, D.C., 1966).
2. Carey McWilliams, *Southern California Country* (New York, 1946), p. 135.

Chapter 14

1. V. O. Key, *Southern Politics* (New York, 1949), p. 11.
2. *Ibid.,* p. 7.
3. On the relationship between the black belts and the Dixiecrat vote, see Alexander Heard, *A Two-Party South?* (Chapel Hill, N.C., 1952), pp. 251–78; David M. Heer, "The Sentiment of White Supremacy: An Ecological Study," *American Journal of Sociology* (May 1959).
4. James Jackson Kilpatrick, *The Southern Case for School Segregation* (New York, 1962), p. 43.
5. See Charles O. Lerche, *The Uncertain South* (Chicago, 1964).
6. William C. Havard, ed., *The Changing Politics of the South* (Baton Rouge, La., 1972), p. 25.

7. See Melvin L. Greenhut and W. Tate Whitman, eds., *Essays in Southern Economic Development* (Chapel Hill, N.C., 1964), especially essays by Henderson, Fulmer, and Hanna.

Chapter 15

1. *The Congressional Record,* 83rd Congress, 2nd Session, p. 16001.
2. Barry Goldwater, *The Conscience of a Conservative* (Shepardsville, Ky., 1960), p. 34.
3. *Ibid.,* p. 37.
4. For poll results, see George H. Gallup, *The Gallup Poll: Public Opinion 1935–1971,* 3 vols. (New York, 1972), Vol. 3, for dates indicated.
5. Robert D. Novak, *The Agony of the G.O.P. 1964* (New York, 1965), pp. 209–10.
6. For election results, see the Republican National Committee, *The 1964 Elections* (Washington, D.C., 1965).
7. See Bernard Cosman, *Five States for Goldwater* (Kingsport, Tenn., 1966).

Chapter 16

1. See George H. Gallup, *The Gallup Poll: Public Opinion 1935–71,* 3 vols. (New York: 1972), Vol. 3, for dates indicated. For dates after 1971, see *Gallup Opinion Index* for month indicated.
2. William F. Buckley, Jr., "Say It Isn't So, Mr. President," *New York Times Magazine,* August 1, 1971, p. 9.
3. Kevin Phillips, *The Emerging Republican Majority* (New Rochelle, N.Y., 1969), p. 37.
4. *Ibid.,* pp. 83–84.
5. Richard Nixon, *RN: The Memoirs of Richard Nixon* (New York, 1978), pp. 16–17.
6. *Ibid.,* p. 17.
7. *Ibid.,* p. 48.
8. *Ibid.,* p. 88.
9. *Ibid.,* p. 214.
10. *Ibid.,* p. 226.
11. Patrick Buchanan, *The New Majority* (Philadelphia, 1973), p. 7.
12. *Public Papers of the Presidents of the United States, Richard Nixon, 1969* (Washington, D.C., 1971), pp. 905–6.
13. *Ibid.,* p. 546.
14. Richard Nixon, "Asia After Viet Nam," *Foreign Affairs,* October 1967, p. 118.
15. Nixon, *RN,* pp. 270–71.

16. John R. Coyne, Jr., *The Impudent Snobs: Agnew vs. the Intellectual Establishment* (New Rochelle, N.Y., 1972), pp. 258–59. This book contains the texts of ninety-three Agnew speeches.

17. *Ibid.,* p. 266.

18. *Ibid.,* p. 43.

Chapter 17

1. Arthur M. Schlesinger, Jr., *A Thousand Days: John F. Kennedy in the White House* (New York, 1965), p. 625.

2. Harry S. Dent, *The Prodigal South Returns to Power* (New York, 1978), p. 210.

3. *Public Papers of the Presidents of the United States, Richard Nixon, 1970* (Washington, D.C., 1971), pp. 345–46.

4. *Ibid.,* p. 409.

5. Congressional Quarterly, *Nixon: The Second Year of His Presidency* (Washington, D.C., 1971), p. 62.

6. See *Intelligence Activities and the Rights of Americans,* Final Report of the Select Committee To Study Government Operations with respect to Intelligence Activities, Book II (Washington, D.C., 1976) and *White House Surveillance Activities and Campaign Activities,* Book VII, Part I, Hearings before the Committee of the Judiciary, House of Representatives, 93rd Congress, 2nd Session.

7. *Intelligence Activities and the Rights of Americans,* p. 95.

8. William Safire, *Before the Fall* (New York, 1975), pp. 321–22.

9. *Ibid.,* p. 319.

10. John R. Coyne, Jr., *The Impudent Snobs: Agnew vs. The Intellectual Establishment* (New Rochelle, N.Y., 1972), p. 360.

11. *Public Papers, Richard Nixon, 1970,* p. 1035.

12. Rowland Evans, Jr., and Robert D. Novak, *Nixon in the White House* (New York, 1972), p. 372.

13. See the account of the "plumbers" in J. Anthony Lukas, *Nightmare: The Underside of the Nixon Years* (New York, 1977).

14. New York *Times, The End of a Presidency* (New York, 1974), p. 109.

15. *Public Papers of the Presidents of the United States, Richard Nixon, 1971* (Washington, D.C., 1972), p. 953.

16. Washington *Star-News,* November 9, 1972.

17. *Ibid.*

18. Richard Nixon, *RN: The Memoirs of Richard Nixon* (New York, 1978), p. 761.

19. Patrick Buchanan, *The New Majority* (Philadelphia, 1973), p. 66.

20. *Public Papers of the Presidents of the United States, Richard Nixon, 1972* (Washington, D.C., 1974), p. 828.

21. *Transcripts of Eight Recorded Presidential Conversations,* May–June 1974, House Committee on the Judiciary, p. 75.
22. See H. R. Haldeman, *The Ends of Power* (New York, 1978); Raymond Price, *With Nixon* (New York, 1977); and Fred D. Thompson, *At That Point in Time* (New York, 1975).
23. James W. McCord, *A Piece of Tape* (Rockville, Md., 1974), endpapers.
24. *Intelligence Activities and the Rights of Americans,* p. 161.

INDEX

357